WORKSHOPS IN COMPUTING
Series edited by C. J. van Rijsbergen

Also in this series

Database Programming Languages (DBPL-4)
Proceedings of the Fourth International
Workshop on Database Programming Languages
– Object Models and Languages, Manhattan, New
York City, USA, 30 August–1 September 1993
Catriel Beeri, Atsushi Ohori and
Dennis E. Shasha (Eds)

**Music Education: An Artificial Intelligence
Approach,** Proceedings of a Workshop held as
part of AI-ED 93, World Conference on Artificial
Intelligence in Education, Edinburgh, Scotland,
25 August 1993
Matt Smith, Alan Smaill and
Geraint A. Wiggins (Eds)

Rules in Database Systems
Proceedings of the 1st International Workshop
on Rules in Database Systems, Edinburgh,
Scotland, 30 August–1 September 1993
Norman W. Paton and
M. Howard Williams (Eds)

Semantics of Specification Languages (SoSL)
Proceedings of the International Workshop on
Semantics of Specification Languages, Utrecht,
The Netherlands, 25–27 October 1993
D.J. Andrews, J.F. Groote and
C.A. Middelburg (Eds)

Security for Object-Oriented Systems
Proceedings of the OOPSLA-93 Conference
Workshop on Security for Object-Oriented
Systems, Washington DC, USA,
26 September 1993
B. Thuraisingham, R. Sandhu and
T.C. Ting (Eds)

Functional Programming, Glasgow 1993
Proceedings of the 1993 Glasgow Workshop on
Functional Programming, Ayr, Scotland,
5–7 July 1993
John T. O'Donnell and Kevin Hammond (Eds)

Z User Workshop, Cambridge 1994
Proceedings of the Eighth Z User Meeting,
Cambridge, 29–30 June 1994
J.P. Bowen and J.A. Hall (Eds)

6th Refinement Workshop
Proceedings of the 6th Refinement Workshop,
organised by BCS-FACS, London,
5–7 January 1994
David Till (Ed.)

**Incompleteness and Uncertainty in Information
Systems**
Proceedings of the SOFTEKS Workshop on
Incompleteness and Uncertainty in Information
Systems, Concordia University, Montreal,
Canada, 8–9 October 1993
V.S. Alagar, S. Bergler and F.Q. Dong (Eds)

**Rough Sets, Fuzzy Sets and
Knowledge Discovery**
Proceedings of the International Workshop on
Rough Sets and Knowledge Discovery
(RSKD'93), Banff, Alberta, Canada,
12–15 October 1993
Wojciech P. Ziarko (Ed.)

Algebra of Communicating Processes
Proceeedings of ACP94, the First Workshop on
the Algebra of Communicating Processes,
Utrecht, The Netherlands,
16–17 May 1994
A. Ponse, C. Verhoef and
S.F.M. van Vlijmen (Eds)

Interfaces to Database Systems (IDS94)
Proceedings of the Second International
Workshop on Interfaces to Database Systems,
Lancaster University, 13–15 July 1994
Pete Sawyer (Ed.)

Persistent Object Systems
Proceedings of the Sixth International Workshop
on Persistent Object Systems,
Tarascon, Provence, France, 5–9 September 1994
Malcolm Atkinson, David Maier and
Véronique Benzaken (Eds)

Functional Programming, Glasgow 1994
Proceedings of the 1994 Glasgow Workshop on
Functional Programming, Ayr, Scotland,
12–14 September 1994
Kevin Hammond, David N. Turner and
Patrick M. Sansom (Eds)

East/West Database Workshop
Proceedings of the Second International
East/West Database Workshop,
Klagenfurt, Austria,
25–28 September 1994
J. Eder and L.A. Kalinichenko (Eds)

Asynchronous Digital Circuit Design
G. Birtwistle and A. Davis (Eds)

continued on back page...

Leslie S. Smith and Peter J.B. Hancock (Eds)

Neural Computation and Psychology

Proceedings of the 3rd Neural
Computation and Psychology
Workshop (NCPW3),
Stirling, Scotland,
31 August – 2 September 1994

Published in collaboration with the
British Computer Society

Springer-Verlag London Ltd.

Leslie S. Smith, BSc, PhD
Department of Computing Science,
University of Stirling, Stirling, FK9 4LA,
Scotland

Peter J.B. Hancock, MA, MSc, PhD
Department of Psychology,
University of Stirling, Stirling, FK9 4LA,
Scotland

ISBN 978-3-540-19948-9   ISBN 978-1-4471-3579-1 (eBook)
DOI 10.1007/978-1-4471-3579-1

British Library Cataloguing in Publication Data
Neural Computation and Psychology: Proceedings of the 3rd Neural Computation and
Psychology Workshop (NCPW3), Stirling, Scotland, 31 August–2 September 1994. –
(Workshops in Computing Series)
    I.   Smith, Leslie S.   II.   Hancock, Peter J. B.   III.   Series
    006.3

Library of Congress Cataloging-in-Publication Data
Neural Computation and Psychology Workshop (3rd : 1994 : Stirling, Scotland)
    Neural computation and psychology : proceedings of the 3rd Neural Computation and
Psychology Workshop (NCPW3), Stirling, Scotland, 31 August–2 September, 1994 /
Leslie S. Smith and Peter J.B. Hancock, eds.
       p. cm. – (Workshops in computing)
    "Published in collaboration with the British Computer Society."
    Includes bibliographical references and index.

    1.   Neural networks (Computer science)–Psychological aspects–Congresses.
I.   Smith, Leslie S., 1952–   .   II. Hancock Peter J.B., 1958–
III.   British Computer Society.   IV.   Title.   V.   Series.
QA76.87.N473 1994   94-47039
006.3– dc20   CIP

© Springer-Verlag London 1995
Originally published by British Computer Society in 1995.

Typesetting: Camera ready by contributors
Printed by Athenæum Press Ltd., Gateshead
34/3830-543210 Printed on acid-free paper

Preface

The papers that appear in this volume are refereed versions of presentations made at the third Neural Computation and Psychology Workshop, held at Stirling University, Scotland, from 31 August to 2 September 1994. The aim of this series of conferences has been to explore the interface between Neural Computing and Psychology: this has been a fruitful area for many researchers for a number of reasons. The development of Neural Computation has supplied tools to researchers in Cognitive Neuroscience, allowing them to look at possible mechanisms for implementing theories which would otherwise remain 'black box' techniques. These theories may be high-level theories, concerned with interaction between a number of brain areas, or low-level, describing the way in which smaller local groups of neurons behave. Neural Computation techniques have allowed computer scientists to implement systems which are based on how real brains appear to function, providing effective pattern recognition systems. We can thus mount a two-pronged attack on perception.

The papers here come from both the Cognitive Psychology viewpoint and from the Computer Science viewpoint: it is a mark of the growing maturity of the interface between the two subjects that they can understand each other's papers, and the level of discussion at the workshop itself showed how important each camp considers the other to be.

The papers here are divided into four sections, reflecting the primary areas of the material.

The first section, on cognition, covers a broad area, reflecting the degree to which neural networks have permeated theories about cognition. Willshaw's paper examines the relationship between symbolic and subsymbolic computing. For a limited range of problems with 0/1 outputs, he finds this to be a question of the level of description: however, for problems with real-valued output, there does appear to be a qualitative difference. Dienes, Altmann and Gao attempt to show transfer of grammatical knowledge elicited using a version of an Elman network. Bullinaria discusses the issue of making conclusions about reaction times from the behaviour of (non-temporal) neural network models. He illustrates the success of his approach with examples from the domain of reading. Slack explores the problem of binding distributed representations and shows that there is a limit of three on the number that may be bound in one step. He presents psychological data that suggest that some aspects of human performance may reflect this limitation. Cartwright and Humphreys describe an experiment to replicate the effect of aging on a trained neural network. The effect seems to be that recall becomes noisy, rather than that complete forgetting of associations occurs, at least for the limited range of networks explored.

The second section deals with how certain aspects of perception can be accomplished using neural networks. This is an area which has grown up particularly since the advent of sophisticated neural network learning techniques. The question of how groups of neurons can come to achieve the processing clearly evident in perception has always been one of major interest to psychologists and is now to computer scientists. The possibility that we may be able to replicate this behaviour has made the area even more attractive. Stone's work extends earlier neural network models of systems which learn invariances; the concept of learning invariancies (functions of the input that change much more slowly than the input itself) is incorporated directly into the function learned by the network. Baddeley uses a Boltzmann machine architecture to investigate topographic map formation: that is, formation of groups of neurons in which nearby neurons are sensitive to similar inputs. By applying some biologically plausible constraints a network can be made to form a topographic map when exposed only to natural images. Fyfe and Baddeley introduce non-linearities into a net normally used to extract principal components, to allow it to find higher-order (third and fourth) moments of an input distribution. Although the net was shown to work on synthetic data, it failed to discover anything of interest in natural images. Herrmann, Bauer and Der propose a neural network model based on Kohonen networks to explain an effect of increased generalisation capacity for vowel perception when the vowels are prototypical. Kohonen nets usually put most units where there is most data: their modification forces it to put more into the decision boundary regions, thereby encouraging categorical outputs (see the paper by Beale and Keil for a demonstration of this effect with face perception). Phillips, Kay and Smyth introduce a context-based neural network classifier with an information theoretically justified objective function. This is used to provide a possible explanation for how real brains produce representations.

The third section considers particular aspects of auditory and visual perception. Griffith's paper considers an aspect of musical perception. Using a pitch tracking net followed by an Elman recurrent network trained using backpropagation, he shows that the representations induced by these models from nursery rhyme tunes are analogous to human perceptions of the degrees in the diatonic scale. Smith investigates early auditory processing of voiced sounds, postulating that the auditory system is particularly sensitive to amplitude modulations in wideband filtered sounds. He suggests a particular neural source for this sensitivity. Beauvois and Meddis describe a computer model which accounts for human perception of alternating tones either as a single stream or as a pair of streams. The model is based on early auditory processing, including the temporal integration of wideband channel excitation. Smith and Humphreys implement a guided search using a Boltzmann machine algorithm. This successfully mimics human performance for displays containing only a single target, but fails to do so with displays containing two targets. Beale and Keil investigate categorical perception of face stimuli finding such effects amongst highly familiar faces, but not in unfamiliar face stimuli.

The last section considers sequence learning in the word domain. Lovatt and Bairaktaris consider word list recall, modelling the complexities found in human performance using a dynamically adaptive network whose input describes the sequence of phonemes of the words in the list. They find similarities between their simulation and human performance in the way that similarities between word sounds affect recall. Glasspool, Houghton and Shallice investigate a dual route (i.e. lexical and phonological) connectionist model of spelling. They consider the error performance of each route: the lexical network displays failure performance similar to human performance on words. The phonological network is still being developed: however, it is intended to account for other effects, such as priming in spelling non-words. They suggest that much of the difficulty in dual-route models centres on combining the outputs of the two systems, rather than the individual designs.

The editors would like to thank all the contributors, session chairs, and referees, particularly Roland Baddeley, Dimitrios Bairaktaris, Michael Beauvois, Vicki Bruce, John Bullinaria, Mike Burton, Ben Craven, Joe Levy, Ray Meddis, Bill Phillips, Roger Watt and David Willshaw.

Leslie S. Smith
Peter J.B. Hancock

Contents

Cognition

Symbolic and Subsymbolic Approaches to Cognition
D. Willshaw 3

Mapping Across Domains Without Feedback: A Neural
Network Model of Transfer of Implicit Knowledge
Z. Dienes, G.T.M. Altmann and S.-J. Gao 19

Modelling Reaction Times
J.A. Bullinaria 34

Chunking: An Interpretation Bottleneck
J. Slack 49

Learning, Relearning and Recall for Two Strengths of Learning
in Neural Networks 'Aged' by Simulated Dendritic Attrition
R. Cartwright and G.W. Humphreys 62

Perception

Learning Invariances via Spatio-Temporal Constraints
J.V. Stone 75

Topographic Map Formation as Statistical Inference
R. Baddeley 86

Edge Enhancement and Exploratory Projection Pursuit
C. Fyfe and R. Baddeley 97

The "Perceptual Magnet" Effect: A Model Based on
Self-Organizing Feature Maps
M. Herrmann, H.-U. Bauer and R. Der 107

How Local Cortical Processors that Maximize Coherent
Variation Could Lay Foundations for Representation Proper
W.A. Phillips, J. Kay and D.M. Smyth 117

Audition and Vision

Using Complementary Streams in a Computer Model of the
Abstraction of Diatonic Pitch
N. Griffith 137

Data-Driven Sound Interpretation: Its Application to
Voiced Sounds
L.S. Smith   147

Computer Simulation of Gestalt Auditory Grouping
by Frequency Proximity
M.W. Beauvois and R. Meddis   155

Mechanisms of Visual Search: An Implementation of
Guided Search
K.J. Smith and G.W. Humphreys   165

Categorical Perception as an Acquired Phenomenon:
What are the Implications?
J.M. Beale and F.C. Keil   176

Sequence Learning

A Computational Account of Phonologically Mediated
Free Recall
P.J. Lovatt and D. Bairaktaris   191

Interactions Between Knowledge Sources in a Dual-Route
Connectionist Model of Spelling
D.W. Glasspool, G. Houghton and T. Shallice   209

Author Index   227

Cognition

Symbolic and Subsymbolic Approaches to Cognition

David Willshaw
Centre for Cognitive Science
University of Edinburgh
2 Buccleuch Place
Edinburgh EH8 9LW

Abstract

As an appropriate topic for a workshop on Neural Computation and Psychology, I discuss the relationships that can be established between conventional, symbolic ("rule-based") and subsymbolic approaches to cognition. I first make some general remarks about symbolic and non-symbolic approaches. I then describe a framework, due to Foster (1992), within which different methods for solving the same computational problem can be compared. I then demonstrate the use of this framework as applied to a specific example. I use this illustrative example to consider whether subsymbolic methods are merely implementations of symbolic ones.

1 Symbolic and Subsymbolic approaches

Influenced by several lines of argument (Newell & Simon, 1981; Fodor, 1975), particularly that there is a Language of Thought, the conventional view of cognition is that it involves the manipulation of a set of entities according to specific rules. These entities refer to objects in the external world and they are manipulated by rules akin to the rules of logic; hence, for semantic and syntactic reasons the entities are called *symbols*. However, it has long been recognised that symbolic systems are subject to many limitations which are not shared by the human cognitive systems that they are intended to model. Such *rule-based* systems suffer from brittleness, inflexibility, difficulty of learning from experience, inadequate generalisation, domain specificity, and inadequacy of serial search through large systems (Smolensky, 1988). As far as the application of symbolic methods to artificial intelligence is concerned, Hofstadter (1980) has commented that *"... the strange flavour of AI work is that people try to put together long sets of rules in strict formalisms which tell inflexible machines how to be flexible"*

In the *subsymbolic* approach (Smolensky, 1988), the basic element is the activity of an individual unit of a neural network. Such elements can be regarded as constituents of the entities of the symbolic approach and thus have been called *subsymbols*. It has been held that subsymbols are not operated upon by symbol manipulation, but participate in numerical computation.

There has been much discussion as to the fundamental differences between the symbolic and subsymbolic approaches (Fodor & Pylyshyn, 1988; Smolensky, 1987; Chater & Oaksford, 1990; Clark, 1989; Willshaw, 1994). This general discussion will not be continued here but instead three specific questions will be addressed:

1. How can different subsymbolic methods for the same task be compared?

2. How can symbolic and subsymbolic methods for the same task be compared?

3. Are symbolic methods formulated on a higher and independent level than subsymbolic ones? Specifically, are subsymbolic methods merely implementations of symbolic ones?

A key consideration is the importance of the levels at which the given task is analysed. The notion that there are different levels at which a problem can be approached is familiar to people from many different disciplines – philosophy and computer science, to take two examples. Many people refer to the framework established by Marr (1982), which contains three levels. What most people understand by this is that at the highest, *computational*, level, the nature of the task is discussed, the *algorithmic* level concerns the method for carrying out the task and the *implementational* level the means for carrying out the task. For example, if the task is long division, one method (discussed at the algorithmic level) is to use successive subtraction and another method is to use a set of look-up tables for how one digit is divided by another. At the implementational level, an abacus, a pocket calculator, pencil and paper or piles of stones are all different types of hardware for carrying out this task.

Whilst most people will agree that analysis of a task in terms of levels is useful, there is disagreement as to how many levels there are and whether they have concrete or abstract form (Dennett, 1971; Newell, 1982; Pylyshyn, 1984; Rumelhart & McClelland, 1985; Haugeland, 1985). For example, in the design of electronic circuits, very many more than three levels can be identified. There is the device level, the logic circuit level, the register-transfer level, and so on (Newell, 1982). At all of these levels it is valid to discuss what computation is to be carried out and how it is done. In neurobiology, what is regarded as the computational, the algorithmic or the implementational level is determined by what questions are being asked and by whom. For example, the pattern of activity in the CA3 pyramidal cells of the hippocampus may represent to a physiologist the computation carried out by the cells, to a psychologist the implementation of a method for the storage of information; the passage of ions under the influence of extracellular calcium in the NMDA receptors in hippocampal nerve cells may represent to a pharmacologist the computation and to a physiologist the implementation of a mechanism for synaptic change.

In neurobiology, at least, the computational/algorithmic/implementational set of levels can be said to form a "floating triumvirate" (Churchland & Sejnowski, 1992; Willshaw, 1994), illustrating the point that in general there are more than three levels. With respect to the symbolic/subsymbolic debate, two important questions are whether the different levels are independent of one another and what the right level is for discussing a particular method for solving a problem.

It is important to realise that this paper addresses the problem of how to carry out the computation *once it has been specified*. The problem of how to specify the computation itself is not discussed.

2 Comparison of different subsymbolic approaches

Many different neural networks can be constructed to solve the same problem. The networks may differ in their basic architecture or they may have the same architecture but different weight values. One way of comparing these networks is to compare the logical functions computed by their component parts. In his MSc thesis Forrest (1987) compared the performance of neural networks in solving various simple binary classification problems. In one set of simulations, a network with two hidden units was run repeatedly on the exclusive-or problem (X-OR), starting from a different set of randomly chosen weights on each occasion. It was found that the network learns this function in two ways, which can be distinguished by the speed of convergence of the weight values in the network. When convergence was fast the weights were found to be arranged *asymmetrically*: the weights from one input unit are negatively valued and those from the other unit have positive weights; one hidden unit has a positive weight to the output unit and the other hidden unit a negative weight. For networks where convergence was slow, the weights were arranged *symmetrically*: each input unit has a positive and a negative weight onto the two hidden units and the two hidden units each have a positive weight to the output unit. Typical patterns of weights seen in these two cases are shown in Figures 1 and 2.

Subsequent analysis of the patterns of activity in these two types of networks revealed characteristically different truth tables for the hidden units in the two cases. One interesting and yet unexplained finding is that not all of the possible ways by which X-OR could be computed are learnt by a neural network when trained by backpropagation. For example, in no case is the problem solved by a combination of conjunctions and disjunctions being computed, even though units are capable of forming conjunctions or disjunctions individually. Table 1 shows the activity values (rounded to the nearest integer) assigned to the hidden units when computing X-OR, for the fast and slow solutions. The states that would be adopted if the hidden units had computed disjunctions and the output unit had computed a conjunction are also shown.

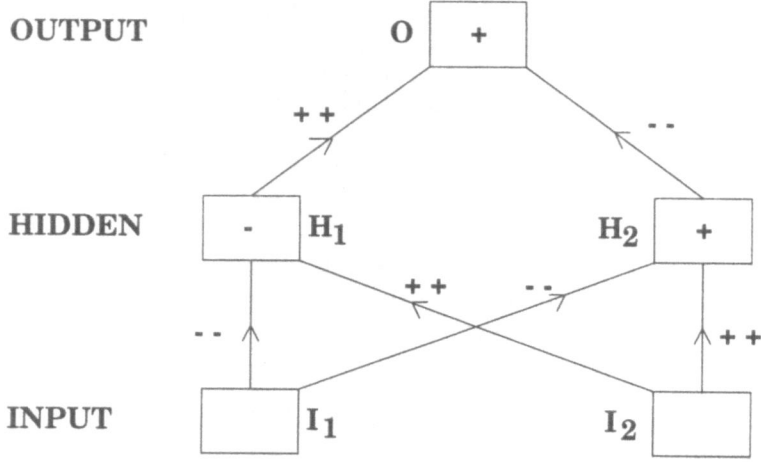

Figure 1: **A network with 2 hidden units that solves X-OR. Fast (asymmetric) solution. The symbols "+", "++", "-", "–" indicate the polarities and relative sizes of the weights and biases in the network**

		Fast		Slow		And/Or		
I_1	I_2	H_1	H_2	H_1	H_2	H_1	H_2	O
0	0	0	1	0	0	0	1	0
0	1	1	1	0	1	1	1	1
1	0	0	0	1	0	1	1	1
1	1	0	1	0	0	1	0	0

Table 1. Three different ways of computing X-OR

Whilst this approach has its uses, it is restricted to analysis at the binary logic level. A more general treatment is required and one possible approach has been developed recently by Foster (1992). She showed how to construct a family of ideal machines which can be used as a framework for comparison between any two methods for solving a problem. It can be applied to symbolic and subsymbolic methods alike, as will be described in the following section.

3   Foster's algorithmic framework

Foster considers the situation where the computational task can be specified in terms of an input/output mapping. While this is a restricted class of computations, it is nevertheless a large and varied one, covering computations which are as simple as binary classifications or as complex as ordering the elements

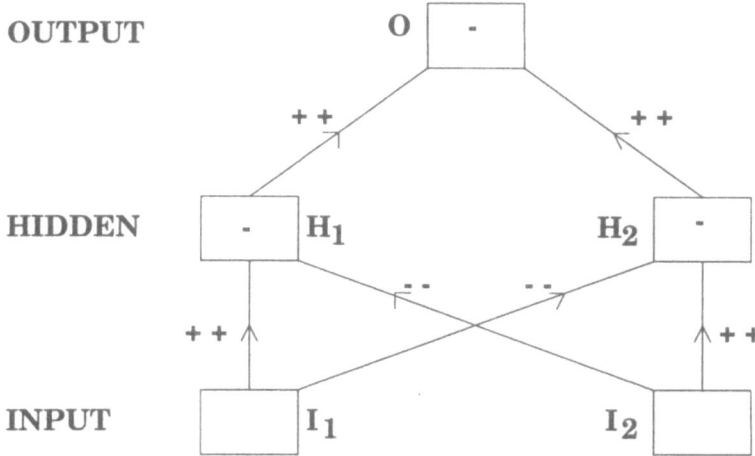

Figure 2: **A network with 2 hidden units that solves X-OR. Slow (symmetric) solution. Conventions as in Fig.1**

of a list. She further assumes that the computation is ultimately constrained by the hardware on which it is to be carried out. In brief, she shows how any method for carrying out the given task can be mapped onto a member of a family of ideal machines. Two different methods for carrying out the same task can be compared by comparing the ideal machines onto which they map.

An ideal machine (called an *algorithm*) is the *description* of the *states* through which the *given physical system* passes through in solving the problem according to the *given method*. The *level of detail* which is used to describe the states depends on the method in question.

Foster gives formal definitions of the following terms:

The task is specified in terms of the input/output mapping that is to be computed on the given physical system.

A state is a set of pairs of labels and associated values (usually relating to the system parameters and their values for the method used) at a particular point in the computation.

An algorithm is the sequence of such state descriptions through which the system passes for all possible input assignments.

Equivalence of two algorithms is defined as the equivalence of the sequences of states through which the two algorithms pass.

Having established a description of the particular algorithm, more *abstract* versions of the same algorithm can be obtained by the application of certain rules. According to one rule, specified states are removed from the algorithm; another rule removes certain pairs of labels and values from all states. The effect of these types of operation is to furnish a less detailed description of the algorithm. In the extreme case, if enough detail is removed all that is left is a description of the input/output relations themselves, ie, a description of the algorithm at the highest, computational level. In the opposite direction of *implementation*, more detailed algorithms can be produced by including (informally speaking) more information about the values of the internal variables of the physical system. Such extra detail that is included is always constrained by the nature of the system itself; that is, the parameters and values to be included always have a physical reality. Having constructed in this way a family of abstractions and implementations of any given algorithm, it will be possible to see the relationships between any two algorithms. One result is that all algorithms for the same computation have a common abstraction. Trivially, this can be at the highest level of abstraction, ie, the input/output relationship itself. What will be less clear *a priori*, and which can be discovered using Foster's method, is whether one particular algorithm is an implementation of another one.

4 Example of the detection of mirror symmetry

I now illustrate how the framework developed by Foster (1992) is used by working through a simple example. This is the task of detecting whether the ones and noughts in a bit string form a mirror symmetrical pattern.

4.1 Comparing symbolic algorithms

One obvious, symbolic method is to check if the value of the first bit is the same as that of the last bit, the value of the second bit is the same as that of the next-to-last bit, and so on. For 4-bit strings, a typical portion of pseudo-code that one might write for this method is shown in Table 2. The variables $X1$, $X2$, $X3$ and $X4$ are read in. The bits in the two halves of the string are compared and used to compute the values of two intermediate variables $Y1$ and $Y2$, on which the value of the output variable Z then depends.

Program A
read $X1$
read $X2$
read $X3$
read $X4$
if $X1 = X4$ then $Y1 = 1$ else 0
if $X2 = X3$ then $Y2 = 1$ else 0
if $Y1 = 1$ & $Y2 = 1$ then $Z = 1$ else 0
write Z
end

Table 2. One method for computing mirror-symmetry

The Foster description for this method is shown in Table 3, for the bit-string 1110 only. There are 9 states in the sequence, and each state contains 8 labels and their associated values, which are written in columnar form. At the beginning of the computation many of the variables have values that are undefined. Strictly speaking, this information should be indicated in the columns of values but here it is omitted for the sake of clarity. Note also that Program A itself becomes just another set of values, each value being the string of characters making up a single instruction.

Program A	X1	X2	X3	X4	Y1	Y2	Z
read $X1$							
read $X2$	1						
read $X3$	1	1					
read $X4$	1	1	1				
if $X1 = X4$ then $Y1 = 1$ else 0	1	1	1	0			
if $X2 = X3$ then $Y2 = 1$ else 0	1	1	1	0	0		
if $Y1 = 1$ & $Y2 = 1$, $Z = 1$ else 0	1	1	1	0	0	1	
write Z	**1**	**1**	**1**	**0**	**0**	**1**	**0**
end	1	1	1	0	0	1	0

Table 3. The Foster description for Program A

A second method for solving the same problem is to regard each half of the bit-string as the unique, binary representation of an integer. To test for mirror symmetry, the method is to reconstruct the two integers (reversing the order of the bits in one of the two halves) and then test to see whether the two integers are the same. The Foster description is shown in Table 4, again for the bit string 1110 only. At state 5 in the sequence the two halves of the bit string are compared and the value of the intermediate parameter Y computed.

	Program B	X1	X2	X3	X4	Y	Z
1	read $X1$;						
2	read $X2$;	1					
3	read $X3$;	1	1				
4	read $X4$;	1	1	1			
5	$Y = 2X1 + X2 - (X3 + 2X4)$;	1	1	1	0		
6	if $Y = 0$ then $Z= 1$ else $Z= 0$;	1	1	1	0	2	
7	**write Z;**	1	1	1	0	2	0
8	end	1	1	1	0	2	0

Table 4. A second method for computing mirror-symmetry

We can now begin to investigate the relations between these two algorithms by constructing more abstract (less detailed) versions of them by using some of the abstracting operations *selection of states, selection of values, rounding* and *duplication*. By *selecting states* (taking just the penultimate rows from Tables 3 and 4 and repeating this for all of the 16 possible input states) and *selecting values* (removing the columns that contain a description of the code) the result is the descriptions for programs A and B shown in Table 5. For reasons of compactness, the values for the labels $X1$, $X2$, $X3$ and $X4$ refer to the descriptions for both A and B.

It is clear that these two algorithms, although now presented in a similar form, are in fact different.

X1	X2	X3	X4	A Y1	Y2	Z	B Y	Z
0	0	0	0	1	1	1	0	1
0	0	0	1	0	1	0	-2	0
0	0	1	0	1	0	0	-1	0
0	1	0	0	1	· 0	0	1	0
1	0	0	0	0	1	0	2	0
0	0	1	1	0	0	0	-3	0
0	1	0	1	0	0	0	-1	0
1	0	0	1	1	1	1	0	1
0	1	1	0	1	1	1	0	1
1	0	1	0	0	0	0	1	0
1	1	0	0	0	0	0	3	0
1	1	1	0	0	1	0	2	0
1	1	0	1	1	0	0	1	0
1	0	1	1	1	0	0	-1	0
0	1	1	1	0	1	0	-2	0
1	1	1	1	1	1	1	0	1

Table 5. Algorithms A and B are different

4.2 Comparing subsymbolic algorithms

It is possible in a similar manner to construct descriptions of neural network algorithms for the same task. Figures 3, 4 and 5 show the architectures and weight values for three neural networks which have learned mirror symmetry. Network P (Figure 3) contains 2 hidden units. Network Q (Figure 4) has just one hidden unit, but there are also direct connections from input to output. Network R (Figure 5) can be thought of as a superposition of Networks P and Q since it has two hidden units and also direct input-output connections. I ran the standard back propagation algorithm on networks of each type. The patterns of weights obtained was the same for all networks with the same architecture. Rumelhart, Hinton, and Williams (1986) point out that networks of type P, with only two hidden units, can compute mirror-symmetry, for any number of input units. It is noteworthy that networks of type Q, which can also perform this computation, contain a smaller number of weights.

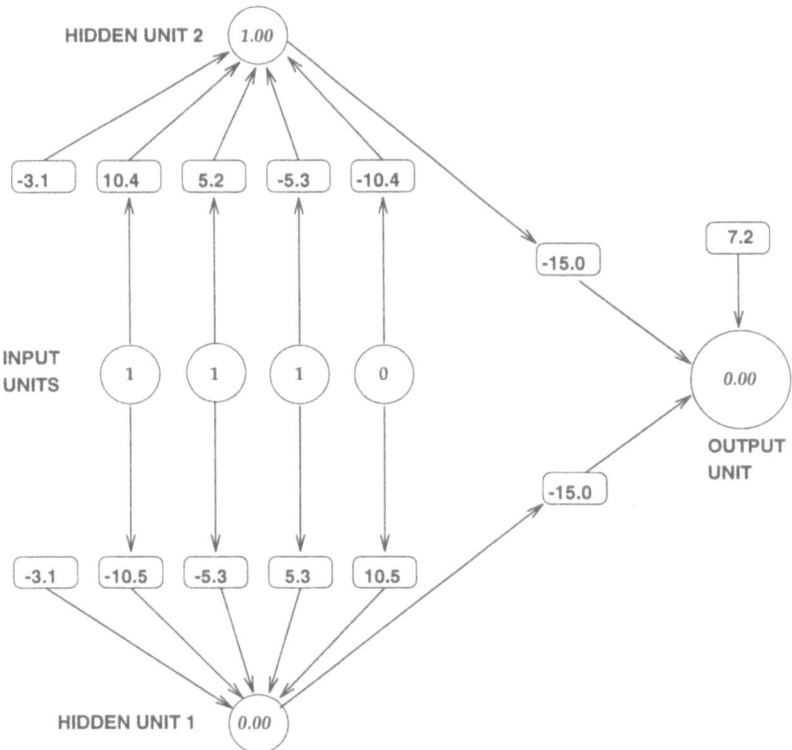

Figure 3: **Net P, with 2 hidden units, which has been trained by back-propagation to compute 4-bit mirror-symmetry. The numbers within the rectangles are weight values; those within the circles are activity values for the input string 1110.**

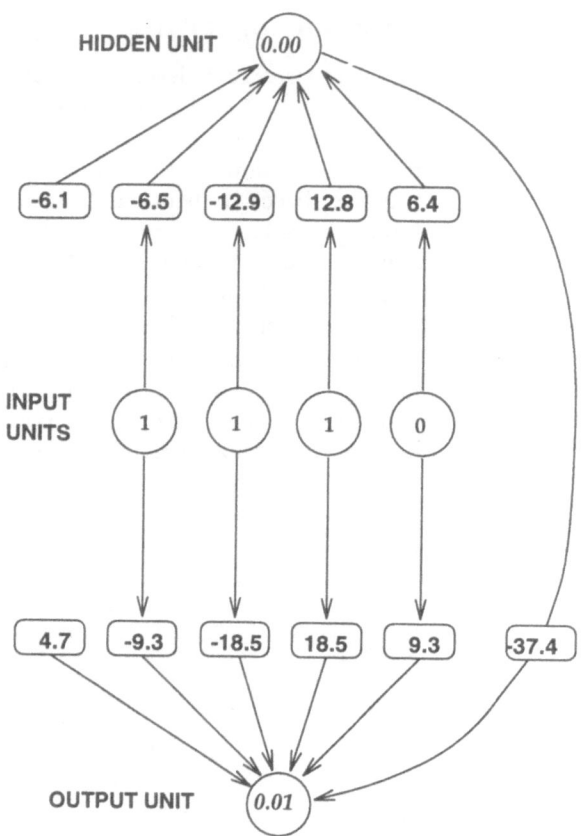

Figure 4: **Net Q, with 1 hidden unit and direct input-output connections, which has been trained to compute 4-bit mirror symmetry. Conventions as for Fig 3.**

Neural network algorithms are usually characterised in terms of their activity values. Table 6 shows, using the condensed format of Table 5, the descriptions for Networks P and Q and R in terms of the activity values of all the units for all possible input assignations. It can be seen straightaway that each network is different and also differs from the algorithms A and B described in Table 5.

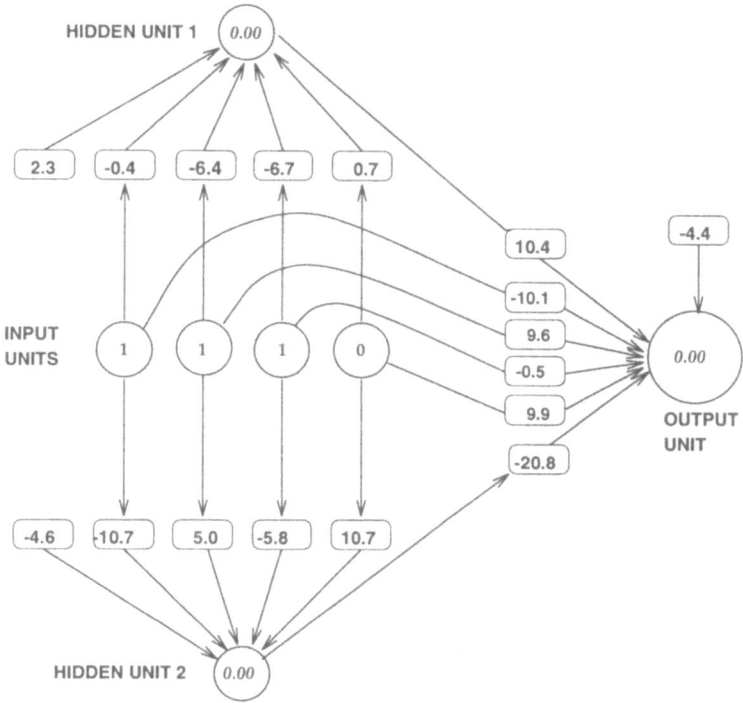

Figure 5: **Net R, with 2 hidden units and direct connections between input and output, which has been trained to compute 4-bit mirror-symmetry. Conventions as for Fig 3.**

					P		Q	R	
X1	**X2**	**X3**	**X4**	**O**	**H1**	**H2**	**H**	**H1**	**H2**
0	0	0	0	1.00	0.04	0.04	0.00	0.91	0.01
0	0	0	1	0.00	1.00	0.00	0.56	0.95	1.00
0	0	1	0	0.00	0.90	0.00	0.99	0.01	0.00
0	1	0	0	0.00	0.00	0.90	0.00	0.02	0.59
1	0	0	0	0.00	0.00	1.00	0.00	0.87	0.00
0	0	1	1	0.00	1.00	0.00	1.00	0.02	0.57
0	1	0	1	0.00	0.89	0.00	0.00	0.03	1.00
1	0	1	0	0.00	0.00	0.89	0.55	0.01	0.00
1	1	0	0	0.00	0.00	1.00	0.00	0.01	0.00
1	1	1	0	0.00	0.00	1.00	0.00	0.00	0.00
1	0	0	1	1.00	0.04	0.04	0.00	0.93	0.01
0	1	1	0	1.00	0.04	0.04	0.00	0.00	0.00
1	1	0	1	0.00	0.00	0.89	0.00	0.02	0.57
1	0	1	1	0.00	0.90	0.00	1.00	0.01	0.00
0	1	1	1	0.00	1.00	0.04	0.56	0.00	0.99
1	1	1	1	1.00	0.04	0.04	0.00	0.00	0.99

Table 6. Network algorithms P, Q and R are all different

4.3 Comparison of algorithms

The relationships between the symbolic and the subsymbolic algorithms are explored by comparing A, B and P. This is done by first constructing algorithm B[1] from B by duplicating the label/parameter value set Y and calling the new sets $Y1$ and $Y2$. We then construct B[2] from B[1] by (i) replacing negative values of $Y1$ by 1 and all other values by 0 and (ii) replacing positive values of $Y2$ by 1 and other values by 0. Finally P[1] is constructed by P by replacing each real value by the nearest integer. These various algorithms are displayed in Table 7. To make it easier to compare the patterns of values for the various algorithms, zero values are omitted from the righthand part of the table. Columns of values relating to labels O and Z also are not shown. The result is that whereas it is clear from the central columns of this table that algorithms A, B and P are different, the righthand side shows that an abstraction of B (B[2]) and an abstraction of P (P[1]) are identical.

	A		B	P		B[1]		B[2]		P[1]	
X1-X4	Y1	Y2	Y	H1	H2	Y1	Y2	Y1	Y2	H1	H2
0000	1	1	0	0.04	0.04						
0001	0	1	−2	1.00	0.00	−2	−2	1		1	
0010	1	0	−1	0.90	0.00	−1	−1	1		1	
0100	1	0	1	0.00	0.90	1	1		1		1
1000	0	1	2	0.00	1.00	2	2		1		1
0011	0	0	−3	1.00	0.00	−3	−3	1		1	
0101	0	0	−1	0.89	0.00	−1	−1	1		1	
1001	1	1	0	0.04	0.04						
0110	1	1	0	0.04	0.04						
1010	0	0	1	0.00	0.89	1	1		1		1
1100	0	0	3	0.00	1.00	3	3		1		1
1110	0	1	2	0.00	1.00	2	2		1		1
1101	1	0	1	0.00	0.89	1	1		1		1
1011	1	0	−1	0.90	0.00	−1	−1	1		1	
0111	0	1	−2	1.00	0.04	−2	−2	1		1	
1111	1	1	0	0.04	0.04						

Table 7. Abstractions of algorithms A, B and P

The network algorithms can be compared in a similar fashion by application of the abstraction operations. For example, applying *selection of values* and *rounding* to algorithm P yields P[2] and then P[3], which is identical to Q[1], itself an abstraction of Q (Table 8).

X1	X2	X3	X4	O	P		Q	P[2]	P[3]	Q[1]
					H1	H2	H	H1	H1	H
0	0	0	0	1						
0	0	0	1	0	1.00		0.56	1.00	1.00	1.00
0	0	1	0	0	0.90		1.00	0.90	1.00	1.00
0	1	0	0	0		0.90				
1	0	0	0	0		1.00				
0	0	1	1	0	1.00		1.00	1.00	1.00	1.00
0	1	0	1	0	0.89			0.89		
1	0	0	1	1						
0	1	1	0	1						
1	0	1	0	0		0.89	0.55			
1	1	0	0	0		1.00				
1	1	1	0	0		1.00				
1	1	0	1	0		0.89				
1	0	1	1	0	0.90		1.00	0.90	1.00	1.00
0	1	1	1	0	1.00		0.56	1.00	1.00	1.00
1	1	1	1	1						

Table 8. Abstractions of subsymbolic algorithms P and Q

These examples are somewhat contrived but this detailed description may help to make the basic points. The relationships between the various algorithms constructed in this way is shown as a graph in Figure 6. The vertical axis denotes the abstract/detailed dimension, 'upwards' indicating the direction of more abstract algorithms. An arrow points from each algorithm towards an algorithm which is an abstraction of it. All arrows point eventually to the highest, computational level description (marked by a star) which is identical to the input/output specification. Below this there are algorithms at many different levels. We started out with five different algorithms, two of which are of the symbolic type and three of which are of the subsymbolic, or neural network, type. Looking at their positions in the graph, it is clear that the symbolic algorithms A and B do not occupy any particular privileged position; furthermore, the subsymbolic algorithms are not at a lower level than the symbolic algorithms. In general, it is impossible to tell whether two specific algorithms are related by one being an implementation of the other. This has to be determined empirically and will depend on, amongst other things, the algorithms being compared and the physical systems on which these algorithms are being implemented.

5 Conclusion

Foster's scheme can be used to construct the relationships between any two algorithms. This is done by mapping each of the two algorithms onto members

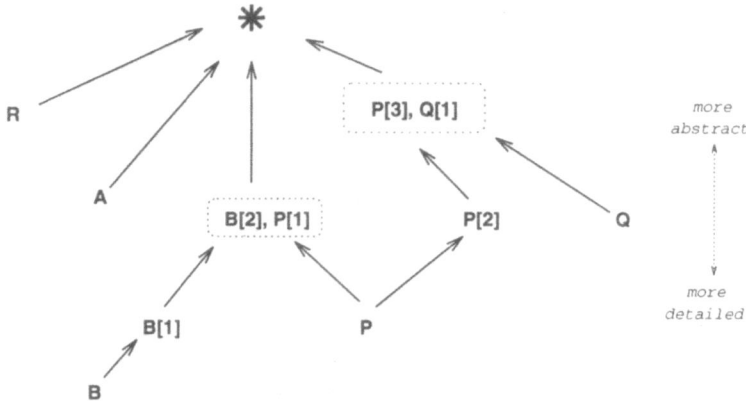

Figure 6: **Showing the relationship between algorithms A, B, P, Q & R and some of their abstractions.** * denotes the top level algorithm

of the family of ideal machines and then comparing the relationships between the particular ideal machines. Unlike procedures which map onto more abstract entities, such as Turing machines, this scheme has the advantage that at any level of abstraction the ideal machines can be related to the physical system on which the computations are carried out. Consideration of Foster's scheme reinforces the view that there are many different levels at which the expecution of a given computational task can be discussed. Symbolic and subsymbolic algorithms are not divided neatly into two distinct classes, with the one being at a "higher" level than the other. However, the description of a neural network in terms of its real-valued activities makes it difficult for it to be compared with any other algorithms without first applying an abstraction operation.

Foster's scheme has been applied so far to only a small number of computations, the most complicated relating to algorithms for sorting out lists of numbers (Foster, 1992). Many aspects remains to be investigated, such as what limits there are to the abstracting operations used, the nature of which defines (and determines) the valid abstractions for a given algorithm. It would useful to apply the method to computations that lend themselves naturally to the subsymbolic approach. Finally, it could be considered how this theoretical framework can be extended to cases where the input-output mapping is not specified completely in advance. Some discussion of this issue, particularly the more general problem of extension to infinite time and space, is given in (Foster, 1992).

Acknowledgements

I thank Carol Foster for many helpful discussions and the Medical Research Council for financial support.

References

Chater, N., & Oaksford, M. (1990). Autonomy, implementation and cognitive architecture: A reply to Fodor and Pylyshyn. *Cognition, 34*, 93–107.

Churchland, P. S., & Sejnowski, T. J. (1992). *The Computational Brain.* MIT Press/Bradford Books, Cambridge, MA.

Clark, A. (1989). *Microcognition: Philosophy, Cognitive Science and Parallel Distributed Processing.* MIT Press/Bradford Books, Cambridge, MA.

Dennett, D. C. (1971). Intentional systems. *The Journal of Philosophy, 68*, 87–106.

Fodor, J. A. (1975). *The Language of Thought.* Crowell, New York.

Fodor, J. A., & Pylyshyn, Z. W. (1988). Connectionism and cognitive architecture: A critical analysis. *Cognition, 28*, 3–71.

Forrest, J. H. (1987). Computations in PDP networks. Master's thesis, University of Edinburgh.

Foster, C. L. (1992). *Algorithms, Abstraction and Implementation.* Academic Press, London.

Haugeland, J. (1985). *Artificial Intelligence: The Very Idea.* MIT Press/Bradford Books, Cambridge, MA.

Hofstadter, D. R. (1980). *Godel, Escher, Bach: an Eternal Golden Braid.* Penguin Books.

Marr, D. (1982). *Vision.* Freeman, San Francisco.

Newell, A. (1982). The knowledge level. *Artificial Intelligence, 18*, 87–127.

Newell, A., & Simon, H. (1981). Computer science as empirical inquiry. In Haugeland, J. (Ed.), *Mind Design.* Bradford Books, Montgomery, VT.

Pylyshyn, Z. W. (1984). *Computation and Cognition.* MIT Press, Cambridge, MA.

Rumelhart, D. E., Hinton, G. E., & Williams, R. J. (1986). Learning representations by back-propagating errors. *Nature, 323*, 533–536.

Rumelhart, D. E., & McClelland, J. L. (1985). Levels indeed! A response to Broadbent. *Journal of Experimental Psychology: General, 114*, 193–197.

Smolensky, P. (1987). The constituent structure of connectionist mental states: A reply to Fodor and Pylyshyn. *The Southern Journal of Philosophy, 26*, 137–159.

Smolensky, P. (1988). On the proper treatment of connectionism. *Behavioural and Brain Sciences, 11*, 1–74.

Willshaw, D. J. (1994). Sub-symbolic and non-symbolic models. *Phil Trans Roy Soc A*, in press.

Mapping across domains without feedback: A neural network model of transfer of implicit knowledge

Zoltán Dienes, Gerry T. M. Altmann, and Shi-Ji Gao
Lab. of Experimental Psychology, University of Sussex
Falmer, Brighton BN1 9QG, U.K.

Abstract

Exposure to exemplars of an artificial grammar allows subjects to decide subsequently whether a novel sequence does or does not belong to the same grammar [1], If subjects are exposed to exemplars of an artificial grammar in one domain (e.g. sequences of tones differing in pitch), subjects can later classify novel sequences in another domain (e.g. sequences of letters). This paper introduces a version of the Simple Recurrent Network (SRN) that can also transfer its knowledge of artificial grammars across domains without feedback. The performance of the model is sensitive to at least some of the same variables that affect subjects' performance in ways not predicted by other theories.

1 Introduction

In a number of studies, Reber and others have shown that asking subjects to memorize strings of letters generated by a finite state grammar (see Figure 1) enables subjects to later classify new strings as obeying the rules or not [2]. Reber regarded this knowledge as having two key properties [1]. First, he argued that the knowledge was _implicit_ because subjects found it very difficult to report what the rules of the grammar were. This claim has aroused a lot of controversy, but all seem to agree that the knowledge is at least difficult to articulate freely, and so is implicit in this minimal descriptive sense (see [3], [1], [4] for reviews). Second, Reber argued that the knowledge was abstract. This paper will focus on this second claim, and in particular on the claim that the knowledge (or a substantial part of it) is not tied to any specific perceptual features. Initially, experimental evidence relevant to the claim that the knowledge is abstract will be overviewed. Then, the application of Elman's Simple Recurrent Network model to artificial grammar learning will be discussed [5]. Finally, our extension of the model to allow more abstract knowledge will be described and fitted to experimental data.

Knowledge can be abstract in different ways, and we need to be clear about which sense of abstractness different data are relevant to [6, 7]. According to one sense, knowledge is abstract if its function is to indicate the relations between features in the input (e.g. training strings) as a whole. Such knowledge can then apply to strings or parts of strings that were not presented during training. For example, the following knowledge is abstract in this sense: 'In the training set, T can immediately repeat itself after an M', 'X cannot start', etc. At first, it may seem that if subjects can classify strings that they were not trained on, then their knowledge must be abstract in this sense. Brooks, however, pointed out that subjects could memorize training strings and then classify test strings on the basis of their similarity to the training strings [8]. To determine whether exemplar-based information was an important determinant of classification performance, Vokey and Brooks attempted to manipulate grammaticality and similarity to studied strings independently [9] (also see [10]). Similarity was measured (inversely) by the smallest number of differences in letter positions to any studied string. Vokey and Brooks defined test strings as being 'near' if they differed from any training string by only one letter, and 'far' otherwise. They showed that both similarity and grammaticality affected the tendency to give a 'grammatical' response. For example, subjects were more likely to classify a nongrammatical string as grammatical if it differed from a grammatical string by only one letter rather than more than one letter. That is, subjects appeared to be sensitive to the properties of individual training strings. However, as we shall see later, this finding may reflect not the explicit storage of training strings but the abstraction of a grammar that reflects the idiosyncrasies of the sample of training strings used.

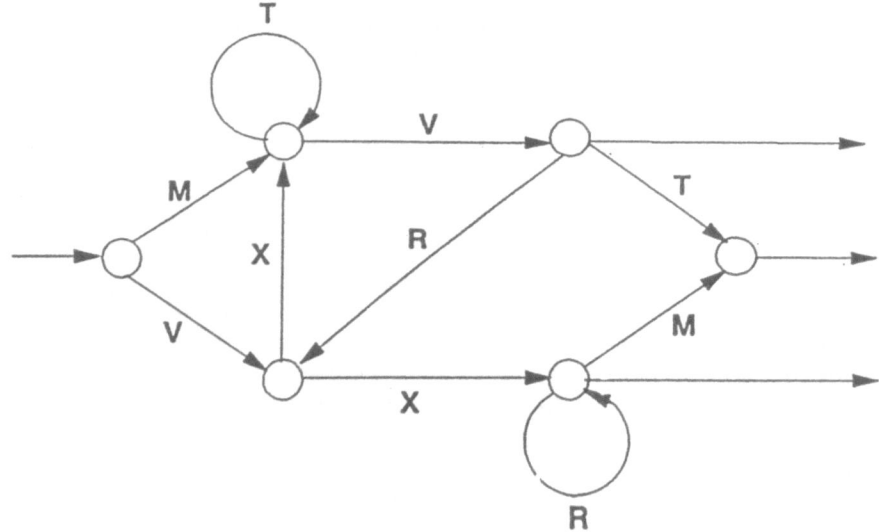

Figure 1. A finite-state grammar. Every time a path is traversed between two nodes a letter is produced.

There is another sense in which knowledge of an artificial grammar can be abstract which has received empirical support: Namely, the knowledge is not strongly tied to specific perceptual features. Reber asked subjects to memorize strings of letters generated by a finite state grammar [11]. The more strings subjects had previously studied, the easier they found it to memorize new strings generated by the grammar. This benefit remained intact even when the new strings were constructed from a different letter set, but the same grammar. That is, subjects could apply their knowledge of the grammar regardless of the letter set. Similarly, Mathews, Buss,

Stanley, Blanchard-Fields, Cho, & Druhan, Brooks and Vokey, Whittlesea and Dorken, Gomez and Schvaneveldt, and Manza and Reber showed that when subjects were exposed to strings constructed from one letter set, they could later classify as grammatical or not strings constructed from another letter set, even though subjects were not told the mapping between the letter sets and were not given feedback on the accuracy of their responses [12, 13, 14, 15, 16]. Altmann, Dienes and Goode, and Manza and Reber extended these findings by showing that subjects trained in one modality (e.g. sequences of tones) can classify in another modality (e.g. sequences of letters), even when the mapping between the domains was arbitrary and no accuracy feedback was given [17, 16].

This paper is primarily concerned with modelling the last type of abstractness, the ability to transfer knowledge of an artificial grammar across different domains. We define two domains as being different if the mapping between the domains is not a priori known to subjects. The process of forming a mapping between two disparate domains is a fundamental aspect of human cognition; indeed, Hofstadter regarded the problem of how analogies are formed as the fundamental problem in cognitive science [18]. We will deal with a small part of that problem: How can an analogy be formed when the domains have already been carved up into the corresponding components and the task is to determine the mapping. Our aim is to provide an account of how that mapping could be established in the context of a plausible model of artificial grammar learning. There are at least three key empirical results that can be used to constrain and test any such model:

i) The amount of transfer to a different domain relative to performance in the same domain. For example, across four experiments, Altmann et al found that, relative to controls, transfer performance was about 70% of same domain performance [17].

ii) Near-far effects. Brooks and Vokey showed that both similarity and grammaticality played a role in determining the tendency to respond 'grammatical' in the different domain [13]. They argued that, just like same-domain performance, transfer could be based on memory for specific training strings. Subjects could make 'abstract analogies' between a test string and a specific training string. For example, MXVVVM and BDCCCB can be seen as similar because of the abstract correspondence of the relations between letters within each string. Consistently, Brooks and Vokey found that in the transfer case near rather than far strings were more likely to be called grammatical regardless of their actual grammatical status. Whether or not this near-far effect is explained as analogy to specific stored exemplars, any model of transfer needs to provide some account of it.

iii) Transfer to stimuli with no repeated elements. Altmann et al showed that transfer occurred to test strings in which every element was different [17]. In this case, abstract analogy cannot be used to produce transfer because the repetition structure is identical in grammatical and nongrammatical strings.

None of the existing computational models of artificial grammar learning can account for these findings. Competitive chunking [19], the exemplar models investigated by

Dienes [20], the classifier system used by Druhan and Mathews [21], and the connectionist models of Cleeremans and McClelland [22] and Dienes [20] all acquire knowledge that is intimately bound up with the perceptual features of the domain in which learning took place. Roussel and Mathews showed how classifier systems (and also exemplar models) could produce transfer by coding the runs structure of a string [23]. However, the finding that, in a new domain, subjects can correctly classify strings with no repeated letters (adjacent or otherwise) indicates that this cannot be the whole story [17]. We will show that a simple extension of the approach used by Cleeremans and McClelland can account for all the transfer phenomena described above [22].

2 Computational models of artificial grammar learning

Cleeremans and McClelland used an architecture introduced by Elman, called a Simple Recurrent Network (SRN), as shown in Figure 2 [22, 5]. The purpose of the SRN is to learn to predict what element should come next in a temporal sequence of elements by means of a learning procedure that is completely local in time. The current element in the sequence is coded by the input units. Activation is passed from the input units and context units through the hidden units to the output units, which attempt to predict the next element in the sequence. At the next step, the input units code the next input, the pattern of activation across the hidden units is directly copied to the context units, and the procedure is repeated in order to predict the next element. At each stage weights are changed using the back propagation algorithm.

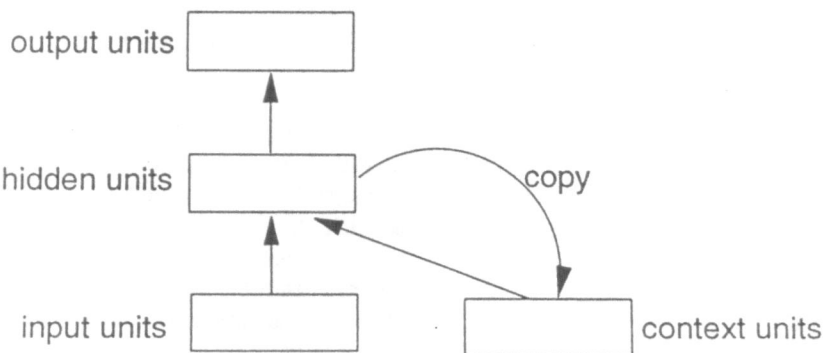

Figure 2. Elman's Simple Recurrent Network [5].

Cleeremans and McClelland used the SRN to model finite state grammar learning in a reaction time task [22]. Subjects saw one of six lights come on, and their task was to press as quickly as possible a corresponding button. Unbeknownst to subjects, the sequence of positions lighting up followed transition probabilities given by a finite state grammar. During the course of 60,000 trials spread over 20 sessions, subjects became progressively more sensitive to the constraints of this grammar: This was shown by subjects becoming relatively faster on trials that were grammatical rather than nongrammatical. Cleeremans and McClelland found that with a version of the SRN, the model could account for 81% of the variance of the subject data.

Dienes showed that the SRN could also be usefully used to simulate subjects learning a finite state grammar by simple exposure to strings of letters [24, 25]. Subjects asked to memorize training strings can later classify new test strings as being grammatical or not. The SRN was exposed to training strings for the same number of epochs as subjects. In the subsequent classification phase, test strings were applied to the network. Because the SRN had learned some of the constraints of the grammar, it predicted successive letters more successfully for grammatical rather than nongrammatical test strings. A classification response was based on the extent to which predicted and actual letters matched. The results showed that the SRN could classify new grammatical and nongrammatical strings at the same level as subjects, and also misclassfied strings in a similar way to subjects (a property that several other models of human learning do not have) [20] .

Cleeremans, D. Servan-Schreiber, and McClelland showed that an SRN could be trained to predict optimally all possible successors of each element of a finite state grammar [26]. This was true even though optimal predictions required more than the immediate predecessor to be encoded. Thus, the activation across the hidden units came to encode the relevant aspects of whole sequences of elements to allow accurate prediction of the next element. On the first trial, the hidden units code information relevant to the first element; so on the second trial when these activations are copied to the context units, the hidden units can come to code information about the previous two elements; and so on, for an indefinite number of elements. Note that this occurs in a procedure that is local in time, in that the complete sequence of elements does not need to be explicitly encoded at once.

The SRN starts by simply learning the bigrams that occur commonly in the training strings, and then building up to trigrams and so on. Cleeremans shows how with extended training the representations that the network develops can, under some conditions, be very close to the abstract representation of the finite-state grammar: each state of the finite state grammar becomes encoded by a pattern (more precisely, by a set of very similar patterns) of activation over the hidden units of the network [27]. Cleeremans argues that although this representation is abstract, in that it has coded relevant underlying dimensions, it is not abstract in that it is intimately bound to the perceptual domain in which the SRN was trained. Cleeremans showed how the SRN could readily transfer to a new task in the same domain where the correct output simply required a different mapping from the hidden units to the output units. But how could the SRN be used to model transfer between different domains, where the input and ouput for one domain can be arbitrarily different from that of another?

3 A connectionist model of transfer

A simple adjustment to the SRN is to add an extra hidden layer (we call this the hidden encoding layer), as shown in Figure 3. One can think of the function of this layer as being to provide an abstract recoding of the domain-dependent coding provided by the input layer. Of course, when people perceive stimuli they also must successively recode the original input. In recognition of the fact that we may wish to consider transfer between two perceptually non-overlapping domains, the input layer has been arbitrarily drawn as two sets of units: One set codes the first domain (the D1 input units) and the other set codes the second domain (the D2 input units). Similarly, the ouput layer can be considered to be one set of D1 output units and a different non-overlapping set of D2 output units.

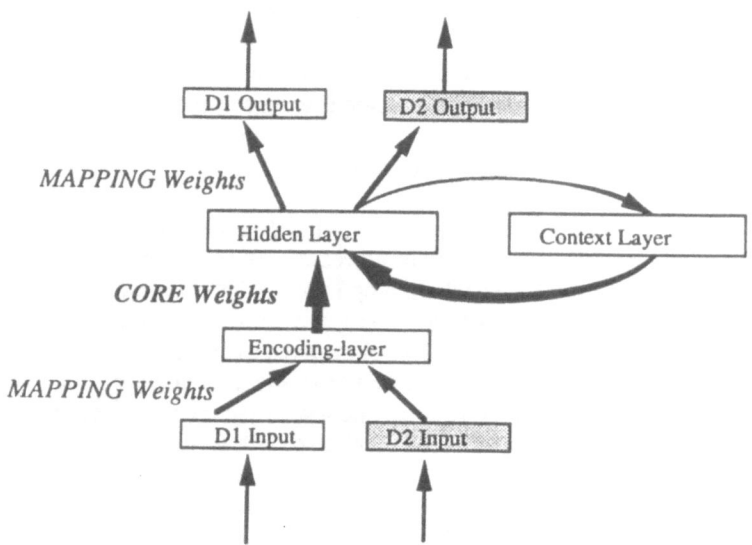

Figure 3. A modified Simple Recurrent Network that can transfer
knowledge across arbitrarily different domains.

3.1 Training

The model can be trained and tested in any one domain just like a normal SRN [24, 5, 26]. Initially, all weights in the network are given small random values by sampling from a uniform distribution with a lower limit of -0.5 and an upper limit of +0.5. Let us say the first domain the model is trained on is melodies (e.g. Altmann et al, experiments one and two), where each melody can be made from combining and repeating any of m tones [17]. The input and output D1 layers would then consist of (m+2) units each, a unit for each tone plus a unit to code the start of a melody and a unit to code the end of a melody. At the beginning of each melody, the 'start' D1 input unit is activated (activation set to 0.9, activation of all other units set to 0.1), and the activation of all units in the context layer is set to 0.5. This pattern of activation is successively recoded by the hidden layers in order to predict the first tone of the melody at the D1 output units (target activation of the unit coding that tone is set to 0.9, the targets for all other units is set to 0.1). Weights are adjusted by backpropagation (with momentum fixed at 0.9, and biases are also adjusted for all output and hidden units). Then the first tone is applied to the D1 input units in order to predict the second tone, and so on. The network is trained on all the melodies subjects were exposed to for the same number as subjects received.

In a subsequent classification phase, test strings are applied to the network (results vary slightly depending on whether the weights are frozen in the test phase or free to vary). If the grammar has been at least partially learned, then the network should more successfully predict successive tones of grammatical rather than nongrammatical melodies when they are applied to D1. Thus, a classification response can be based on the extent to which predicted and actual tones match. Specifically, the procedure used by Dienes was employed [20, 24]. The cosine was found of the angle between the vector of the actual tones in each position of the melody and the vector of predicted tones in each position (if the melody was n tones long, then the predicted and actual vectors would each have length (n+2)*(m+2), with the beginning and end of each melody being coded). The cosine, C, was converted into a probability of saying 'grammatical' by the equation

$$p("g") = 1/(1 + e^{-kC \cdot T})$$

where the parameters k and T were fixed according to the procedure of Dienes [20]. That is, the value of T was set to produce equal numbers of 'grammatical' and 'nongrammatical' resposnes over the whole test phase, and k was set so that the predicted proportion of times the network would classify strings in error twice was 5% higher than the predicted proportion of times the network would classify a string first correctly and then in error (this is a robust property of subjects' data; see Dienes, 1992, and Reber, 1989, for details). The logistic equation for p("g") can be regarded as an example of the Luce choice rule; the logistic has frequently been used for determining classification responses in connectionist networks [28, 29].

3.2 Testing in a new domain

Now let us say the network is tested on a new domain, for example letter strings. The 'core weights' (see Figure 3) are frozen, and only the D2 input and output mapping weights are changed. The freezing could be seen as an approximation to an adaptive learning rate procedure in which the learning rate shrinks as the domain is learned [30]. The D2 mapping weights start at arbitrary random values. The 'start' is activated in the D2 input units, and the network attempts to predict the first letter. Backpropagation changes the mapping weights, and the network then attempts to predict the second letter given the first, and so on. By the time the network has reached the end of the string the mapping weights have changed, so the network can iterate around the string a number of times before moving on to the next test string to make use of mapping information gained from each pass around the string. The number of iterations, I, is a free parameter in the model. As in the same domain case, the network will classify a string as grammatical if on the last iteration around the string it can predict successive letters in the string well, and classification is tested in the same way. The vector of predicted letters is based only on the final iteration around the string.

Because the core weights implicitly encode the structure of the new domain, the network just needs to learn the mapping to and from the abstract encodings formed by the SRN in order to produce transfer.

4 Simulating the key findings

4.1 The amount of transfer to a different domain relative to performance in the same domain

In experiments one and two of Altmann et al (in press), a grammar like that in Figure 1 was used to generate simple melodies or sequences of letters. The letters M, T, V, R, and X were mapped onto the tones c, d, g, e, and a. Subjects were asked to memorize 20 grammatical stimuli - half the subjects memorized strings of letters and the other half memorized melodies. Subjects were exposed to the set of melodies twice in a different random order each time. Subjects were exposed to the letter strings for the same total amount of time. All subjects then classified new test letter strings and new test melodies without feedback. Finally, control groups were run who were trained on randomly generated strings, or who only received the test phase. As shown in Table 1, relative to controls, classification was improved for subjects tested in the same modality as learning (a 9% advantage). Relative to controls, classification was also improved when a switch in modality had occurred (a 6% advantage), even though subjects were not informed of the mapping.

Experiment three of Altmann et al (in press) used a similar design as experiment one, but with a different grammar and different stimuli. Subjects initially listened to sequences of nonsense syllables. The set of nonsense syllables was played to subjects four times in a different random order each time. Next subjects classified sequences of unusual graphics characters. A control group received no training. As shown in Table 1, after a switch in domain classification performance was 11% higher than that of controls.

Table 1 Results from Altmann, Dienes, & Goode [17].

	Controls	Same domain	Different domain
Experiment 1	49 (1)	58 (1)	55 (1)
Experiment 3	47 (2)	--	58 (2)

Note Scores are percentage correct classification. Standard deviations appear in parentheses.

The model was trained on the same training stimuli as people for the same number of epochs (i.e. two epochs for experiment one and four epochs for experiment three). For each set of parameter values an average of 50 runs of the model was calculated, where each run used a different random seed for setting the initial weight values. Figure 4 shows the advantage of training the core weights on the same grammar (The 'transfer' data) as opposed to a different grammar (the 'control' data) to that of the test

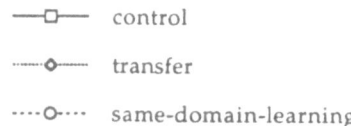

Classification
Performance

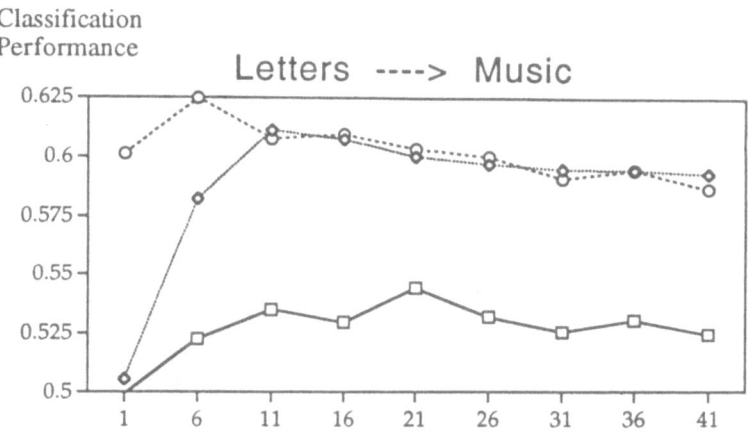

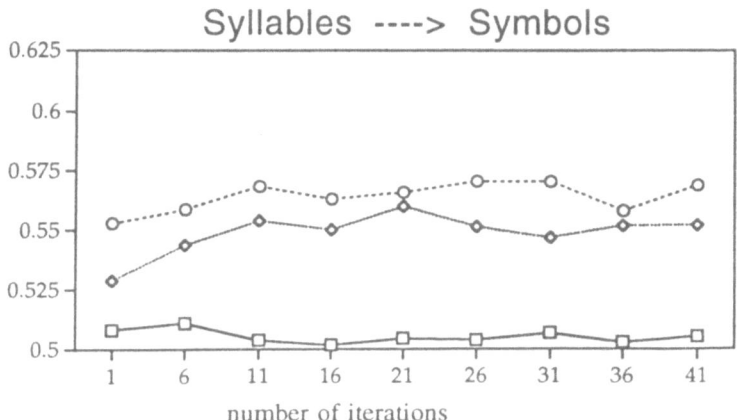

number of iterations

Figure 4. Simulations of Experiments 1 and 3 of Altmann et al.[17].

stimuli. Note that the model could achieve the same classification performance as subjects in the control, same domain, and transfer groups. If we take the same domain performance to define the maximum amount of cross domain transfer that could in principle be shown, then the model, like people, can perform in transfer at 70% or more of the maximum possible (see Figure 4).

This pattern of results was relatively insensitive to learning rate over the range 0.5 to 1.5, and relatively insensitive to the number of hidden units over the range 7 to 35.

4.2 Near-far effects

Brooks and Vokey showed that both similarity and grammaticality played a role in determining the tendency to respond 'grammatical' in both the same and different domains [13]. Figure 5 shows the mean proportion of grammatical responses to test stimuli cross classified by grammaticality and whether they are near (i.e. only one letter different to a training string) or far (i.e. at least two letters different to any training string).

The model was trained for 10 epochs on the same stimuli as subjects learned. (Subjects were not trained for a fixed number of epochs.) Figure 6 shows the proportion of grammatical responses to the test stimuli in the same and different domains. Consider first the same domain. The model reproduces the effects of similarity and grammaticality of the same magnitude as subjects. Note that whenever the subject showed any learning it also showed a specific similarity effect. So the existence of a similarity effect with these materials is a falsifiable prediction of the model. The similarity effect does not occur because the model has simply explicitly memorized the training strings; as Cleeremans has shown, the SRN acquires abstract knowledge of the training stimuli [27]. However, it is sensitive to the peculiarities of sample of strings on which it has been trained. The model also reproduces the effects of similarity and grammaticality of the same magnitude as subjects in the different domain. Although the model may well be sensitive to the repetition structure of stimuli, the effect of similarity in the different domain is not because the model simply implements the 'abstract analogy' strategy suggested by Brooks and Vokey [13]. As shown in the next section, the model can correctly classify stimuli with no repetition structure.

The pattern of results as shown in Figure 6 is relatively insensitive to learning rate at least over the range 0.7 to 1.3, and to numbers of hidden units at least over the range 15 to 25.

4.3 Transfer to stimuli with no repeated elements

Altmann et al showed that transfer occurred to test strings in which every element was different [17]. Specifically, 34 of the 80 test strings used in experiment three had no repetition structure, but about half of these strings were grammatical and half nongrammatical. The difference in classification performance of these strings

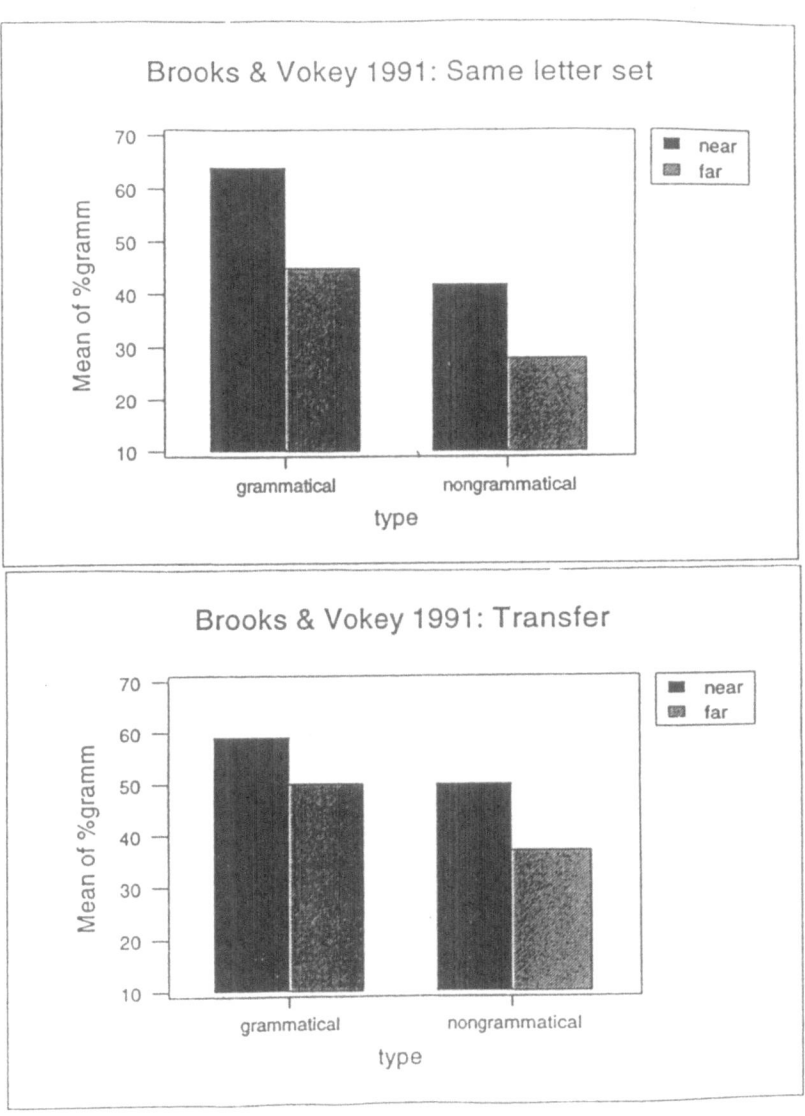

Figure 5. The experimental findings of Brooks and Vokey [13].

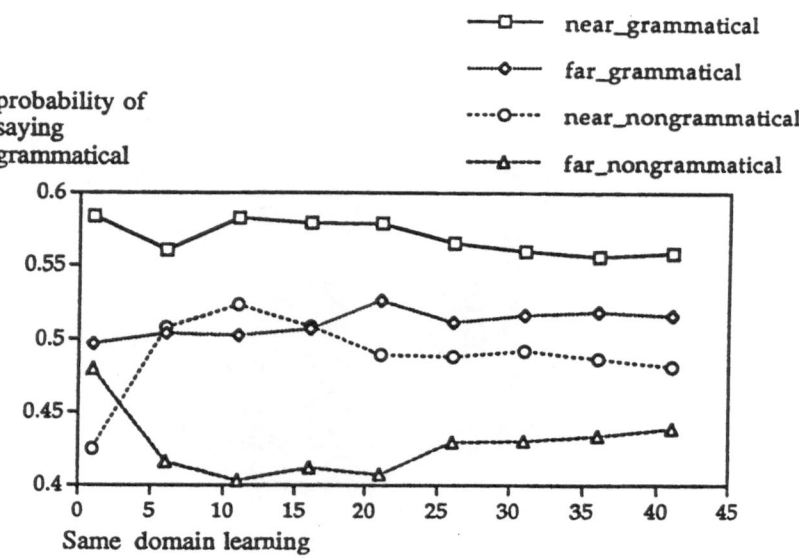

Same domain learning

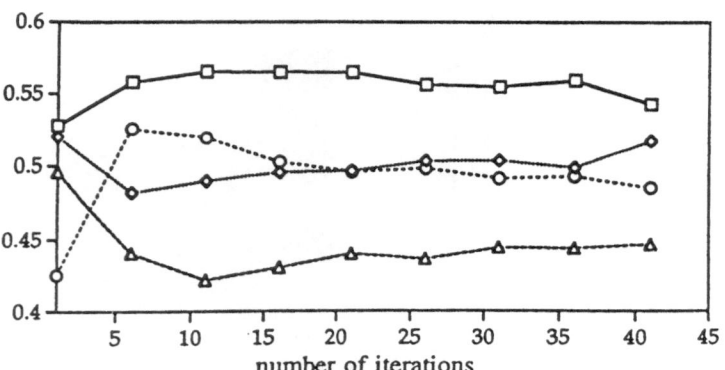

number of iterations

Transfer learning

Figure 6. Simulations of the findings of Brooks and Vokey [13].

between transfer and control subjects was 9%. Over a range of parameters, the model could consistently produce an advantage of the transfer over the control group of about 6%. As the model classifies test stimuli it induces a correct mapping in the mapping weights, enabling the network to classify stimuli with no repetition structure. Note that whenever the model showed learning, it also classified at above chance rates stimuli with no repetition structure.

5 Conclusion

The purpose of this paper has been to explore the type of model that could apply knowledge of the structure of one domain to another in the same way as people. Simply adding an extra layer to the SRN enables it to transfer knowledge of a finite state grammar between two different domains, to be responsive to both the grammaticality of the test strings and their similarity to training strings, and to classify test strings with no repetition structure, all to the same degree as subjects. The success of the SRN in modelling this data illustrates how abstract knowledge of an artificial grammar can be understood simply in terms of sensitivity to statistical structure. It also illustrates how knowledge of artificial grammars can be seen as implicit (see Dienes & Perner, for a discussion of the relation between connectionist networks and implicit knowledge) [3].

References

1. Reber A.S. Implicit learning and tactic knowledge. Journal of Experimental Psychology: General 1989; 118: 219-235.
2. Reber, AS. Implicit learning of artificial grammars. Journal of Verbal Learning and Verbal Behaviour 1967; 6: 855-863.
3. Dienes Z. & Perner J. Implicit knowledge in people and connectionist networks. In G. Underwood (Ed) Implicit cognition. Oxford University Press. (in press)
4. Shanks DR. & St. John MF. Characteristics of dissociable human learning systems. Behavioural and Brain Sciences.(in press)
5. Elman J. Finding structure in time. Cognitive Science 1990; 14: 179-211.
6. Mathews RC. Abstractness of implicit grammar knowledge Comments on Perruchet and Pacteau's analysis of synthetic grammar learning. Journal of Experimental Psychology: General 1990; 119: 412-416.
7. Mathews RC. The forgetting algorithm: How fragmentary knowledge of exemplars can abstact knowledge. Journal of Experimental Psychology: General 1991; 120: 117-119.
8. Brooks L. Nonanalytic concept formation and memory for instances. In E. Rosch & B.B. Lloyd (Eds.) Cognition and Categorization. Hillsdale, N.J.: Erlbaum, Hillsdale, N.J., 1978, pp.169-211.
9. Vokey JR. & Brooks LR. Salience of item knowledge in learning artificial grammars. Journal of Experimental Psychology: Learning, Memory, and Cognition 1992; 18: 328-344.
10. McAndrews MP. & Moscovitch M. Rule-based and exemplar-based classification in artificial grammar learning. Memory & Cognition 1985; 13:

469-475.

11. Reber AS. Transfer of syntactic structures in synthetic languages. Journal of Experimental Psychoogy 1969; 81: 115-119.

12. Mathews RC., Buss RR., Stanley WB., Blanchard-Fields F. Cho JR. & Druhan B. The role of implicit and explicit processes in learning from examples: A synergistic effect. Journal of Experimental Psychology: Learning, Memory, and Cognition 1989; 15: 1083-1100.

13. Brooks LR. & Vokey JR. Abstract analogies and abstracted grammars: Comments on Reber (1989) and Mathews et al. (1989). Journal of Experimental Psychology: General 1991; 120: 316-323.

14. Whittlesea BWA. & Dorken MD. Incidentally, things in general are particularly determined: An episodic-processing account of implicit learning. Journal of Experimental Psychology: General 1993; 122: 227-248.

15. Gomez RL. & Schvaneveldt RW. What is learned from artificial grammars? Transfer tests of simple association. Journal of Experimental Psychology: Learning, Memory, and Cognition 1994; 20: 396-410.

16. Manza L. & Reber AS. Representation of tacit knowledge: Transfer across stimulus forms and modalities. Unpublished manuscript, 1994.

17. Altmann GTM., Dienes Z. & Goode A. On the modality independence of implicitly learned grammatical knowledge. Journal of Experimental Psychology: Learning, Memory, and Cognition (in press).

18. Hofstadter DR. Metamagical themas: Questing for the essence of mind and pattern. Middlesex: Penguin, Middlesex, 1985.

19. Servan-Schreiber E. & Anderson J.R. Learning artificial grammars with competitive chunking. Journal of Experimental Psychology: Learning, Memory, and Cognition 1990; 16: 592-608.

20. Dienes Z. Connectionist and memory array models of artificial grammar learning. Cognitive Science 1992; 16: 41-79.

21. Druhan B. & Mathews R. THIYOS: A classifier system model of implicit knowledge of artificial grammars. Proceedings of the Eleventh Annual Conference of the Cognitive Science Society. NY: Lawrence Erlbaum, New York, 1989.

22. Cleeremans A. & McClelland JL. Learning the structure of event sequences. Journal of Experimental Psychology: General 1991; 120: 235-253.

23. Roussel L. & Mathews R. THIYOS: A synthesis of rule-based and exemplar-based models of implicit learning (submitted).

24. Dienes Z. Computational models of implicit learning. In DC. Berry & Z. Dienes, Implicit learning: theoretical and empirical issues. Lawrence Erlbaum, Hove, 1993.

25. Berry DC. & Dienes Z. Implicit learning: Theoretical and empirical issues. Lawrence Erlbaum, Hove, 1993.

26. Cleeremans A., Servan-Schreiber D. & McClelland, JL. Finite state automata and simple recurrent networks. Neural Computation 1989; 1: 372-381.

27. Cleeremans A. Mechanisms of implicit learning: Connectionist models of sequence processing. MIT Press, Cambridge, 1993.

28. Gluck MA. & Bower GH. Evaluating an adaptive network of human learning. Journal of Memory and Language 1988; 27: 166-195.

29. McClelland JL. & Elman J. Interactive processes in speech perception: The TRACE model. In JL. McClelland & DE. Rumelhart (eds.), Parallel distributed processing. Explorations in the microstructure of cognition. Cambridge, MA: MIT Press, Cambridge, 1986.
30. Jacobs R. Increased rates of convergence through learning rate adaptation. Neural Networks 1988; 1: 295-308.

Modelling Reaction Times

John A. Bullinaria

Department of Psychology, University of Edinburgh
7 George Square, Edinburgh EH8 9JZ, UK

Abstract

We discuss the simulation of reaction times in connectionist systems. The obvious way to do this involves thinking in terms of neural activations building up towards some threshold in cascaded systems, but it has also been suggested that the output activation error scores in standard back-propagation networks should also be correlated with response times. The idea is that in the more realistic cascaded processing systems, the clearer the outputs (i.e. the lower the errors), the lower the time taken to reach the threshold. If this is correct and we can consider our simple feedforward networks to be reasonable approximations to these cascaded systems, then we have an easy way to simulate reaction times. However, the validity of this has been questioned. I will discuss these issues in some detail, suggest a more principled way of extracting simulated reaction times from back-propagation networks and show how this relates to the corresponding cascaded networks.

1 Introduction

Often when connectionist modelling we wish to simulate reaction times, i.e. the time taken to produce an output after being given an input. These may take many forms: naming latencies in models of reading, times taken to recognise particular sounds in models of hearing, and so on. The obvious way to model these involves thinking in terms of neural activations building up towards a threshold in some form of cascaded system [1-6]. The basic assumption is that the response depends on a series of sub-processes and that activation cascades through these levels eventually activating the appropriate output units. Any activation at one level will feed through to the next at a rate depending on the connection weights (i.e. synaptic strengths) between the levels: there is no need for processing at one level to be completed before the next begins [1].

The natural system of equations to describe such a build-up of activation is:

$$Out_i(t) = Sigmoid(Sum_i(t)) \tag{1}$$

$$Sum_i(t) = Sum_i(t-1) + \sum_j w_{ij} Prev_j(t) - \lambda Sum_i(t-1) \tag{2}$$

so that at each timeslice t the output $Out_i(t)$ of each unit is the sigmoid of the sum of the inputs into that unit at that time. The sum of inputs $Sum_i(t)$ is the existing sum at time $t-1$ plus the additional weight w_{ij} dependent contribution fed through from the activation $Prev_j(t)$ of the previous layer and a natural exponential decay of activation depending on some decay constant λ. This can be rewritten as:

$$Sum_i(t) = \lambda \sum_j \frac{w_{ij}}{\lambda} Prev_j(t) + (1 - \lambda)Sum_i(t-1) \qquad (3)$$

which with $\lambda \to \tau$ and $w/\lambda \to w$ corresponds exactly with the equivalent formulation of Cohen et al. [5]. In the asymptotic state $Sum_i(t) = Sum_i(t-1)$ so:

$$Sum_i(t) = \sum_j \frac{w_{ij}}{\lambda} Prev_j(t). \qquad (4)$$

It follows that the asymptotic state of our cascaded network is the same as a standard feedforward network with weights w/λ. Assuming the right way to train the cascading network is to adjust the weights so that it produces the right asymptotic output for each input, we can obtain exactly the same results by training the standard feedforward network in the conventional manner, e.g. by back-propagation. It would seem that any back-propagation network can be trivially re-interpreted as a cascaded network and we can easily extract response times from it in this manner.

If our neural network consists only of input and output units with no hidden layers, the process is easy to analyse (for an application see [6]). $Prev_j(t)$ becomes the constant input and the differential equation (2) is easily solved to give:

$$Sum_i(t) = \sum_j \frac{w_{ij}}{\lambda} Input_j + \left(Sum_i(0) - \sum_j \frac{w_{ij}}{\lambda} Input_j \right) e^{-\lambda t}. \qquad (5)$$

The initial condition $Sum_i(0)$ may be some resting or reset value (e.g. zero) or simply that value corresponding to the previous input configuration. We shall discuss this further in the section on priming effects. Figure 1 shows typical plots of $Sum_i(t)$ for four output units with different asymptotic activations. The unit which reaches some threshold activation first may be deemed to indicate the correct network output and the time taken to reach that threshold is the reaction time. It is therefore easy to read off response times from graphs such as these and, since the curves never cross, we can tell almost immediately which output unit is going to reach the threshold first.

Once we start introducing hidden layers to give proper cascaded networks with non-linear activation functions, everything becomes much more complicated (cf. [1]). The previous layer activation $Prev_j(t)$ is no longer a constant input but a varying hidden layer activation. As we can see from Figure 1, the activations of hidden units can change radically over time and hence the rate at which the various output activations build up can have complicated time and unit dependence. It becomes possible for output activation curves to cross each other and we have to be

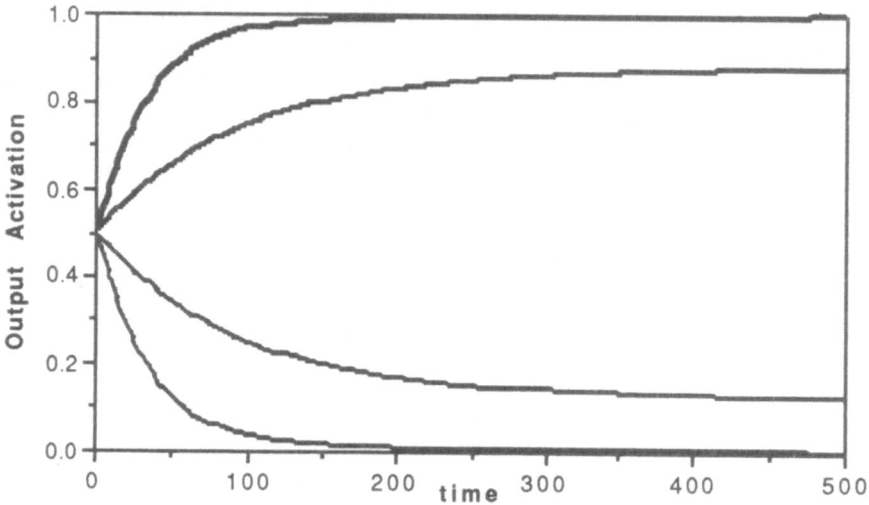

Figure 1: The build up of the Sum in the simplest cascade network with constant inputs and no hidden layer.

very careful about choosing thresholds if the outputs of our cascaded system are to agree with the feedforward network on which it is based. Rather than attempting to derive general solutions to the differential equations here, we shall illustrate the kind of things that can happen by looking at a specific reasonably realistic model.

2 Naming Latencies in a Reading Model

The system we shall look at in detail is a simple model of reading aloud, i.e. text to phoneme conversion, in which the response times are naming latencies. Most of what we say, though, will be applicable quite generally. A complete reading system might look something like shown in Figure 2. Here we will only attempt to model the section from the "letter buffer" to the "phoneme buffer". This sub-system has been described in some detail by Bullinaria [7]. It is basically a NETtalk style model [8] with a modified learning algorithm that obviates the need to pre-process the training data. It uses simple localist representations for its inputs (i.e. one unit for each of 26 letters) and outputs (i.e. one unit for each of 38 phonemes including a phonemic null). The complete input layer consists of a moving window of 13 blocks of 26 units and the output layer consists of two blocks of 38 units. The most highly activated unit of each output block gives the phonemes corresponding to the letter in the central input block in the context of the letters in the other input blocks. We shall concentrate on one such network with a single hidden layer of 300 units trained by back-propagation on the extended Seidenberg & McClelland [9] corpus of 2998 mono-syllabic words. This network achieved 100% performance on its training data and 98.8% generalization performance on a standard set of non-words.

Following the discussion above, it is easy to treat this feedforward network as a cascaded system and plot the build up of output activations for each input letter. To

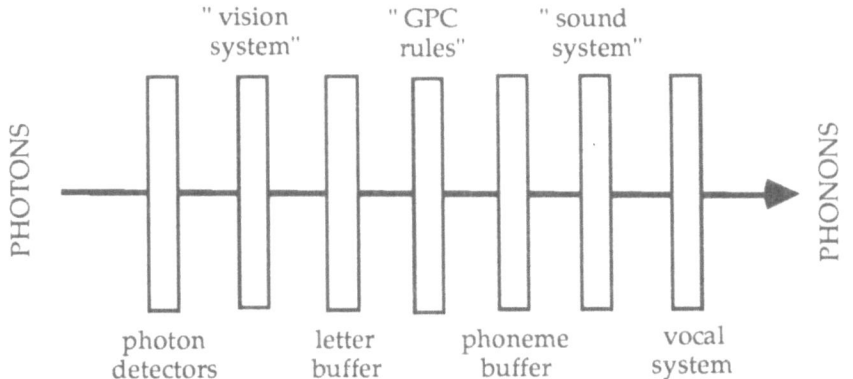

Figure 2: Possible levels in a cascaded system of reading aloud.

illustrate the problems involved in choosing the appropriate thresholds we present a few well chosen examples. The first graph of Figure 3 shows the build-up of output activations for the 'd' in 'dog'. This is what typically happens for regular letter to phoneme correspondences. Initially all the outputs fall until the appropriate hidden unit activations build up and then the correct phoneme output activation rises to its high value and all the others decay to their low values. The second graph of Figure 3 shows what can happen for a less regular case. The 'oo' in 'spook' is pronounced as an exception to a sub-rule and also occurs infrequently in the training data. Three things complicate this case: First, the asymptotic winner /U/ doesn't take the lead until after about 150 time slices; second, it has a relatively close rival /u/; and third, the final activation is relatively low. Indeed, it is quite possible for the maximum asymptotic activation to be less than the starting activation.

Given the complications introduced by the hidden layer, how do we now read off the reaction times? We cannot simply impose a reasonably high threshold and wait for the first output unit to reach that threshold because there is no guarantee that any unit will reach that threshold. If we impose a too low threshold it is possible that the wrong output unit will reach it first. Similarly, we cannot look for the first unit to start increasing again after the initial decrease because this does not necessarily happen for the right unit. Finally, since all the output activations will generally get multiplied by different weights in the next layer, it is not clear that imposing equal thresholds for all units makes sense anyway.

In a complete cascaded system it is the integrated activations of each layer that power the next, so it seems reasonable that the threshold we should be imposing is not on the activations themselves but on the time integrals of these activations. Figure 4 shows the time integrated activations corresponding to the graphs of Figure 3. We note several important features: first, since the activations are all greater than zero, any output will eventually reach any threshold however low the activation is; second, the complicated effects that occur at small times will contribute to the time taken to reach the threshold but do not interfere with a straightforward implementation of the threshold; and third, we can see how regularity effects could arise in the response times. Note that, even if this is not *technically* the right thing

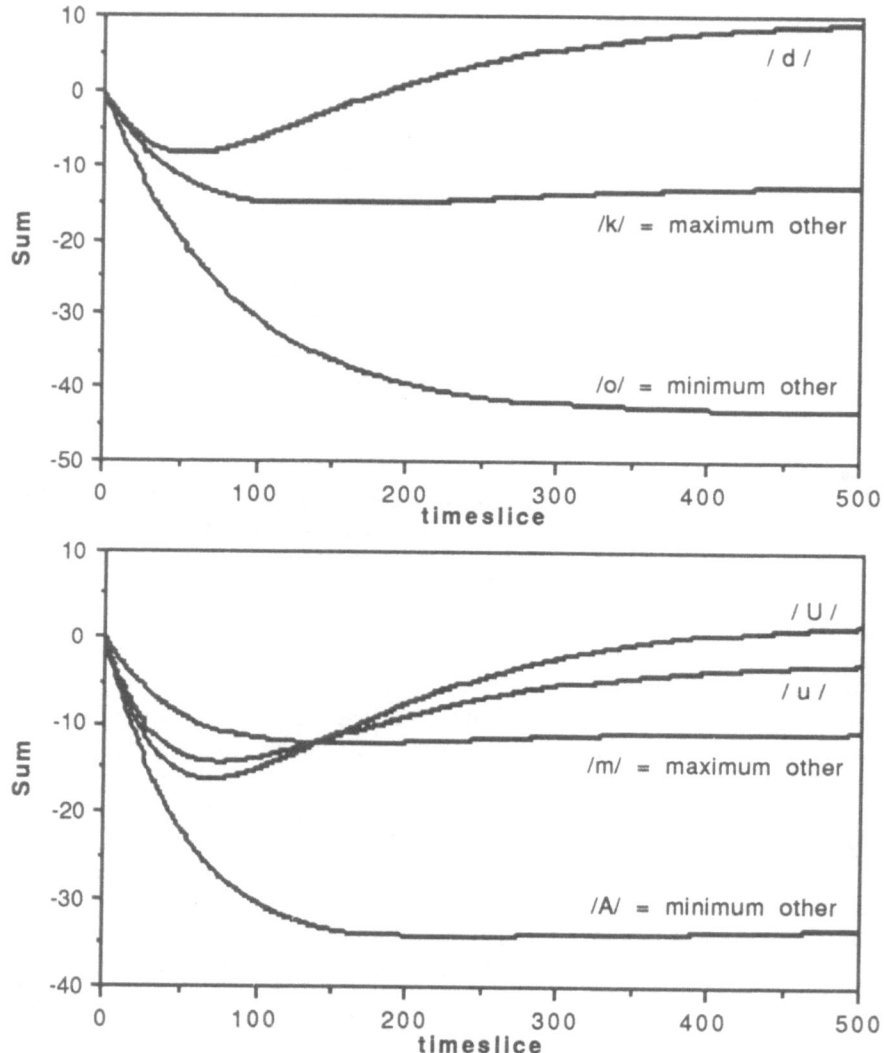

Figure 3: The build up of Sum in the reading model for the regular 'd' in 'dog' and the irregular 'oo' in 'spook'.

to do, we see from the graphs that it does give a much fairer and unambiguous indication of the time taken to process each letter.

To simulate response times for whole words we have to decide if they should be the sum of the response times for the individual letters or if we should assume that parallel processing takes place and the overall response time is that taken for the slowest letter. Experimental evidence suggests that (for mono-syllabic words at least) we should take the naming latency to be given by the longest response time of the constituent letters (i.e. otherwise our simulated response times bear little relation to human naming latencies). In a complete system we will clearly have to worry

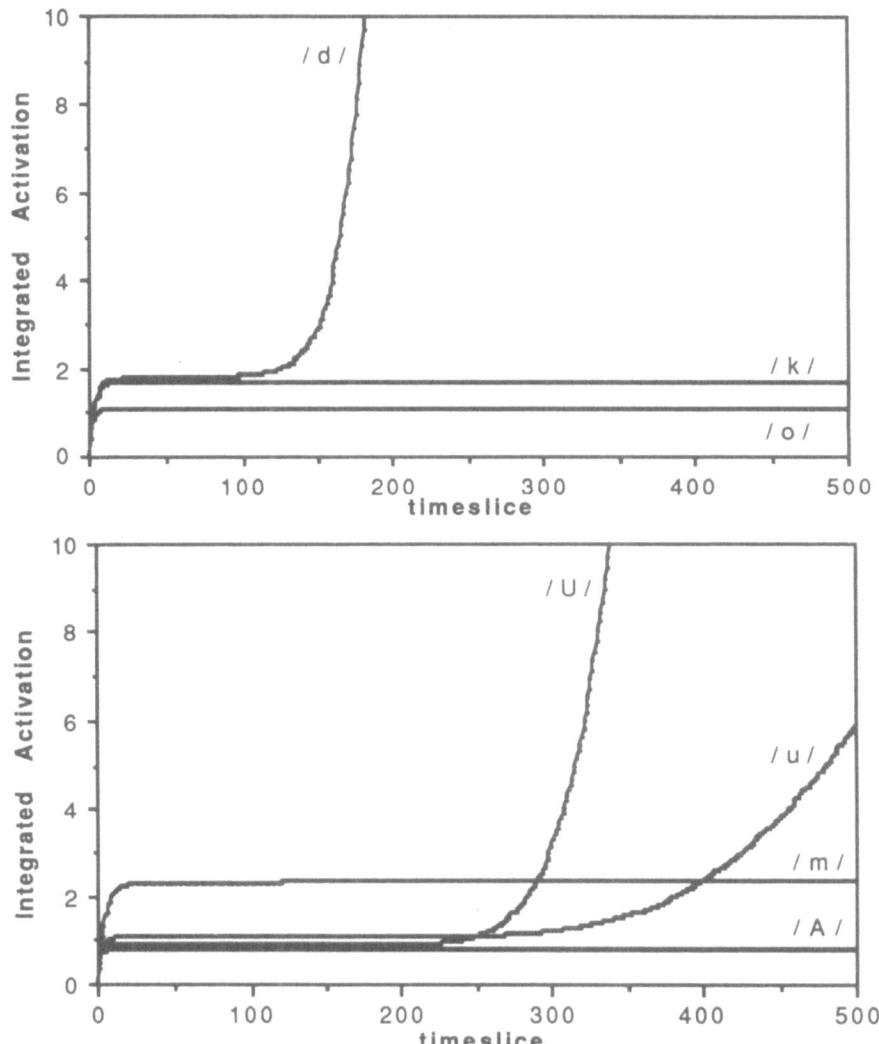

*Figure 4: The build up of integrated output activation in the reading model
for the regular 'd' in 'dog' and the irregular 'oo' in 'spook'.*

about the details of this parallelization process and it will be quite likely that
different phonemes will require different integrated activations to drive the process
to completion. However, the best we can do here is assign each phoneme unit the
same simple threshold.

Applying this cascading procedure to the reading model we can obtain naming
latencies for all the words in the training data. The timescale λ and the threshold
have to be chosen carefully: The timescale must be small enough that the stepwise
build-up of activation is a reasonable approximation to a realistic continuous build-
up, yet large enough that the simulations do not take too long to run. The threshold

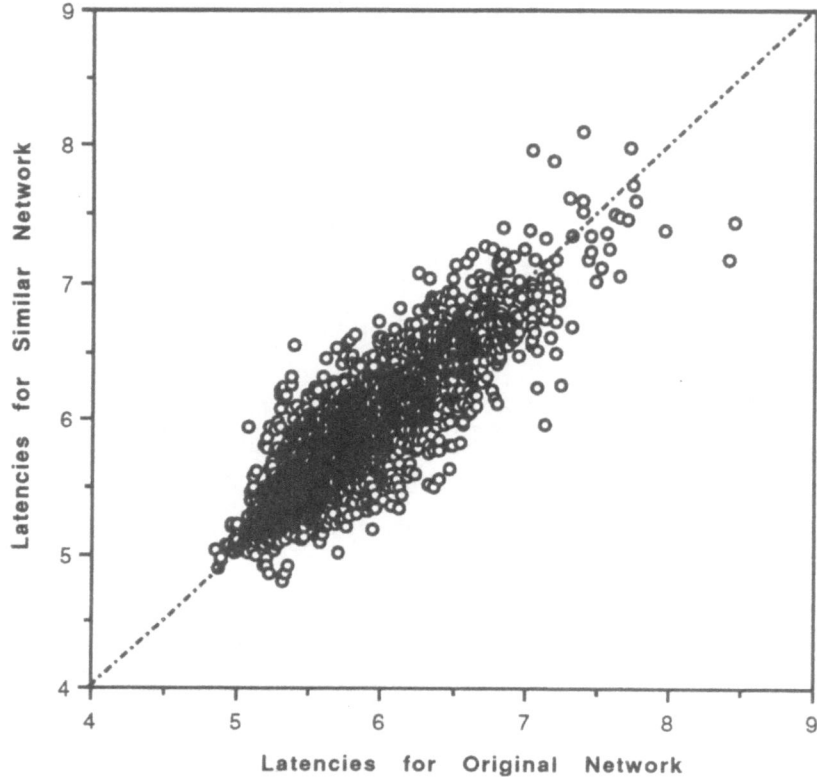

Figure 5: Variation in naming latencies between different networks.

must be small enough that low activation units do not take an unreasonably long time to reach it, yet not too low that the wrong unit reaches it first (e.g. the /m/ in Figure 4). We found that a timescale of $\lambda = 0.2$ and an integrated activation threshold of 20 were appropriate for our model. The output phonemes produced for each input word corresponded exactly to the training data and we obtained a reasonably realistic distribution of naming latencies that could be compared with the experimental results for humans. These latencies correlated extremely well (Pearson $r = 0.9998$, Spearman $\rho = 0.9996$) with those obtained using $\lambda = 0.1$ instead, indicating that $\lambda = 0.2$ was an acceptable value to use.

For both the Taraban & McClelland [10] and Waters & Seidenberg [11] exception words and controls we found a significant regularity effect as observed in humans ($F = 175.5$, $p < 0.0001$ and $F = 52.9$, $p < 0.0001$) but no frequency nor interaction effects ($p > 0.1$). A separate t-test on the Waters & Seidenberg exception words did show a frequency effect ($t = 3.6$, $p < 0.0019$). The lack of significant frequency effects, apart from this, is in conflict with experiment but easily understood. To get the network to train in a reasonable time we had to logarithmically compress the word frequency distribution. There is good reason to suppose that training with a more realistic frequency distribution will produce a more realistic frequency effect in the naming latencies.

We might ask if the simulated reaction times we obtain are consistent across networks. Figure 5 shows how the latencies compare for the training words for two identical networks starting with different random initial weights and having the words presented in different random orders. We see that there is a reasonable correlation ($r = 0.87$, $\rho = 0.85$) but find a spread similar to the inter-subject differences found in humans.

The situation is slightly more complicated for non-word data. The network actually generalizes quite well, but still the outputs are rather marginal with very low activations for some non-words (i.e. those based on exceptional words). This results in some unrealistically large simulated naming latencies. We can hope that these problems will go away in more realistic networks that incorporate basins of attraction in the output layer or simple lateral inhibition between output units. In the meantime, we simply imposed a time cut-off (of 10) on the troublesome non-words. For the Glushko [12] non-words and controls we then found a significant non-word effect ($F = 65.5$, $p < 0.0001$), regularity effect ($F = 15.7$, $p = 0.0011$) and interaction effect ($F = 9.6$, $p = 0.0023$). However, unlike in humans, we found no significant difference between the regular words and regular non-words ($t = 0.80$, $p = 0.43$) and no pseudohomophone effect ($t = 0.73$, $p = 0.46$).

The various discrepancies between the network's naming latencies and those found in humans were discussed in some detail by Bullinaria [7]. These problems, together with problems modelling certain types of dyslexia, led us to conclude that the model still required the incorporation of an additional semantic route between the text and phonemes. Activation flowing into the output units via this route will clearly have an effect on the simulated naming latencies. We also expect reaction time effects to arise from the other levels in Figure 2, e.g. common strings of letters may be easier to recognise than others, common strings of phonemes may be easier to pronounce. It is therefore premature to expect our simulated naming latencies to be totally realistic at this stage, but our results so far give us good reason to expect this approach will work well given more realistic back-propagation networks.

3 Priming Effects

Thus far we have taken all the $Sum_i(0)$ to be zero. In this section we consider what happens if they are non-zero, i.e. the system is primed.

The most natural values to use for the $Sum_i(0)$ are whatever values the $Sum_i(t)$ happen to be due to the previous letter processed. This is likely to result in the well known priming effects found in humans (e.g. [13, 14]). An obvious potential problem with this is that, if the previous output is strongly activated (e.g. as is the /d/ in 'dog'), then we need that activation to be reduced sufficiently quickly once the phoneme is spoken lest it triggers the output mechanism again and produces a form of stutter. This can easily be achieved for our model by choosing the threshold sufficiently high. Another problem is that, if we are assuming a certain amount of parallel processing, it is not immediately obvious which should be taken as the previous letter to be processed. Table 1 shows the effect of various priming letters on the speed of output for the 'oo' in 'spook'. We see that priming with the word 'spook' itself and the closely related word 'spoof' both produce a significant

Prime	time	Sum(0)	time
spoof	3.87	+2.0	8.10
spook	4.12	+1.0	7.79
food	4.46	0.0	7.39
bed	5.54	−1.0	6.88
spot	5.80	−2.0	6.23
book	6.24	−3.0	5.58
dog	6.47	−4.0	5.18
tip	6.79	−5.0	5.02
tip	7.15	−6.0	4.97
tip	7.23	−7.0	5.01
-	7.39	−8.0	5.09
bat	7.42	−9.0	5.17
bat	7.74	−10.0	5.25

Table 1: The effect on the speed of phoneme production for the 'oo' in 'spook' of priming with particular previous inputs and various values of Sum(0).

reduction in the naming latency. Priming with certain unrelated words can produce an increased latency. Interestingly, many apparently unrelated words can also reduce the latency.

Choosing all the $Sum_i(0)$ to be zero would seem to be a fair way to average over these priming effects. However, Table 1 also shows that setting all the $Sum_i(0)$'s to be uniformly less than zero can also improve the naming latencies. (This corresponds to resetting all the $Out_i(0)$ to some low value after each output is produced.) The precise value that minimises the naming latency varies from word to word, but setting $Sum_i(0) = -3.0$ gives a good overall reduction. Figure 6 illustrates how this occurs. It is feasible that such a reset mechanism may also be an efficient way for real brains to operate as well. This introduces yet another free parameter into our simulations. If changing this parameter simply re-scales the reaction times, it would not pose too much of a problem. Figure 7 shows that, although the speed up is far from uniform, there is a some degree of correlation ($r = 0.79$, $\rho = 0.74$), the type effect found previously still remains ($F = 59.9$, $p < 0.0001$ and $F = 13.2$, $p < 0.001$) and it introduces no additional frequency nor interaction effects ($p > 0.1$). If we allow the network to be primed by the previous letter in each word, the correlation is poorer ($r = 0.73$, $\rho = 0.67$) which is not surprising since that letter is essentially random.

Throughout our discussion so far we have treated the network processing unit thresholds as just another network weight ($\theta_i = - w_{io}/\lambda$) and when we set $Sum_i(0)$ we are effectively balancing the sum of weighted inputs against this threshold. One could argue that it would be more reasonable to take the threshold out of the $Sum()$ and into the $Sigmoid()$. This is equivalent to using $Sum_i(0) = -\theta_i$ instead of 0 in our existing formulation. In fact, for our model, the thresholds are all quite small (mean output threshold 0.9, s.d. 1.0; mean hidden unit threshold 1.3, s.d. 0.6), so the new naming latencies correlate quite well with the old ($r = 0.93$, $\rho = 0.91$). A related

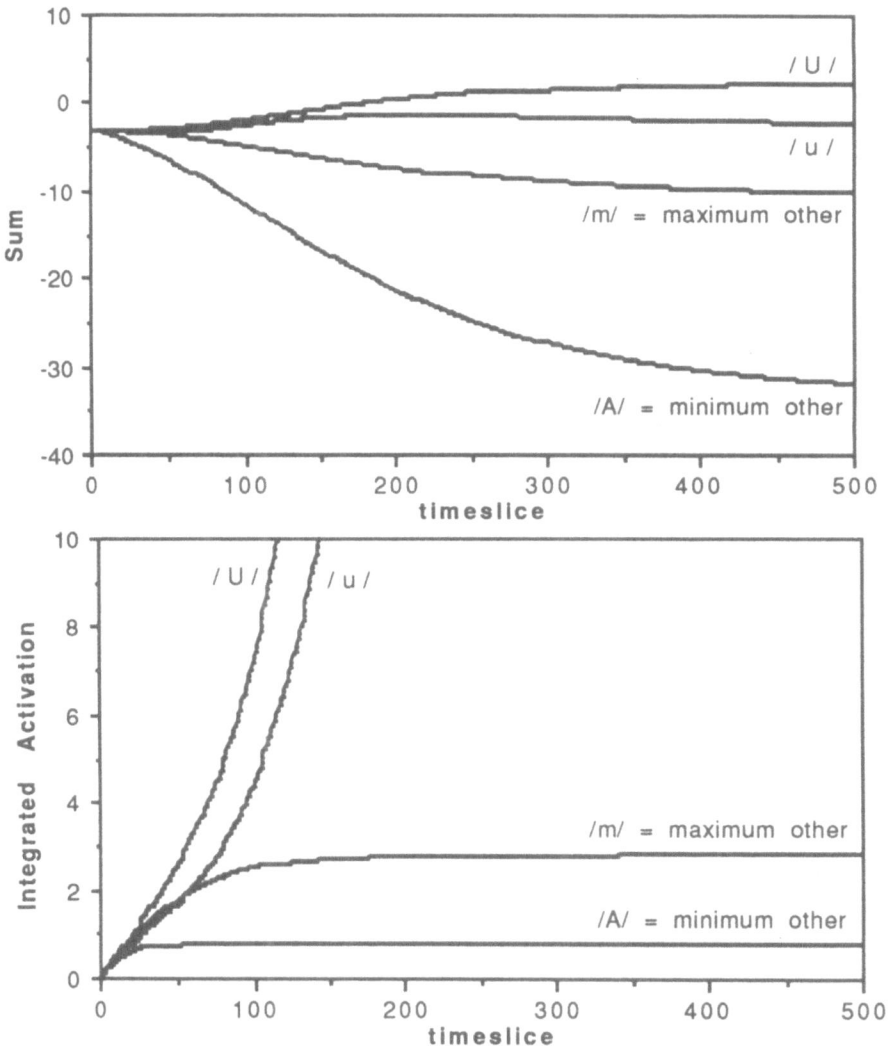

Figure 6: The changes in performance on the 'oo' in 'spook' brought about by having Sum(0) = –3.0 rather than 0.0 .

variation, that also needs to be checked, takes into account the fact that in the natural resting state the hidden unit activations are non-zero and hence we really have non-zero inputs into the output units. Incorporating this into our model we get yet another set of naming latencies that correlate well with both our new set (r = 0.98, ρ = 0.98) and the original set (r = 0.96, ρ = 0.95).

A final point that may have a bearing here, is that real brains operate with limited precision and so it is quite possible that very high and low $Sum_i(t)$'s will never get learnt. This will clearly be yet another effect on the speed of response when the input is changed.

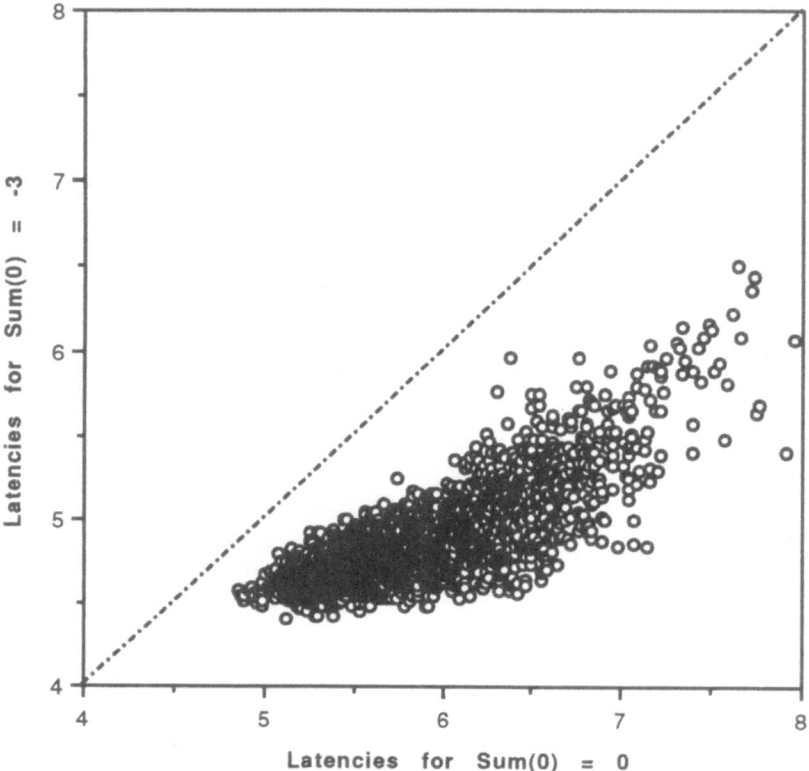

Figure 7: Comparison of simulated naming latencies for two values of Sum(0).

In summary then, we have seen how various priming effects can be modelled easily in this kind of cascaded system and that resetting all units to the same negative *Sum(0)* can result in a general overall improvement in speed. The results from numerous plausible variations of the basic approach are all quite highly correlated and all result in the significant type effects found in humans.

4 Rushing and Other Detrimental Effects

Another well known effect found in human readers is that they make more mistakes when they are required to operate under time constraints, i.e. when they are rushed. In fact, such speed-accuracy trade-offs occur quite generally [15, 1]. In our model, this corresponds to setting the threshold to a lower value so that the outputs are produced more quickly than normal. Figure 8 shows that for sufficiently large thresholds we have a simple linear relation between the thresholds and mean reaction times. Using successively smaller thresholds eventually introduces errors into the network outputs. Fortunately, Figure 8 also shows that our speed-accuracy trade-off curve compares well with those of humans [1, 15]. The first errors are generally regularized vowels followed by wrong vowels and other regularizations.

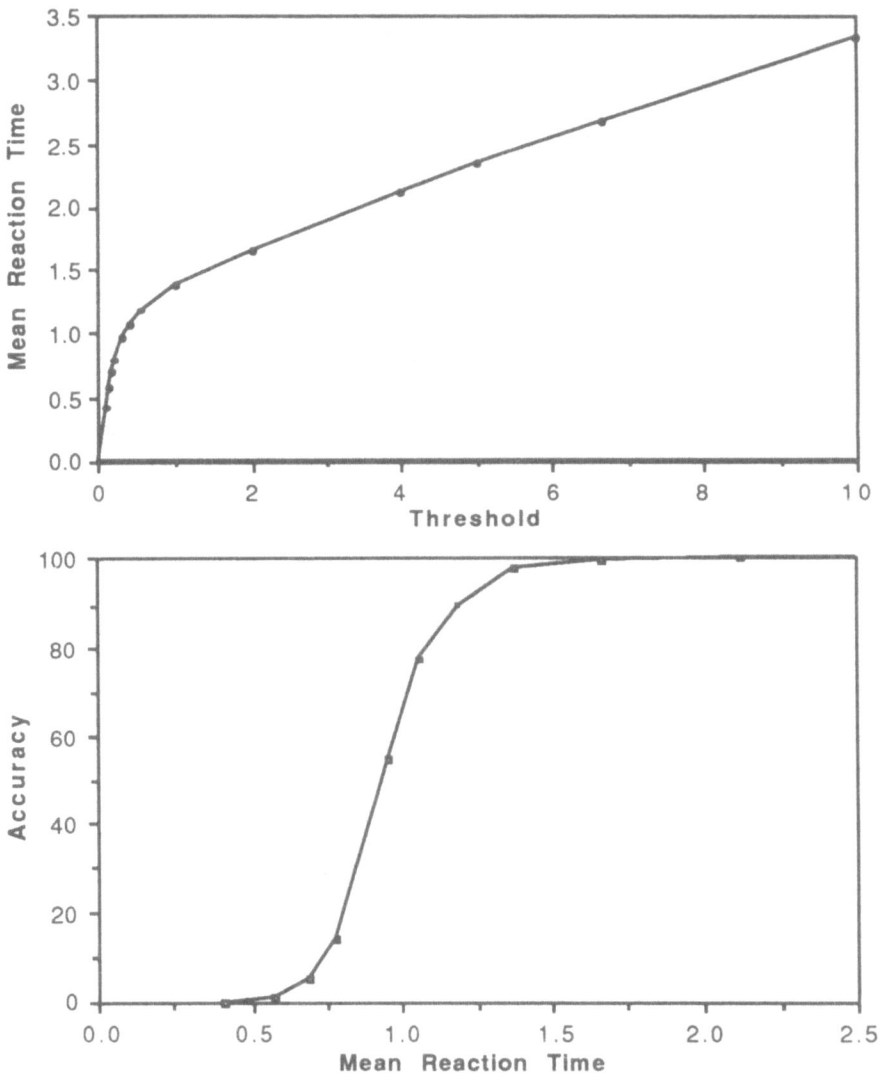

Figure 8: The speed versus accuracy tradeoff for the Sum(0) = −3 case.

It is easily checked that, as long as our thresholds are set sufficiently high, the precise values have little effect on the simulated latencies (for thresholds 20 and 10 we have r = 0.997, ρ = 0.999; for 20 and 4 we have r = 0.986, ρ = 0.994). Real brains will presumably normally operate in this region where the error rate is reliably low.

Finally, one might argue that for total consistency we should also have our input activations building up over time. Doing this uniformly, scatters the naming latencies yet again (r = 0.86, ρ = 0.82). Given the likelihood that some letters will be detected more rapidly than others and at rates depending on their contexts, we

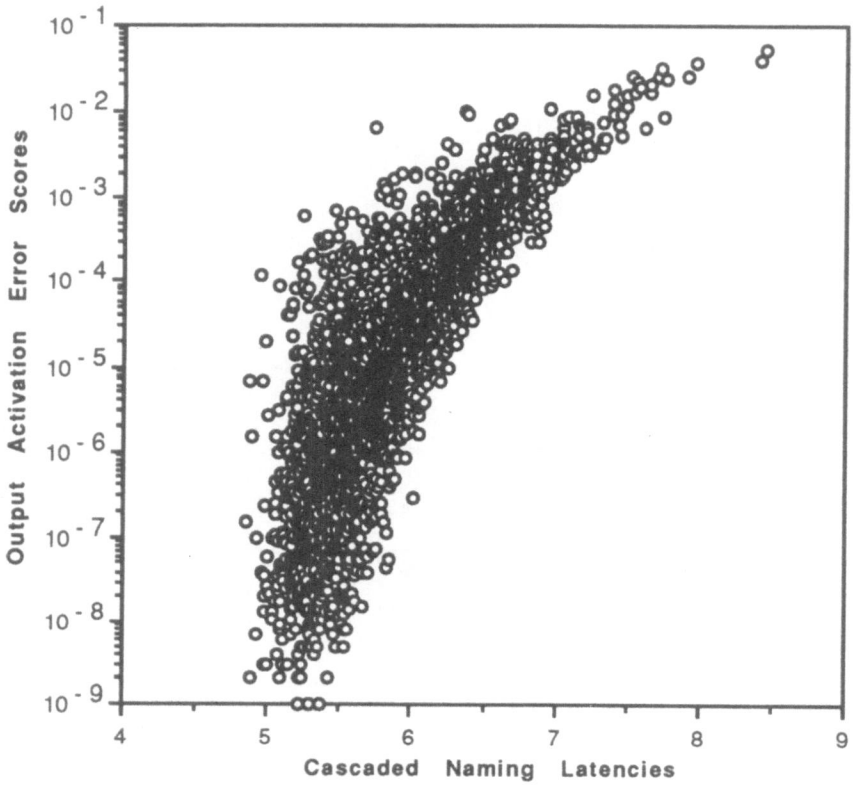

Figure 9: The relationship between our cascaded naming latencies and standard output activation error scores.

can expect even more scattering than this in a completely realistic system. Taking this one step further, it is easy to imagine how other manipulations of the input activations might be used to simulate the effects of reading degraded type faces, "bad light" and so on.

5 Non-cascaded Response Times

It has been suggested (by Seidenberg & McClelland [9] and many others since then) that the output activation error scores in standard back-propagation networks should also be correlated with response times. The idea seems to be that in the more realistic cascaded processing systems we have been considering, the clearer the outputs (i.e. the lower the errors), the lower the time it should take to reach the threshold. If this is correct, then we have an easy way to simulate reaction times. However, the validity of this has been questioned and it has been demonstrated explicitly for our model of reading that changing the precise mathematical relation used to relate the error scores to the simulated response times can have quite significant effects on the results [7].

The first thing to notice is that, if the procedure we have adopted here to simulate reaction times is correct, then it is only the activation of the winning output unit of the slowest parallel process that matters. Taking into account the error score contributions due to faster parallel processes or other units having not quite zero activation seems to be the wrong thing to do. Indeed, Figure 9 shows that the relationship between the error scores and the cascaded latencies for our reading model is far from simple. In particular, we see that the error score distribution is excessively skewed. There *is* a significant correlation ($\rho = 0.72$) and the high cascaded latencies *do* correspond to high error scores, so we still get the strong type effect, but apart from that we cannot say much. The various other non-cascaded estimations of naming latencies suggested by Bullinaria [7] do not do much better: Inverse Log Errors $r = 0.75$, $\rho = 0.72$; Log Sum Luce Ratios $r = 0.68$, $\rho = 0.67$; Sum Inverse Inputs $r = 0.56$, $\rho = 0.56$.

We see from Figures 3, 4 and 6 that there are two main contributions to the time taken to reach threshold. First, the time taken for the output activations to build up to near their asymptotic values and second, the asymptotic slope of the curve which is trivially related to the critical asymptotic output activation. In fact, even the inverses of these critical output activations are surprisingly poor indicators of the cascaded results ($r = 0.63$, $\rho = 0.76$), so it is hard to see what other than our full cascaded approach could do much better than the simple output error scores.

6 Conclusions

We have seen how it is easy to re-interpret simple feedforward back-propagation networks as cascaded systems. This provides a principled procedure for simulating reaction times complete with independent priming and rushing effects that are rather difficult to model in non-cascaded systems.

Looking at a particular reading model, we find significant correlations between the simulated naming latencies of virtually any two variations of the basic approach and strong word type effects seem to be obtained whatever we do. The standard supposed relationship between reaction times and the output activation error scores seems to have some basis but must clearly be treated with caution and we will have to be much more careful when looking for weaker effects in our models.

References

1. McClelland, J.L. (1979). On the time relations of mental processes: An examination of systems of processing in cascade. *Psychological Review*, **86**, 287-330.
2. Dell, G.S. (1986). A Spreading-Activation Theory of Retrieval in Sentence Production, *Psychological Review*, **93**, 283-321.
3. McClelland, J.L. and Rumelhart, D.E. (1981). An Interactive Activation Model of Context Effects in Letter Perception: Part 1. An Account of Basic Findings, *Psychological Review*, **88**, 375-407.
4. Rumelhart, D.E. and McClelland, J.L. (1982). An Interactive Activation Model

of Context Effects in Letter Perception: Part 2. The Contextual Enhancement Effect and Some Tests and Extensions of the Model, *Psychological Review*, **89**, 60-94.

5. Cohen, J., Dunbar, K. & McClelland (1990). On the control of automatic processes: A parallel distributed processing model of the Stroop task, *Psychological Review*, **97**, 332-361.

6. Norris, D. (1993). A quantitative model of reading aloud, Technical report, MRC APU, Cambridge.

7. Bullinaria, J.A. (1994). Representation, Learning, Generalization and Damage in Neural Network Models of Reading Aloud, Submitted.

8. Sejnowski, T.J. and Rosenberg, C.R. (1987). Parallel Networks that Learn to Pronounce English Text, *Complex Systems*, **1**, 145-168.

9. Seidenberg, M.S. & McClelland, J.L. (1989). A distributed, developmental model of word recognition and naming, *Psychological Review*, **96**, 523-568.

10. Taraban, R. & McClelland, J.L. (1987). Conspiracy Effects in Word Pronunciation, *Journal of Memory and Language*, **26**, 608-631.

11. Waters, G.S. & Seidenberg, M.S. (1985). Spelling-sound effects in reading: Time-course and decision criteria, *Memory & Cognition*, **13**, 557-572.

12. Glushko, R.J. (1979). The Organization and Activation of Orthographic Knowledge in Reading Aloud, *Journal of Experimental Sciences: Human Perception and Performance*, **5**, 674-691.

13. Meyer, D.E., Schvaneveldt, R.W. & Ruddy, M.G. (1974). Functions of graphemic and phonemic codes in visual word-recognition. *Memory & Cognition*, **2**, 309-321.

14. Tanenhaus, M.K., Flanigan, H.P. & Seidenberg, M.S. (1980). Orthographic and phonological activation in auditory and visual word recognition. *Memory & Cognition*, **8**, 513-520.

15. Wickelgren, W.A. (1977). Speed-accuracy tradeoff and information processing dynamics, *Acta Psychologica*, **41**, 67-85.

Chunking: An Interpretation Bottleneck

Jon Slack

Department of Psychology

University of Kent

Canterbury, United Kingdom

email: J.M.Slack@ukc.ac.uk

Abstract

The interest of psychologists in elucidating the constraints on human information processing dates from Miller's (1956) paper in which he identifies his famous magic number seven, plus or minus two. Miller's paper
was set in the theoretical context of Information Theory, but his approach
is equally applicable to more contemporary theoretical frameworks, such
as connectionism and symbolic information processing. The notion of
constraint has come to play a key role in our understanding of the computational architecture underlying human cognition. One such constraint
on our ability to process information relates to the bounds on short-term
memory. The capacity of this system is generally measured by means of
a procedure such as digit span, the measure being the length of the string
of digits that can be accurately recalled on at least half the trials. This
measure requires the subject to remember both the individual digits and
their 'places' in the string. Research in this area has led us away from
simple numerical limits to relatively complex processing models and architectures. The aim of this paper is to add another dimension to this
developing theoretical framework based on a crucial distinction between
representational genera. The different categories of representation have
different bounds on their informational capacity. The paper derives an
important *representational constraint* that arises from the restricted capacity of distributed representations for encoding composed, structured
objects. This constraint is shown to be related to some key properties of
human short-term memory.

1 Representational Genera

Classically, two representational genera have been distinguished; *language-like*
or *logical* as against *image-like* or *iconic* representations. The former includes
natural languages, logical calculi, and computer programming languages, while
the latter genus encompasses maps, scale models, analog computers, and the
like.

A key characteristic of logical representations is that they have *compositional semantics*. This means that complete logical tokens, such as sentences,
production rules, well-formed formulae, and so on, are *complex objects*. As
such, they have a recursively specifiable structure and determinate atomic constituents allowing the semantic significance of the whole to be determined by the

structure and semantic significance of its constituents. While such languages arbitrarily fix the contributions of the possible structures and constituents, the significance of a compound object is not at all arbitrary given a particular set of atomic elements.

Iconic representations, in contrast, are not compositional, but represent their contents through some form of *isomorphism*. In some cases the isomorphism is obvious, as in the case of pictures and scale models, but in other cases, such as graphs and wiring diagrams, the common structure they represent is more abstract. Different forms of structure preserving mapping can be employed in iconic representations.[1] While the choice of mapping is initially arbitrary or conventional, once it has been fixed, the contents of particular iconic tokens are not arbitrary.

Haugeland (1991) argues that it is not the form of the *representing relation* between representations and what they represent that distinguishes genera, but the *contents* of such representations. The categories of representation outlined are associated with distinctive forms of representing relation; logical representations are characterised by compositional semantics, and iconic representations by structural isomorphism, but Haugeland demonstrates that these relations are merely indicative of the representational genera. More important are the contents of the representations. In brief, the representational genera identified can be characterised as follows:

- *Logical representations* are built from *absolute* elements.

- *Iconic representations* have contents specified through *relative* elements.

The property that distinguishes the contents of logical representations is that their elements are *absolute*. This means that the primitive elements of logical contents, be they objects and properties, conditions and actions, or whatever, always function as separate and individual atoms. It is this property of 'selfstandingness' that supports the capacity of *systematicity* exhibited by logical representations. For example, the proposition that *The ball is white* can exist as a fact quite independently of any preconditions. That is, the proposition does not carry with it some pre-existing system of other objects and properties.

While the contents of logical representations encode 'structure' and support 'systematicity', the contents of iconic representations capture the notion of 'shape'. Iconic contents can be conceived as variations of values along certain dimensions with respect to locations in certain other dimensions. For example, a 'grey-scale image' as a representation in an image understanding system is iconic in that it encodes the variation in 'light intensity' as a point on a 'grey-scale', with respect to the structured 2D coordinate space of the image frame. The contents of the icon are the shapes of the variations in light intensity, and the concept of 'shape' only makes sense in terms of relative locations in

---

[1]The class of iconic representations should not be confused with the notion of Iconic memory. The latter may be based on codes that might be classified as iconic representations, but the class also encompasses non-visual forms of representation.

structured spaces. The dimensions of the space are not necessarily continuous. For example, a typical grey-scale in an IU system might comprise a 7-point interval scale. The point is that the notion of 'shape' can only be supported by the concept of a 'space' in which locations are identifiable with respect to intrinsically ordered dimensions. To contrast with his use of the term 'absolute,' Haugeland (1991) refers to the dimensionally placed elements of iconic contents as *relative* elements. This contrast between 'shape' and 'structure' provides a clear basis for distinguishing iconic and logical representations.

2   Encoding iconic representations

Most models of short-term memory are based on iconic representations of item information. For example, Baddeley's model of working memory (1981, 1983) incorporates a distinction between a 'central executive' and its 'slave' systems, the latter being memory systems based on iconic representations. One such system, the visuo-spatial scratchpad, encodes the 'shape' of visual information relative to a 2-D image space. A second system, the articulatory loop, encodes the 'shape' of phonetic information relative to the temporal dimension. These systems incorporate an 'isomorphism' between the form of the stimulus information, visuo-spatial and auditory, and the bases of the encoding media, a 2-D image space and a temporally-ordered loop, respectively.

A different form of iconic-based encoding is employed by Lee and Estes (1977) in their model of short-term memory based on a control mechanism that configures the representations of input items into a control loop that regularly cycles activation around them. In this model, an individual item is associated with a *time-tag* on the basis of which its position in the input sequence can be derived. The time-tags specify the discrete 'shape' of input information relative to the dynamics of the control mechanism. In other words, the time-tags do not constitute 'absolute' content elements, but must be interpreted relative to the temporal organisation of the memory system.

In memory systems based on iconic representations, item information is 'bound' to 'places' defined within an encoding medium which is isomorphic to the organisation of the information in space or time. The importance of distinguishing between iconic and logical representations is that the corresponding memory encodings tend to be limited in different ways and by different factors. The constraints on iconic-based memory systems are space-time constraints. For example, the bounds on the articulatory loop are determined by the temporal parameters of the process (Baddeley, Thomson & Buchanan, 1975). In contrast, logical representations are limited by the way composed, structured objects are encoded as composed memory traces.

3   Encoding logical representations

Ordered lists of items, such as digit span lists, can also be encoded as logical representations. This is because they are composed, structured objects in that they comprise (i) a set of constituents, the individual items, and (ii) a particular configuration of those constituents, the particular order of the items in the list. This representation of a list is independent of the sensory encoding of the items that comprise it. One way of formalising this description of structures such as lists is by defining a *composition operator* which when applied to two structured objects produces a third composed object of the same kind. Formally, if we let S denote the set of structured objects that function as logical representations then we can define an operator, denoted $\diamond$, such that

$$a \diamond b = c \tag{1}$$

where $a, b, c \in S$. In other words, the set S is closed under the composition operation $\diamond$. For example, if S is the set of logical representations of ordered lists and $\diamond$ is realised as the binary operation of *concatenation*, denoted '.', then if a and b are two lists

$$a.b = ab \tag{2}$$

and ab is a composed list that is also an element of S. An operator of this type can be applied recursively to build ever more complex structures.

The concept of a 'place' is defined in a different way for logical representations than for iconic representations. A 'place' is not specified relative to an underlying isomorphism but through the application of a composition operator. One way of viewing the operator in Equ. [2] is as a sequence of two sub-operations, the first sub-operation defines a 'place' relative to the first argument, and the second sub-operation 'binds' the second argument to this 'place'. For example, in Equ. [2], the first sub-operation generates the 'place' denoted by the underscore in $a\_$, and the argument b is then bound to it producing $a\underline{b}$. In this way, complex structures are composed through 'binding' arguments to 'places' that are generated through the application of a composition operator.

It is conventional to denote concatenated structures by means of spatial juxtaposition, but this convention is not the source of the operator's capacity for generating 'places', it is merely a convenient way of representing the concept. The real source of the concept is the operator's property of being *non-commutative*, that is, concatenation is a binary operator for which the following is true,

$$a \diamond b \neq b \diamond a \tag{3}$$

This property allows the two arguments of the operator to be distinguished, enabling the second argument to defined as a 'place' relative to the first.[2] For this class of non-commutative, binary operator, a 'place' is designated by the symbolic token identifying the operator and the corresponding token of one of

---

[2] It could be argued that the operator generates two 'places', one for each argument and then 'binds' the two arguments to their respective 'places'. However, in the case of concatenation, the configural structure generated by the operator is 'relative' in that its outcome is a particular structural relation holding between the two arguments. It does not fix the 'places' of the arguments in an absolute sense, only their relative positioning. This means that the operator generates a 'place' relative to one of its arguments.

its arguments. Elsewhere, I have referred to such 'places' as *structural addresses* and the privileged argument relative to which a 'place' is defined as the *origin* of the address (Slack, 1994). The structural relationship between any two 'places', or constituents, within a complex symbol can be specified as a structural address by tracing the 'path' of composition operations that link them. Thus, a structural address comprises an 'origin' argument, or constituent, and a string of operator tokens.[3]

One way of encoding a list as a composed object is to compose a memory trace based on *item-address* bindings. For example, the digit list, 47286, might be encoded as the set of bindings

$$\{4 \star head, 7 \star s(head), 2 \star s(s(head)), 8 \star s(s(s(head))), 6 \star s(s(s(s(head))))\}$$

where 'head' identifies the first element of the list, and 's' is interpreted as the relation *successor_of*. In this encoding, the structural addresses specify 'places' relative to the same significant element, the 'head'. Realising the logical representation of the list as a composed memory trace of this form allows the individual items to be accessed via their structural addresses within the representation. The number of 'places' that can be encoded within a composed trace is not inherently bounded by the nature of the representation. The bounds on 'places' arise when such representations are realised as distributed representations, that is, as vectors.

4   Logical representations as vectors

Fodor and Pylyshyn (1988) have argued that mental representations need to be complex structured objects with articulated internal structure. Their argument is, in part, based on two key properties characteristic of human cognition, *productivity* and *systematicity*. The first property states that, in theory, human cognitive capacities result from an unbounded competence that is realised by a mechanism, the brain, that has finite resource limitations. The second property states that if a cognitive system can generate and interpret certain types of mental representations then it must be capable of generating and interpreting other systematically related representations. For example, if the system can produce a representation for the sentence *John hits Mary* it must also be able to represent *Mary hits John*. For these two properties to characterise human cognitive capacities, Fodor and Pylyshyn (1988) argue that it must be the case that mental representations have a combinatorial structure and are recursively composed. On the basis of this they go on to argue that Connectionism cannot give an account of cognition as a 'language of thought' and, at best, provides an implementation framework for Classical cognitive architecture.

Connectionism as an implementation framework cannot explain our unbounded productive capacity but it does speak to the issue of finite processing resources. In particular, Connectionism is proving a valuable approach

---

[3]Each application of a composition operator results in a particular structural relation between its two arguments and this allows a structural address to comprise either a string of operator tokens or the corresponding string of structural relation tokens.

in explaining the nature of the capacity limitations typical of human memory (Schneider, 1993). One source of limitations relates to the way in which composed objects are encoded on connectionist networks. Different mappings between the elements of structured objects and the components of networks can be used, but a key distinction is between mapping symbol tokens onto units, a *local representation* scheme, and mapping them onto patterns across units, a *distributed representation* scheme. In general, local representations are incompatible with the recursive composition of structured objects. In contrast, Pollack (1990) has shown how distributed representations can be composed and decomposed as a way of encoding recursively-defined structures such as lists and trees. The obvious bounds on such representations are (i) the number of elements comprising a pattern as a ratio of the number of patterns stored on the set of elements, and (ii) the granularity of the patterns. However, a more limiting bound on distributed representations arises from the fact that their composition is not isomorphic to composed structured objects.

Distributed representations are formalised as points in a vector space. Implementing structured objects as distributed patterns over a network requires a *faithful* mapping between the set of structures, S, and the elements of a vector space, V.[4] However, there are no formal operators on vector spaces that can provide a basis for such a mapping as a point in a vector space has no unique decomposition into constituent vectors.[5] While it is possible to identify operators that will allow vectors to be composed to form composite vectors, such vectors cannot be decomposed into their original constituent vectors in a reliable way. To circumvent this problem it is necessary to devise systems that implement *functional composition* (van Gelder, 1990) enabling vectors to be composed and decomposed in a reliable way, thereby providing the basis for a faithful representation mapping.

Pollack (1990) designed a connectionist architecture for encoding symbolic structures based on two mechanisms, a *compressor*, and a *reconstructor*. The compressor encodes lists as left-branching binary trees by merging the patterns of activity representing the first two list items to form a new pattern over a fixed-size vector. This vector is then merged recursively with the pattern representing the next item in the list until all the list item vectors have been composed into a single pattern. For example, the digit-span list, 47286, is encoded by compressing the patterns encoding 4 and 7 to generate a new vector, L_1, which is then compressed with the pattern for the third digit, 2, to generate the vector L_2. Intermediate composite vectors are built up in this way until the vector L_3 is merged with the pattern for the digit 6 to produce the final composite pattern encoding the sequence. The reconstructor mechanism operates in the opposite direction, decoding composite vectors into their constituent patterns. For a pattern, such as L_4, the network generates two new patterns representing L_3 and the digit 6. Composite patterns are recursively

---

[4] A faithful representation mapping, $\Psi : S \rightarrow V$, is a one-to-one mapping such that no element of S is mapped onto the zero vector.

[5] This problem with connectionist representations was first identified by Fodor and McLaughlin (1990).

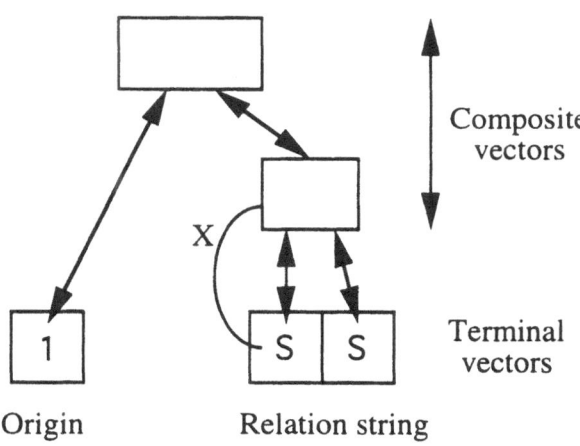

Composite vectors

Terminal vectors

X

1   S S

Origin   Relation string

Figure 1: A general connectionist architecture for composing/decomposing structural addresses. In this instance, the terminal vectors encode the string [1]ss, but longer strings can be composed, or decomposed, via the recursive loop labeled 'X'.

decomposed by cycling them round the mechanism. In this way, the recursive auto-associative memory (RAAM) architecture provides a method for building representations of ordered lists from representations of their constituents and has a reliable operation for decoding such representations.[6]

Consider the general architecture for composing and decomposing vector encodings of structural addresses shown in figure 1. The terminal vectors at the lowest level of the network encode the primitive elements of structural addresses. The leftmost vector is the 'origin' of the address, and the two vectors on the right encode the string of operator, or structural relation, tokens. Figure 1 shows the encoding of the address [1]ss, or $s(s(1))$, where s denotes the relation of rightward adjacency.[7] Vectors are composed as you move up through the levels of the network and the vector at the highest level is the composite pattern encoding the entire address string. Similarly, composite vectors are decomposed by moving down through the levels. The subnetwork incorporating the loop labeled 'X' can be implemented as a RAAM (Pollack, 1990) as the loop allows terminal strings of arbitrary length to be composed, or decomposed, recursively. Basically, the network computes a reliable and invertible mapping between the symbol token vectors at the terminal level and the composite vector at the top level, and as such, implements a general form of functional

---

[6]Pollack's architecture could be developed as a model of memory for sequences, but notice that individual list items cannot be accessed independently of the representation of the entire sequence. As such, it falls into the class of 'chaining' models. Moreover, the chaining is implicit in that adjacency relations between items can only be determined by cycling through the decomposition operation. However, the architecture can also be used for encoding structural addresses.

[7]The successor function, s, can also be used to token the structural relation of 'rightward adjacency.'

composition (van Gelder, 1990). It is general in the sense that it is compatible with any form of invertible, vector composition process. For example, it might be implemented using RAAMs (Pollack, 1990) or Tensor Product operators (Smolensky, 1990).

The key properties of the architecture in figure 1 are that it is finite and fixed. That is, the composition/decomposition mapping is computed by finite means. Moreover, the architecture is fixed in that additional components are not required for it to accommodate arbitrarily complex representations. However, it also embodies an important constraint, namely, that only *three* vectors are distinguished at the lowest level. The patterns at the terminal level are directly interpretable as symbolic tokens, whereas the composite vectors are only accessible symbolically through decomposition. When the network encodes structural addresses of more than three elements, the middle vector at the lowest level encodes a composite symbolic string and requires decoding before it can be interpreted symbolically. This means that the network can encode composite vectors at the 'top' level which are not directly accessible as symbol tokens at the terminal level. Decomposing the vector representation of a structural address longer than three elements requires one or more of the terminal vectors to be stored 'outside' the network in which case its configural role within the address is lost. Each of the terminal elements within the network has a distinguished role within an address; the connections that instantiate the 'X' loop distinguish between the two relational components.[8] The configural role of a terminal vector stored outside the network cannot be related to the component organisation of structural addresses as configured within the network. The architecture embodies an *interpretation bottleneck*; it can encode structural addresses of arbitrary length as composed vectors, but it can only interpret addresses comprising, at most, three elements, an 'origin' vector plus two relational vectors.

This constraint is a general representational bound in that it does not derive from properties peculiar to the architecture, but holds for all forms of functional composition irrespective of the nature of the mechanisms that implement it. The 'interpretation bottleneck' is characteristic of any reliable, invertible composition mapping that can be applied to strings of arbitrary complexity and which is implemented on a fixed and finite architecture. The main consequence of the 'bottleneck' is that relative to a given 'origin' constituent only three 'places' can be distinguished, the 'place' of the 'origin', and the two 'places' signified by the addresses comprising one and two relational tokens. More complex structural addresses cannot be interpreted symbolically, although they can be encoded and processed as composite vectors. The 'interpretation bottleneck' can be re-stated as a general representational constraint as follows:

Logical representations encoded as distributed patterns within a connectionist system are constituted from locally interpretable units or 'chunks'. Each 'chunk' comprises a primitive 'origin' constituent

---

[8]The 'X' loop connections can be used to order the two relational elements; the component with the connections encodes the 'first' of the two terminal vectors.

plus two 'places' configured relative to it. The 'places' correspond to interpretable, configural roles which have other constituents, either atomic or composed, bound to them.

4.1 Psychological support for chunks

Given that the interpretation 'bottleneck' is an inherent characteristic of logical representations encoded within connectionist architectures, the question arises as to how it might emerge as a property of human cognition. The concept of interpretable chunks determines the granularity of composed objects as mental representations, and Slack (1994) has shown how this granularity accounts for the structure of phrasal elements within natural languages. If digit-span lists are encoded as structured objects in memory then the chunking of items should be reflected in the retrieval of information from such traces.

It is important to stress that the interpretation 'bottleneck' is a restriction on the encoding of logical representations. It is not a limitation of the retrieval processes operating on such representations, except to the extent that such processes are constrained by the form and content of the encodings. One interpretation of the representational constraint is that the basic chunk size for composed objects is *three* and that chunks are encoded relative to special constituents that function as 'origins'. The question is how are these concepts and limits related to the constructs used to explain immediate memory phenomena.

In a list of items, the only 'special' constituents that can be distinguished in terms of their position are the end items and these nodes provide a basis for building chunks (Shiffrin & Cook, 1978). However, a list of arbitrary length can be reconfigured as multiple lists by grouping the items in some way. This enables multiple end nodes to be distinguished. It is a robust finding in human experimental psychology that dividing strings of items into shorter groups improves their handling and that performance is optimal with groups of size three (Wickelgren, 1964; Ryan, 1969; Broadbent & Broadbent, 1973). This is consistent with the notion of 'chunks' as defined by the representational constraint.

While strings of items may be optimally encoded as chunks of size three, this is not the only factor that determines short-term memory span. A list of items can be represented either logically, as a composed object, or as some form of iconic representation, or both. For example, Baddeley's (1983) articulatory loop system stores and maintains a phonological representation of a list. This type of representation is iconic in that it is specified relative to the underlying temporal structure of the string. The bounds on iconic representations relate to their iconic bases. Accordingly, the bounds on the phonological representation of a list are determined by the temporal parameters of the storage and maintenance mechanism(s). In general, the bounds on logical representations are more severe than the corresponding bounds on iconic representations. Digit span is often more than seven items reflecting the temporal bounds on the phonological representation. Memory span only reflects the limits of the logical representation of a list when the iconic representation is unavailable. This situation arises when the phonological representation of a list either cannot be generated or is inaccessible to the retrieval processes.

When a list of items is presented via the visual modality, subjects translate the stimuli into their corresponding phonological codes through articulation (Baddeley, 1983). However, not all visual stimuli have associated phonological codes. For example, Zhang and Simon (1985) investigated the capacity of short-term memory using Chinese linguistic elements some of which, the set of radicals, have no familiar pronounceable name. This means that the phonological system cannot be used to encode radicals and their short-term memory span should reflect a different capacity constraint to that underlying the span for other types of linguistic item, such as, characters and words. Zhang and Simon (1985) found that short-term memory capacity for material encoded non-phonologically is no greater than three items, whereas acoustical short-term memory has a capacity of up to seven items. This capacity for non-phonological material is consistent with the limit expected on the basis of the representational constraint. Zhang and Simon (1985) suggested that the reduced capacity for such material might reflect the bounds on a different 'slave' system within Baddeley's model, namely, the visuo-spatial scratch pad. However, the capacity of this system as measured by span-type procedures, such as the memory span for visual matrix patterns, is generally far greater than three elements (Ichikawa, 1983; Wilson, Scott & Power, 1987).

Another source of supporting evidence is to be found in the deficits of patients with damaged short-term memory systems (Vallar & Shallice, 1990). A number of such patients have been studied that appear to have a phonological storage deficit but intact articulatory rehearsal (see Shallice & Vallar, 1990). Vallar and Baddeley (1984) have suggested that these patients do not utilise articulatory rehearsal as a strategy because their reduced phonological storage capacity makes such a strategy ineffective. In this case, the patients are forced to rely on an alternative representation, and might be sensitive to the capacity bounds indicative of the representational constraint. In general, it is found that such patients have an immediate memory span of about three items. For example, Vallar and Baddeley (1984) studied a patient, P.V., whose auditory memory span was grossly defective; the probability of recalling a sequence correctly fell sharply for sequences of more than three items. Also, Martin (1987, 1990) has studied a brain-damaged patient, E.A., with the same short-term memory pattern and a span of two to three words for auditory presentation. Material presented via the auditory modality is necessarily encoded phonologically and if the 'slave' system that stores the iconic representation of the list is ineffective then a patient has no choice but to rely on the logical representation which is subject to the interpretation 'bottleneck'. In this case, chunk size (i.e., three) should be an important determinant of the patients' short-term memory span.[9]

---

[9]Interestingly, both patients have a span of about four items for visually-presented material. This might reflect the use of the visuo-spatial scratch pad suggesting that its capacity is greater than three items thereby contradicting the explanation of the reduced capacity for non-phonological material suggested by Zhang and Simon (1985).

A different type of evidence is to be found in the notion of 'perfect span' which is the length of span which can be reliably recalled at a very high level of accuracy.[10] The length of perfect span is about three items and is unaffected by the nature of the items (Cardozo & Leopold, 1963). This suggests that short-term memory span generally reflects the bounds of both the iconic and logical representations of a list.

A final source of evidence derives from a study that investigated memory for symbolic circuit drawings (Egan & Schwartz, 1979). The recall of both skilled technicians and novices showed a marked degree of 'chunking', or grouping, by functional units. Moreover, in both cases the maximum number of symbols per 'recalled chunk' never exceeded three. For technicians, the size of recalled chunks varied between 2.87 and 1.68 with the larger chunks being recalled earlier in the recall output sequence and the smaller chunks later. It would seem that rather than using the visuo-spatial scratch pad to encode the configurations of symbols, the subjects decomposed the drawings into chunks of functionally related units encoded as structurally composed objects.

5 Conclusions

The main conclusion to be drawn from this work is that structured information encoded in memory as distributed patterns representing composed objects is subject to an interpretation 'bottleneck'. This constraint forces structured objects to be broken down into smaller chunks and these chunks are independently accessible within memory. However, the constraint only applies to composed memory objects and does not limit our capacity for encoding information iconically.

This analysis of representational genera is important for psychological theorising as it identifies a source for the concept of 'chunking' which has played a crucial role in our understanding of short-term memory. The analysis also derives a precise measure for the size of unit resulting from this process. Psychologists have generated a large body of data suggesting the existence of a process such as chunking, but to date, there has been no theoretical rationale linking chunking to the categories of representation characteristic of human cognition. The hope is that the rationale provided here might provide a useful basis for (i) explaining the existing corpus of data relating to chunking, (ii) generating further data to clarify the nature of the process, and (iii) relating short-term memory constraints to the constraints characteristic of other cognitive processes.

References

[1] Baddeley, A. D. (1981) The concept of working memory: A view of its current state and probable future development. **Cognition**, 10, 17-23.

---

[10]The span of immediate memory normally reported is the number of items which can be recalled on 50% of trials.

[2] Baddeley, A.D. (1983) Working memory. **Philosophical Transactions of the Royal Society, London**, B302, 311-324.

[3] Baddeley, A. D., Thomson, N., & Buchanan, M. (1975) Word length and structure of short-term memory. **Journal of Verbal Learning and Verbal Behavior**, 14, 575-589.

[4] Broadbent, D.E., & Broadbent, M.H.P. (1973) Grouping strategies in short-term memory for alpha-numeric lists. **Bulletin of the British Psychological Society**, 26, 135.

[5] Cardozo, B.L., & Leopold, F.F. (1963) Human code transmission. Letters and digits compared on the basis of immediate memory rates. **Ergonomics**, 6, 133-141.

[6] Egan, D.E., & Schwartz, B.J. (1979) Chunking in recall of symbolic drawings. **Memory & Cognition**, 7, 149-158.

[7] Fodor, J., & McLaughlin, B.P. (1990) Connectionism and the problem of systematicity: Why Smolensky's solution doesn't work. **Cognition**, 35, 183-204.

[8] Fodor, J., & Pylyshyn, Z. (1988) Connectionism and cognitive architecture: A critical analysis. **Cognition**, 28, 3-71.

[9] van Gelder, T. (1990) Compositionality: A connectionist variation on a classical theme. **Cognitive Science**, 14, 355-384.

[10] Haugeland, (1991) Representational genera. In W. Ramsey, S. P. Stich, & D. E. Rumelhart (eds.), **Philosophy and Connectionist Theory**. Hillsdale, N.J.: Erlbaum.

[11] Ichikawa, S. (1983) Verbal memory span, visual memory span, and their correlations with cognitive tasks. **Japanese Psychological Research**, 25, 173-180.

[12] Lee, C.L., & Estes, W.K. (1977) Order and position in primary memory for letter strings. **Journal of Verbal Learning and Verbal Behavior**, 16, 395-418.

[13] Martin, R.C. (1987) Articulatory and phonological deficits in short-term memory and their relation to syntactic processing. **Brain & Language**, 32, 137-158.

[14] Martin, R.C. (1990) Neuropsychological evidence on the role of short-term memory in sentence processing. In G. Vallar & T. Shallice (Eds), **Neuropsychological impairments of short-term memory**. Cambridge: Cambridge University Press.

[15] Miller, G. A. (1956) The magical number seven, plus or minus two: Some limits on our capacity for processing information. **Psychological Review**, 63, 81-97.

[16] Pollack, J., (1990) Recursive distributed representations. **Artificial Intelligence**, 46, 77-107.

[17] Ryan, J. (1969) Grouping and short-term memory: Different means and patterns of grouping. **Quarterly Journal of Experimental Psychology**, 21, 137-147.

[18] Schneider, W. (1993) Varieties of working memory as seen in biology and in connectionist/control architectures. **Memory & Cognition**, 21, 184-192.

[19] Shallice, T., & Vallar, G. (1990) The impairment of auditory-verbal short-term storage. In G. Vallar & T. Shallice (Eds), **Neuropsychological impairments of short-term memory**. Cambridge: Cambridge University Press.

[20] Shiffrin, R.M., & Cook, J.R. (1978) Short-term forgetting of item and order information. **Journal of Verbal Learning and Verbal Behavior**, 17, 189-218.

[21] Slack, J. (1994) Structured objects as mental representations. (under review).

[22] Smolensky, P. (1990) Tensor product variable binding and the representation of symbolic structures in connectionist systems. **Artificial Intelligence**, 46, 159-217.

[23] Vallar, G., & Baddeley, A. (1984) Fractionation of working memory: Neuropsychological evidence for a phonological short-term store. **Journal of Verbal Learning & Verbal Behavior**, 23, 121-142.

[24] Vallar G., & Shallice T. (1990), **Neuropsychological impairments of short-term memory**. Cambridge: Cambridge University Press.

[25] Wickelgren, W.A. (1964) Size of rehearsal group and short-term memory. **Journal of Experimental Psychology**, 68, 413-419.

[26] Wilson, J.T.L., Scott, J.H., & Power, K.G. (1987) Developmental differences in the span for visual memory for pattern. **British Journal of Developmental Psychology**, 5, 249-255.

[27] Zhang, G., & Simon, H.A. (1985) STM capacity for Chinese words and idioms: Chunking and acoustical loop hypotheses. **Memory & Cognition**, 13, 193-201.

Learning, Relearning and Recall for Two Strengths of Learning in Neural Networks 'Aged' by Simulated Dendritic Attrition.

Cartwright, R. and Humphreys, G.W.
School of Psychology, The University of Birmingham,
Birmingham, England.

Abstract

Two exploratory experiments used backpropagation networks to simulate the effects of: 1) aging by 'dendritic attrition' on the networks' speed of learning and recall performance, and 2) 'strength of learning' on the networks' ability to relearn, or transfer prior learning after aging. In the first experiment dendritic attrition was simulated by random connection pruning and the extent of pruning was progressively increased to simulate aging. In the second experiment dendritic attrition was simulated by pruning connections in descending weight order. Also: 1) the networks were pretrained to 'Minimally Learnt' and 'Well Learnt' strengths of learning, aged progressively (by stepwise increases in the extent of pruning), and finally retrained to both strengths of learning, 2) recall was tested after pretraining, aging and retraining, 3) recall was scored for both correctly recalled pattern elements and for 'noise' on patterns recalled. In the first experiment, and after pretraining in the second experiment, 'age-related' changes in speed of learning and recall scores were qualitatively similar to general patterns of change found in human population and cohort studies (i.e. gradual but accelerating age-related declines in mean performance with corresponding increases in the range of scores). In the second experiment age-related declines in correct recall of pattern elements were similar for both strengths of pretraining, and subsequent aging: 1) resulted in 'noisy recall' (rather than forgetting), and 2) recall of the 'Well Learnt' networks was noisier. When finally retrained 'Well Learnt' networks took longer to relearn, recalled less and their recall was noisier. Explanations for these results and implications for future work are discussed.

1 Introduction

Research in progress aims to test and develop explanatory theories of aging which causally relate age-related changes in cognitive performance and neurophysiology. Connectionist networks offer a plausible and theory driven means for doing this.

1.1 General Patterns of Change in Cognitive Task Performance with Advancing Age.

Cognitive task performance shows little decremental change until late in life, when general population trends show gradual, but accelerating, decline and an associated increase in the range of within cohort and within individual scores [1]. The related neurophysiological changes may include: increased system noise, reduced speed and strength of transmission, and reductions in neuronal populations and connectivity [2].

1.2 Progress on Methods for Modelling Aging using Neural Networks

Aging characterized as neuronal attrition has been simulated by reducing the number of hidden units in successive populations of backpropagation networks. As network 'age' increased, the changes in mean learning speeds and recall, and the ranges of these scores, qualitatively reflected the general patterns found in human populations [3]. The work reported in this paper developed: 1) methods to simulate dendritic attrition and to distinguish 'forgetting' from 'noisy recall'; and 2) a learn-age-relearn paradigm for exploring how transfer of prior learning affects relearning in networks that are 'aged'.

1.3 Investigating 'Learning Transfer' Within Aging Networks

Learning transfer has been investigated in the contexts of catastrophic forgetting [4] [5] and of transfer between networks [6] [7], but there have not previously been studies of transfer within networks subjected to gradual attrition of nodes or connections. This form of transfer is interesting because, despite age-related changes in human neuronal populations and connectivity, some 'crystallized' aspects of human cognitive performance seem relatively resistant, but not impervious, to loss [8][9].

One possible explanation for this resistance to aging is that the preserved capacities relate to aspects of cognition which are well learnt, and/or frequently practised [9] [10]. This implies: a) 'well learnt' capacities are impervious to neurophysiological change, and b) frequently practised capacities necessarily require some relearning to take place when there is change.

This relearning could involve the formation of new memory structures in parallel with the degrading old memory structures. However, if it is assumed that relearning occurs as changes take place in the residual weight space of the existing memory structures, then several questions emerge, including: 1) 'How is learning within a single neural system affected by these neurophysiological changes?', 2) 'Do the residual components of learning in the system assist relearning (positive transfer) or hinder it (negative transfer)?', and 3) 'How are recall and relearning affected by the strength of learning acquired before age-related changes?'.

The two experiments described explored these questions using autoassociative pattern learning tasks. In the first experiment networks were aged by random connection pruning and were trained to convergence from the initialized and randomized state. The aim was to test whether the general patterns of change in mean scores and range/variance for learning speed and recall, previously found for reducing numbers of hidden units [3], could also be shown for connection pruning. In the second experiment: 1) aging was by largest weight first pruning (to test whether the consequences of systematically scaled pruning were different from random pruning), 2) networks were retrained and retested on the original training file after aging and 3) both prelearning and relearning were conducted to two strengths of learning. Strengths of learning were defined operationally as convergence criteria of .05 rms ('Minimally Learnt'), which was sufficient for recall to approach 90%, and .01 rms ('Well Learnt'), which trained the network well beyond the level necessary to obtain 100% recall.

1.4 Predictions

Three predictions were made: 1) Aging by both random connection pruning and greatest weight first order of pruning would cause network learning and recall performance to degrade gracefully (and this would apply to prelearning and to relearning in the second procedure); 2) As performance degraded the range of associated scores would increase; 3) Networks pretrained to the 'Well Learnt' strength of learning would relearn more rapidly and have better recall than those pretrained to the 'Minimally Learnt' strength of learning (subject to the former failing to learn at lower levels of 'dendritic' attrition when subsequently retrained after aging).

2 Network Configurations

Standard feedforward networks, backpropagated by the delta rule and with sigmoidal transfer function, were used. Both experiments were conducted on 8-6-8 networks (8 input, 6 hidden and 8 output units). The random connection pruning experiment was also performed on 24-6-24 networks. Prior to training all networks were initialized and their connection weights were randomized in the range + 0.1 to - 0.1. Learning rate and momentum were set to 0.9 and 0.6 respectively.

3 Training Files

Two training files were constructed. All input and output pairings were auto-associative. To prevent generalization of micro-features, each pattern comprised only two 1-elements (and six 0-elements). Given this an exhaustive set of 28 possible combinations of two 1-elements from an 8-bit array was derived.

For the first experiment the training file included 14 patterns drawn from the set of 28. As far as possible, these were chosen to counterbalance the frequency of presentation of 1-elements at each position in the array over the training epoch.

For the second experiment all 28 patterns were included. Counterbalancing of the frequency of presentation of each 1-element at each array position over the training epoch was implicit, since this was an exhaustive set of possible combinations.

4 Experiment 1 (Random Connection Pruning)

4.1 Method

Eight 8-24-8 networks and five 8-6-8 networks were randomized, initialized and saved as base networks. Each base network was trained to convergence at .05 rms and tested for recall: 1) with no connections pruned; and 2) after pruning connections to simulate increasing ages of network.

At each step increase in age the unpruned base networks were reloaded and pruned, with the extent of pruning increasing progressively at each age step. Connections were pruned at random (using predetermined random schedules to ensure continuity in the connections removed at each age level). In the 8-24-8 network trials pruning increased in 10% and 15% steps until networks failed to converge, when a further trial was made for a single connection increase in pruning. In the 8-6-8 network trials, the increase in pruning was gradually reduced from eight-connection (8.3%) to single-connection steps and trials were terminated when networks failed to converge over two successive single-connection steps.

4.2 Results and Discussion

Both scales of network showed some evidence of gradual degradation and of increase in range of scores as 'age' increased (see figures 1, 2 and 3).

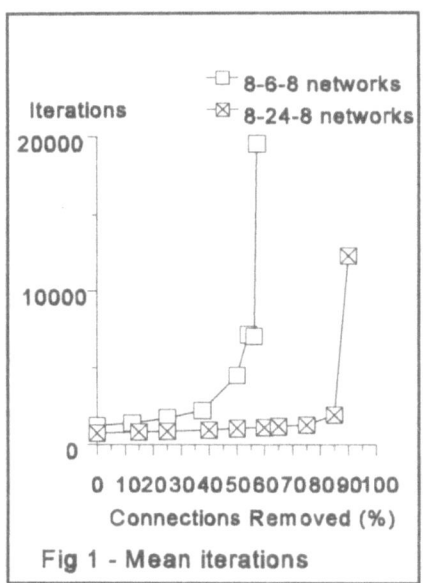

Fig 1 - Mean iterations

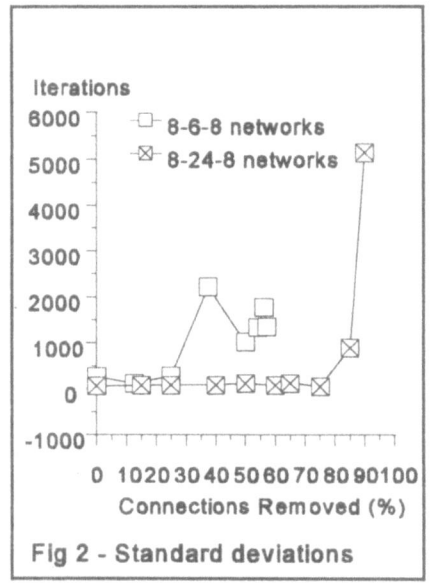

Fig 2 - Standard deviations

Figures 1 & 2 - Mean numbers of iterations (Fig 1) and standard deviations about the means (Fig 2) for different ages of untrained network to learn to convergence at .05 rms

The level of pruning at which the networks failed to learn was generally lower in the 8-6-8 network. In addition there was a large variability in the level of pruning at which failure occurred and this contrasted with the 8-24-8 networks in which the levels of pruning for failure were similar for different networks.

The patterns of change appear to be closer to what might be termed "graceful degradation" for the 8-6-8 networks than for the 8-24-8 networks. However, this is anomalous because early failures of some 8-6-8 networks to converge meant that their effect was removed from the means for these networks. Loss of the worst cohort member then resulted in 'improved' mean cohort performance. This cohort effect has been identified in at least one large scale human study in which the least intelligent cohort members died first, giving an increase in mean cohort intelligence as cohort age increased [11].

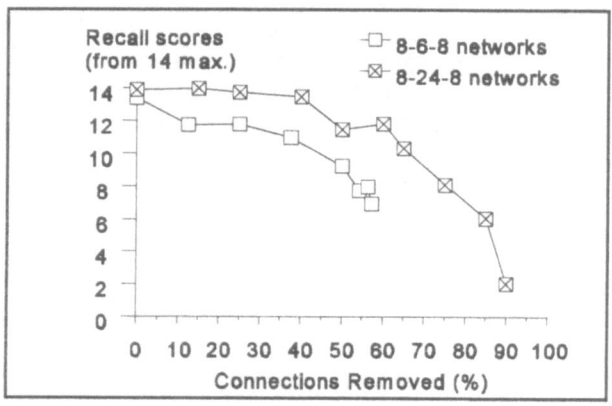

Figure 3 - Recall scores (number of correct patterns) for different age networks trained to convergence at .05 rms.

Whilst the terminal effects of aging on the 8-24-8 networks' speed of learning appear rapid (figure 1) this can be related to these networks tolerating a much higher level of attrition. Consequently: 1) failure occurred at a point where the gradient would be steeper, because nearer 100 % loss there is less latitude for gradual loss, and 2) the relative 'grain' of pruning was coarser.

5 Experiment 2 (prune by greatest weight first, train to 'Minimally' and 'Well Learnt' strengths of learning)

In Experiment 2: 1) only 8-6-8 networks were used, and 2) and the frequencies of 1-element presentation at all array positions over the training epoch were fully counterbalanced by including the exhaustive set of 28 patterns in the training file.

5.1 Procedure

Three randomized and initialized base networks were: 1) pretrained to two levels of learning criterion ('Minimally Learnt' (.05 rms) and 'Well Learnt' (.01 rms)); 2) tested for recall; and 3) saved. A pruning schedule was derived for each network in which connections were ordered by descending strengths (strength was difference from zero regardless of the weight's sign). Each pretrained network was then aged by connection pruning to progressively greater ages (the change in number of connections pruned being gradually reduced as for the 8-6-8 networks in Experiment 1). For each increase in age the pretrained network was reloaded.

At each 'age': 1) the networks were retrained on the original training file to both 'Minimally Learnt' and the 'Well Learnt' convergence criteria, and 2) recall and noise scores, and the number of iterations to convergence, were recorded.

As controls, the three base networks were aged by pruning 62.5% of the connections and were then: 1) tested for recall without being trained, and 2) trained and tested without any pretraining.

5.2 Results

5.2.1 Speed of Learning

Networks pretrained to .01 rms were able to relearn to the .05 rms level, but beyond 62.5% pruning they failed to converge reliably (so the last two points plotted are derived from only two networks) and they were unable to relearn at all at the .01 rms level (figure 4). In contrast figure 4 shows that .05 rms pretrained networks relearned to .05 rms at greater levels of pruning (80%) and to .01 rms up to 52% pruning.

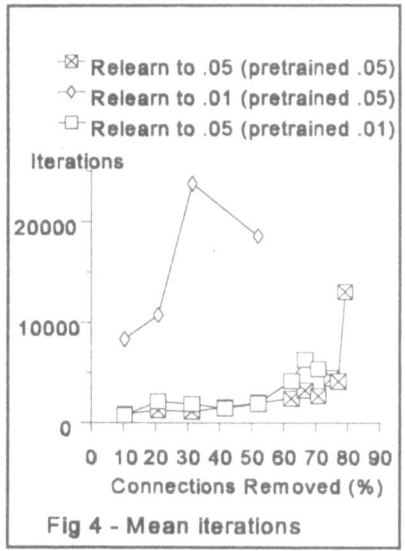 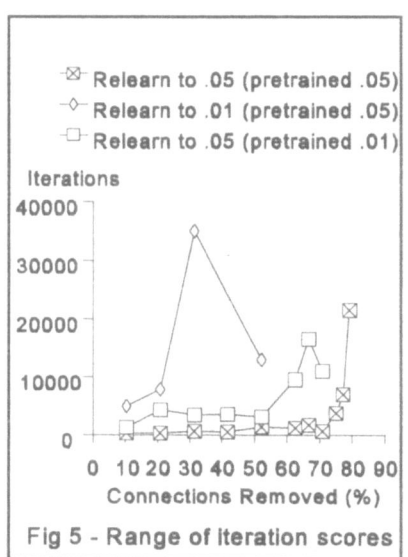

Figures 4 & 5 - Mean iterations (Fig 4) and range of scores about the mean (Fig 5) for pretrained and aged networks to relearn

However, even when not pretrained, networks subjected to 62.5% pruning also failed to learn to .01 rms. Failure to learn at this age level was, therefore, related to a system capacity determined by the number of connections in the system, and was not related to prelearning effects.

As predicted (see 1.4, predictions 1 and 2) speed of learning and speed of relearning generally showed gradual, but accelerating, declines with aging (figure 4) and associated increases in the range of scores (figure 5).

5.2.2 Recall and Noise

Recall scores were defined as the sum total of correct 1-element responses over the whole test epoch; noise scores are the sum total of false 1-element responses (i.e. in place of 0-elements) over the whole test epoch; and signal to noise ratios are recall scores/noise scores.

After Pretraining and Before Aging. Recall scores, as percentages, and signal to noise ratios were respectively 87.5% and 73 for the 'Minimally Learnt' networks and 100% and infinity (zero noise score) for the 'Well Learnt' networks.

After Aging and Before Relearning. Recall after aging, and before relearning, was as predicted (see 1.4, predictions 1 and 2). The patterns of decline in recall scores were similar for both .05 rms and .01 rms pretrained networks (figure 6a). The corresponding ranges of recall scores for correct elements in patterns were also similar for the two levels of training, but these showed no reliable pattern of change with increase in 'age'.

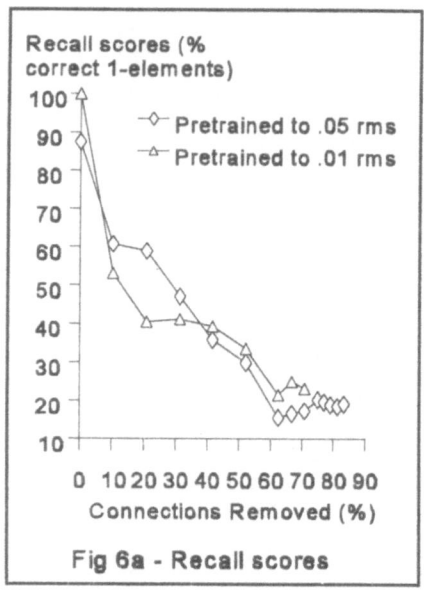

Fig 6a - Recall scores

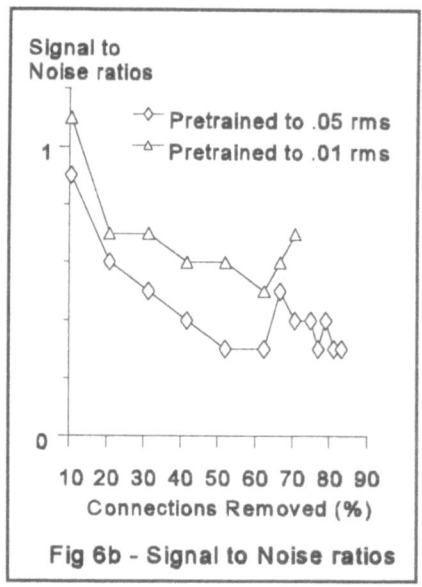

Fig 6b - Signal to Noise ratios

Figures 6a and 6b - Recall scores (Fig 6a) and Signal to Noise ratios (Fig 6b) for test before relearning (after prelearning and aging).

Mean signal to noise ratios fell (figure 6b) from 1.1 at 10% pruning to 0.5 at 64% pruning in the .01 pretrained networks and fell from 0.9 at 10% pruning to 0.3 at 78% pruning in the .05 pretrained networks. Mean signal to noise ratios were higher for the 'Well Learnt' then 'Minimally Learnt' pretrained networks, though after aging these were low across both degrees of training. Allowing for absent values at the 66.7 and 70.8% levels of connections pruned, a one-way within subjects analysis of variance for the effect of pretraining, comparing signal to noise ratios over all of the common range of ages for the two levels of pretraining, showed that even on a sample size of three networks this effect was statistically significant ($F(1, 46) = 4.94$, $p = .031$, $MSe = 3.556$).

After Aging and Relearning. With 62.5% of connections removed the recall scores and noise scores of both .05 rms and .01 rms pretrained networks prior to retraining were no better than those of untrained control networks.

After relearning, recall scores of .05 pretrained networks were substantially greater than those of .01 rms pretrained networks at all levels of pruning (figure 7a), given that the .01 rms pretrained network could not achieve convergence for relearning to .01 rms. The signal to noise ratios for relearning to .05 rms were also greater for the .05 rms pretrained networks, by a factor of at least 2 , for all network 'ages' (figure 7b). When the extreme values of signal to noise ratios for the .05 rms pretrained networks (at the 10.4, 62.5 and 66.7% levels of connections pruned) were adjusted down to the means of the non-extreme values, a one-way within subjects analysis of variance for the effect of pretraining, comparing signal to noise ratios over all of the common range of ages for the two levels of pretraining, showed that this was statistically significance ($F(1, 46) = 35.81$, $p < .001$, $MSe = 3453.8$).

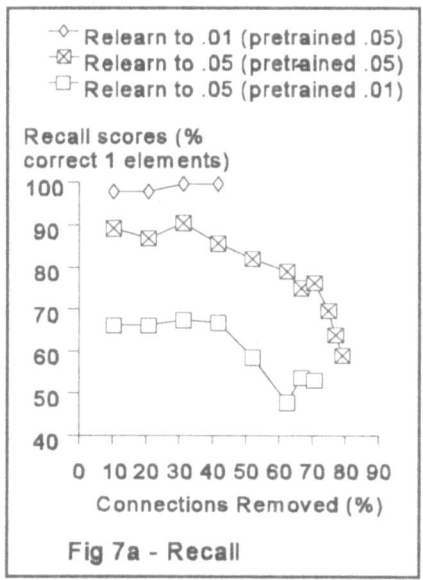

Fig 7a - Recall

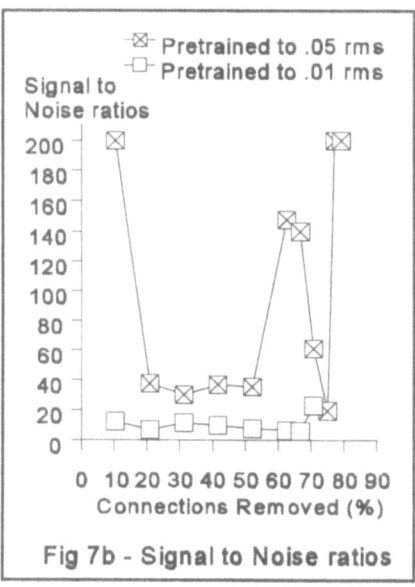

Fig 7b - Signal to Noise ratios

Figures 7a and 7b - Recall Scores (Fig 7a) and Signal to Noise ratios (Fig 7b) for test after relearning (following prelearning and aging)

5.3 Discussion

Aging resulted in 'Noisy Recall' rather than forgetting. Pruning only 10% of the connections from the pretrained networks caused dramatic increases in noise scores for both 'Well Learnt' and 'Minimally Learnt' pretrained networks whilst the corresponding recall scores for correct elements were fairly well preserved (fig 6a), given that the biggest fall in recall scores occurs between 0 and 10% pruning. Subsequent aging resulted in minimal changes in noise scores so that further graceful degradations in signal to noise ratios are effects of gracefully degrading recall scores for correct elements. 'Noise' therefore resulted from any loss of connections, more or less regardless of extent, and 'forgetting' related to the extent of connection loss.

Prelearning to the 'Well Learnt' strength gave better recall scores in the later stages of aging (fig 5, 35% to 70 % pruning) and better signal to noise ratios over all stages of aging. However: 1) there were insufficient trials to show that differences in recall scores were significant (given the closeness of the two sets of recall scores beyond 35% pruning), 2) beyond age 62.5% pruning, 'recall' was no better than that of untrained control networks, and 2) signal to noise ratios were low in all cases. Hence, though the degree of learning here preserved recall to some degree, such savings were slight with respect to overall magnitude of aging effects.

Relearning performance after aging was worse for 'Well Learnt' than for 'Minimally Learnt' networks. These results run counter to the intuitive predictions (see 1.4, prediction 3) but may reflect: 1) negative transfer of prior learning, which was greater in the 'Well Learnt' pretrained networks, and 2) the characteristics of weight space topography which rendered the 'Well Learnt' pretrained networks more liable to entrapment in local minima after aging.

6 Conclusions and Further Discussion

The results suggest that both random pruning and greatest weight first pruning gave the predicted patterns of change for speed of learning and recall when networks were trained from their untrained states. Both methods showed patterns of change that qualitatively reflect the general patterns of change evident in the psychological literature [1]. How comparable they are to one to another and to least weight first pruning remains to be confirmed by further experiments using otherwise identical methodology.

The results for networks that were trained, aged and retrained at different strengths of learning are less easily interpreted. It is suggested that: 1) rather than simply forgetting, recall became noisier, and 2) recall and noise were respectively related to the general topography of weight space and changes in local minima. An analysis of weight space may be desirable in future work.

One final and intriguing question follows on from the above, which is: if the above were to hold, what would happen if connection weights were degraded by multiplicative decay (i.e. $w_{t+1} = w_t .n$). Intuitively, the scale of topography would reduce without the appearance of local minima. In this instance the prediction that networks pretrained to the 'Well Learnt' strength of learning will relearn more rapidly and have better recall than those pretrained to the 'Minimally Learnt' strength of learning would hold. If such a dissociation in network performance for 'Well learnt' learning were to be shown, then this would imply that it might be possible to tell from the pattern of human learning performance whether decrements were consequences of localised dendritic loss or of more general and proportional reductions in the strength of dendritic transmission.

References

1. Rabbitt PMA. Does it all go together when it goes? The Nineteenth Sir Frederick Bartlett lecture to the Experimental Psychology Society. QJEP, 1993; 46a: 1-50

2. Ivy GO, MacLeod CM, Petit TL, Markus EJ: A Physiological framework for perceptual and cognitive changes in aging. In: Craik FIM & Salthouse TA (eds) The Handbook of Aging and Cognition. Lawrence Erlbaum Assoc, Hillsdale, New Jersey, 1992, pp 273-314

3. Cartwright R. Prospects for a Connectionist Account of Ageing. MSc (Cognitive Science) dissertation, School of Psychology, University of Birmingham, England, 1993

4. Hetherington PA, Sedienberg MS: Is there "catastrophic interference" in connectionist networks? In: Proceedings of the Eleventh Annual Meeting of the Cognitive Science Society. Lawrence Erlbaum Assoc, Hillsdale, New Jersey, 1989, pp 26-33

5. McRae K, Hetherington PA: Catastrophic Interference is Eliminated in Pretrained Networks. In: Proceedings of the Fifteenth Annual Meeting of the Cognitive Science Society. Lawrence Erlbaum Assoc, Hillsdale, New Jersey, 1993, pp 723-728

6. Pratt LY. Transferring Previously Learned Back-Propagation Neural Networks to New Learning Tasks. Technical Report No. ML-TR-37. Computer Science Dept, Rutgers University, New Jersey, 1993.

7. Sharkey NE & Sharkey AJ. Adaptive Generalisation. In press, to appear in: Artificial Intelligence Review, 1993, 6: 91-110

8. Horn JL, Donaldson G. On the myth of intellectual decline in adulthood. American Psychologist, 1976; 31: 701-719

9. Salthouse T.A: Effects of aging on verbal abilities: Examination of the psychometric literature. In: Light L.L & Burke D.M (eds) Language, Memory and Aging. Cambridge University Press, Cambridge, UK, 1988, 17-35

10. Rabbitt PMA: Crystal quest: a search for the basis of maintenance of practised skills into old age. In: Baddeley A & Weiskranz L (eds) Attention: Selection, Awareness and Control - a Tribute to Donald Broadbent. Oxford Science Publications, Oxford, UK., 1993, pp 188-230

11. Seigler IC, Botwinick J. A Long-Term Longitudinal Study of Intellectual Ability of Older Adults: The Matter of Selective Subject Attrition. Journal of Geront, 1979; 34: 242-245

Perception

Learning Invariances Via Spatio-Temporal Constraints

James V Stone*
Cognitive and Computing Sciences, University of Sussex, UK.
jims@uk.ac.sussex.cogs

Abstract

A model for unsupervised learning of visual invariances is presented. The learning method involves a linear combination of anti-Hebbian and Hebbian weight changes, over short and long time scales, respectively. The model is demonstrated on the problem of estimating sub-pixel stereo disparity from a temporal sequence of unprocessed image pairs. After learning on a given image sequence, the model's ability to detect sub-pixel disparity generalises, without additional learning, to image pairs from other sequences.

1 Introduction

The ability to learn high order visual invariances - surface orientation, curvature, depth, texture, and motion - is a prerequisite for the more familiar tasks (e.g. object recognition, obstacle avoidance) associated with biological vision. This paper addresses the question: What strategies enable neurons to learn these invariances from a spatio-temporal sequence of images, without the aid of an external teacher?

The model to be presented is, in certain respects, similar to the IMAX models[2, 1, 14]. Unfortunately, the IMAX models suffer from several drawbacks. The IMAX merit function has a high proportion of poor local optima. In [2] this problem was ameliorated by using a hand crafted weight-sharing architecture which which could not be used for other problem domains. In [1] temporally related input vectors were learned in a shift-invariant manner, and the tendency to become trapped in poor local optima was addressed by introducing a user-defined regularisation parameter to prevent weights from becoming too large. The IMAX models require storage of unit outputs over the entire training set, whereas a biologically plausible model should only use quantities that can be computed on-line. The stored outputs are required to evaluate the IMAX merit function and its derivative. This computationally expensive process requires large amounts of CPU time, which increases with the cube of the number of independent parameters implicit in the input data[14].

---

*The author is a joint member of the Schools of Biological Sciences, and Cognitive and Computing Sciences at the University of Sussex.

Although the model described in this paper is substantially different from the IMAX models, it shares with them a common assumption: *Generic solutions to problems of modelling perception are derivable from an analysis of the types of spatial and temporal changes immanent in the structure of the physical world (see [12]).* That is, a learning mechanism can discover high order parameters by taking advantage of quite general properties (such as spatial and temporal smoothness) of the physical world. These properties are not peculiar to any single physical environment so that such a mechanism should be able to extract a variety of high order parameters (e.g. size, position, 3D orientation and shape) via different sensory modalities (vision, speech, touch), and in a range of physical environments.

2 Learning Via Spatio-Temporal Constraints

Consider a sequence of images of an oriented, planar, textured surface which is moving relative to a fixed camera (see Figure 1c). Between two consecutive image frames, the distance to the surface changes by a small amount. Simultaneous with this small change in surface depth, a relatively large change in the intensity of individual pixels occurs. For example, a one-pixel shift in camera position can dramatically alter the intensity of individual image pixels, yet the corresponding change in the depth of the imaged surface is usually small. Thus *there is a difference between the rate of change of the intensity of individual pixels and the corresponding rate of change of parameters associated with the imaged surface.* A high order parameter is therefore characterised by variability over time, but the rate of change of the parameter is small, relative to that of the intensity of individual image pixels. More importantly, this sequence of images defines an ordered set in which consecutive images are derived from similar physical scenarios. That is, contiguous images are associated with similar parameter values. Thus, the temporal proximity of images provides a *temporal binding* of parameter values. This temporal binding permits us to cluster temporally proximal images together, as a means of discovering which invariances they might share.

It is possible to constrain the outputs of a model so that the learning process gives rise to outputs which posses the general characteristics of a high order parameter. *An 'economical' way for a model to generate such a set of outputs is to adapt its connection weights so that the outputs specify some high order parameter implicit in the model's inputs.* That is, it is possible to place quite general constraints on the outputs, such that the 'easiest' way for a model to satisfy these constraints is to compute the value of a high order parameter. Such constraints determine neither which particular parameter should be computed, nor the output value for any given input. Instead, *they specify only that particular types of relations must hold between successive outputs.*

The rate of change of the output of a model can be measured in terms of the 'temporally local', or *short term*, variance associated with a sequence of output values. If it is to reflect the value of a high order parameter then the output value has to vary, and vary *smoothly* over time. Thus its short term variance should be small, relative to its *long term* variance.

3 The Learning Method

The general strategy just described can be implemented using a multi-layer neural network model with a single linear output unit u. The output of u at each time t is z_t. The cumulative output $\tilde{z}_t$ of u is a temporal exponentially weighted sum of outputs z_t. We can obtain the desired behaviour in z by altering the connection weights such that z has a large long-term variance V, and a small short-term variance U. Thus, maximising V/U maximises the variance of z over a long interval, whilst simultaneously minimising its variance over relatively short intervals.

These requirements can be embodied in a merit function F, which can then be maximised with respect to the inter-unit connection weights of the model. The output of an output unit is $z_t = \sum_j w_{ij} y_j$, where w_{ij} is the value of a weighted connection from the jth to the ith unit, and y_j is the output of the jth unit. The merit function F is defined as:

$$F = log \frac{V}{U} = log \frac{\sum_{t=1}^{T}(\bar{z} - z_t)^2}{\sum_{t=1}^{T}(\tilde{z}_t - z_t)^2} \qquad (1)$$

Where V is the variance of z, and U is the short-term variance of z. The cumulative output $\tilde{z}_t$ of a unit is an exponentially weighted sum of outputs z over a period ϕ preceding t:

$$\tilde{z}_t = \sum_{\tau=t-\phi}^{t-1} \lambda^{t-\tau} z_\tau \qquad (2)$$

The long-term variance was set to the variance of z (effectively setting the half-life of the 'long-term' λ to to infinity). Thus, $\bar{z}$ is the mean output is of a unit. The sum of λ's is normalised such that, $\sum_{\tau=t-\phi}^{t-1} \lambda^{t-\tau} = 1$, where $0 \leq \lambda \leq 1$.

The derivative of F with respect to weights of output units results in a learning rule which is a linear combination of *Hebbian* and *anti-Hebbian* weight update, over long and short time scales, respectively[1] (For weights of hidden units, this rule incorporates an additional term which is the derivative of the hidden unit input/output function).

$$\frac{\partial F}{\partial w_{jk}} = V^{-1} \sum_t (\bar{z}_{kt} - z_{kt})(\bar{z}_{jt} - z_{jt})$$
$$-U^{-1} \sum_t (\tilde{z}_{kt} - z_t)(\tilde{z}_{jt} - z_{jt}) \qquad (3)$$

The learning algorithm consists of computing the derivative of F with respect to every weight in the model to locate a maximum in F. The required derivatives of F with respect to weights between successive layers of units are computed using the chain rule (but not the learning method) described in [9].

Note that the function F, and the derivatives of U and V can be computed incrementally at each time step. Thus the quantities required to alter weights (in order to maximise F) can be computed on-line.

---

[1] Thanks to Harry Barrow and Alistair Bray for pointing this out.

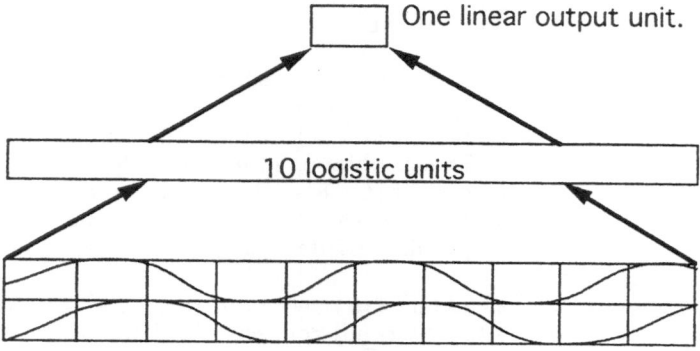

Two one-dimensional images of 10 pixels each.

Figure 1: The neural network model architecture.

3.1 Model Architecture

As shown in Figure 1, the model consists of three layers of units. Every unit
in each layer is connected to every unit in the following layer. The first layer
consists of 20 linear input units, arranged in two rows of 10 units. The second
layer consists of 10 units, each of which has an output $y = tanh(X)$, where X is
the total input to a second-layer unit from units in the input layer. The input
to the ith unit is $X_i = \sum_j (w_{ij} x_j + \theta_j)$, where w_{ij} is the value of a weighted
connection from the jth to the ith unit, and x_j is the output of the jth input
unit. All and only units in the second layer have a bias weight θ from a unit
with constant output of 1. This bias weight is adapted in the same way as all
other weights in the model. The output layer consists of a single linear unit, as
described in the previous section.

3.2 The Input Data

The input consisted of a temporal sequence of stereo images with *sub-pixel
disparities*. The sequence was derived from a planar surface which was both
translating and oscillating in depth in a sinusoidal manner (see Figure 2). This
moving surface was used to generate an ordered set of 1000 stereo pairs of
one dimensional 10-pixel images. The disparity of successive images in this set
varied sinusoidally between ±1 according to the depth of the imaged surface.
The sinusoid had a period of 1000 time steps to correspond with the set of 1000
image pairs.

The grey-level of surface elements was chosen randomly from the range
(0,1). The surface grey-levels were smoothed (using a Gaussian with a standard
deviation of 10 surface elements), and normalised to have zero mean and unit
variance.

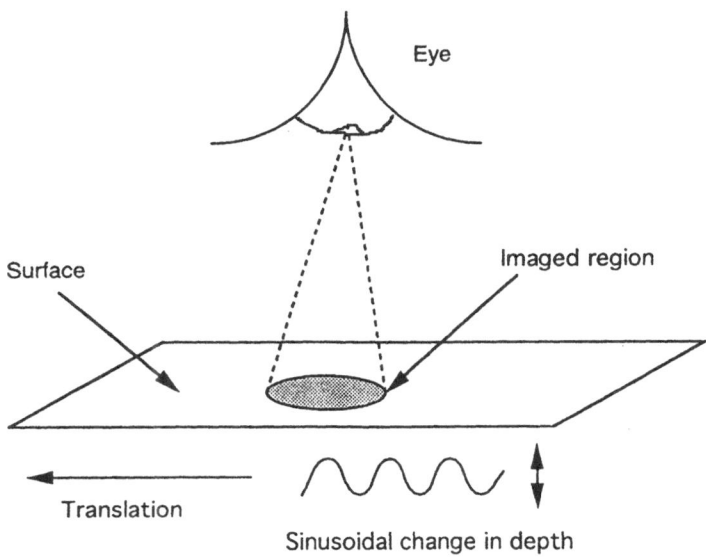

Figure 2: Schematic diagram of how surface moves over time. The surface depth varies sinusoidally as the surface translates at a constant velocity parallel to the image.

At each time step t (see Figure 2), each image pair was constructed by sub-sampling the intensity values on the moving surface. The grey-level of each image pixel was derived from the mean of 10 contiguous surface elements. This allows image pairs with sub-pixel disparities to be generated. For example, if members of a pair sample from surface regions which are separated by one surface element (=0.1 of a pixel width) then the images have a disparity of 0.1 pixels. For disparities in the range ± 1 this means that image pairs with a total of 21 disparities can be obtained. Note that adjacent pixel grey-levels were derived from adjacent, non-overlapping surface regions.

In order to simulate the translation of the surface, the first image $I1_t$ of a pair was moved along the surface by 20 surface elements (=2 image pixels) at each time step. The second image $I2$ of a pair was aligned with $I1$, and then shifted along the surface according to the current disparity value.

4   Results

The model was tested on stereo pairs of images (see Figures 1..3). The value of λ was set such that the half-life h of λ was 32 time steps, and $\phi = 4h$. The long-term variance was set to the variance of z. Thus, $\bar{z}$ is the mean state of a unit. The initial weights varied randomly between ± 0.3.

For results reported here, the function F was maximised using a conjugate gradient technique. The more conventional iterative method associated with Hebbian learning was slower, though no less reliable. The system converges

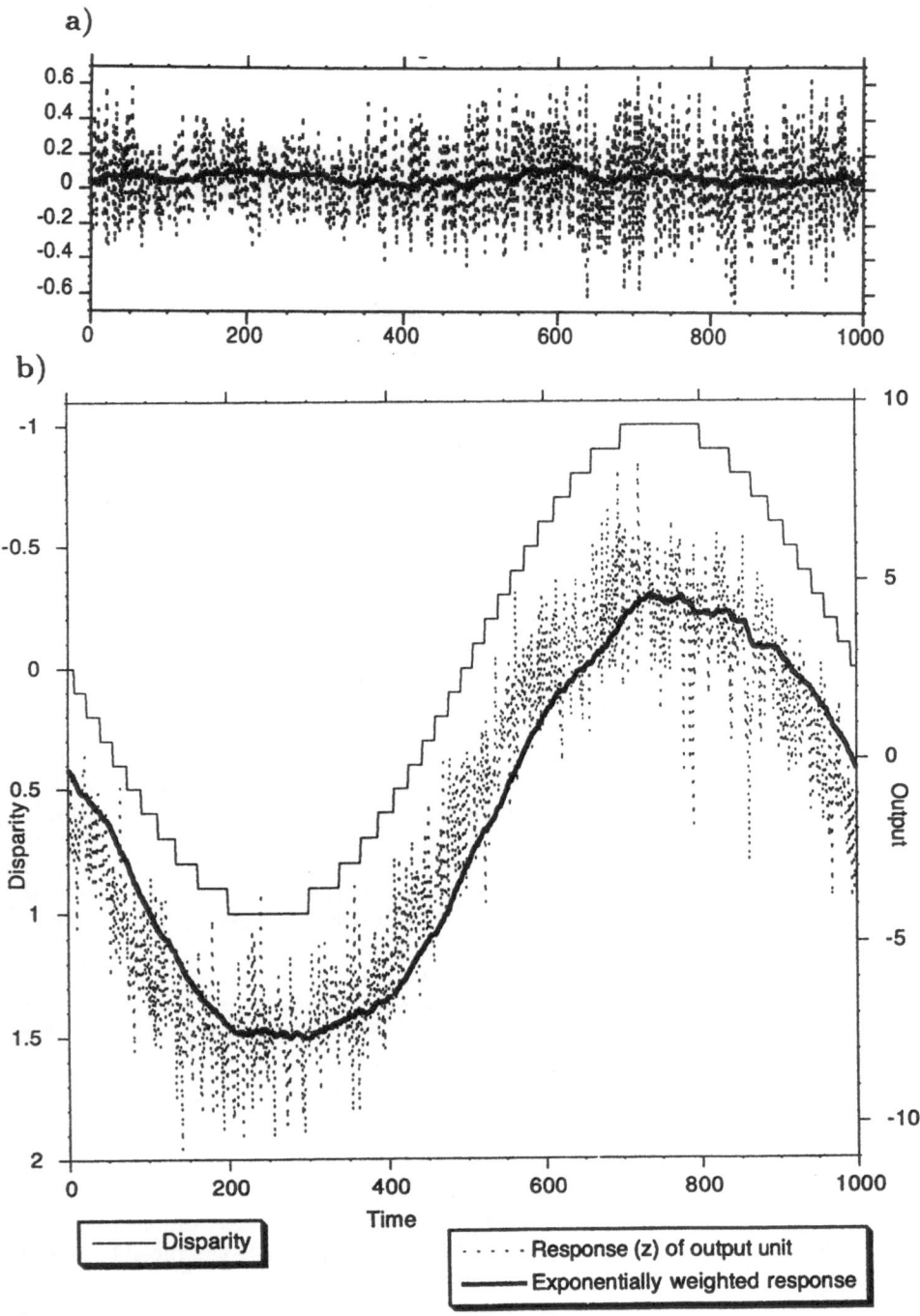

Figure 3: Graphs of time t versus output z (a) before and (b) after learning.

reliably, giving correlation magnitudes between output z and disparity of not less than 0.9. After 100 conjugate gradient iterations the correlation r between the output z and disparity was $r = -0.957$ (see Figure 4). The number of hidden units was not critical, though learning was slower with less than five hidden units. Similar results were obtained with as few as four units in the middle layer.

Note that the correlation r is negative for the results shown here. It is not necessary, nor even desirable, that r should be positive. If we consider the output unit as part of an integrated system which computes the values of different invariances then it is only necessary that a unit's output is able to signal some aspect of the input to other units. This can be achieved equally well with either a high magnitude negative or positive value of r.

4.1 Generalisation

If the model has learned disparity (and not some spurious correlate of disparity) then it should generalise to new stereo sequences, *without any learning of these sequences*. Accordingly, the model was tested with a sequence consisting of 1000 stereo pairs. These were obtained from a new surface constructed in the same manner as was used for the original data set. During testing, the disparity varied sinusoidally between ± 1 as before. However, rather than deriving consecutive image pairs from neighbouring surface regions, each image pair was derived from a random point on the surface. This tested the ability of the system to estimate disparity independently of the particular grey-level profiles in each image pair. Using these data the correlation was $r = -0.916$.

Note that the *rate* at which disparity varies has no effect on this test correlation. This is because, whilst learning depends upon current and previous states, the state z at any time depends only upon the current input. Thus, the model can detect disparity which varies at non-sinusoidally.

4.2 Convergence

The magnitude of the correlation between unit output and disparity was $|r| < 0.9$ only for simulations with a half-life $\lambda < 2$ time steps (see Figure 3). For $\lambda \geq 2$ the rate of convergence, defined as $1/$(the number of iterations required such that $|r| > 0.5$), was proportional to h^2, where h is the half-life of λ.

These results indicate that the function F has a very low proportion of poor local maxima. This, in turn, suggests that the 'energy landscape' defined by F is relatively smooth, allowing it to be traversed by simple search techniques. Simulations using simple gradient ascent produce comparable results in about 500 iterations. More importantly, it suggests that maxima are reliably associated with model weight values which enable the detection of high order parameters of inputs.

4.3 Unit Receptive Fields

An analysis of the response characteristics of units revealed the following observations. Units in the middle layer have stable outputs only over a small range of disparities. This is consistent with the response properties of disparity-sensitive neurons in the primary visual cortex with narrow tuning profiles[8].

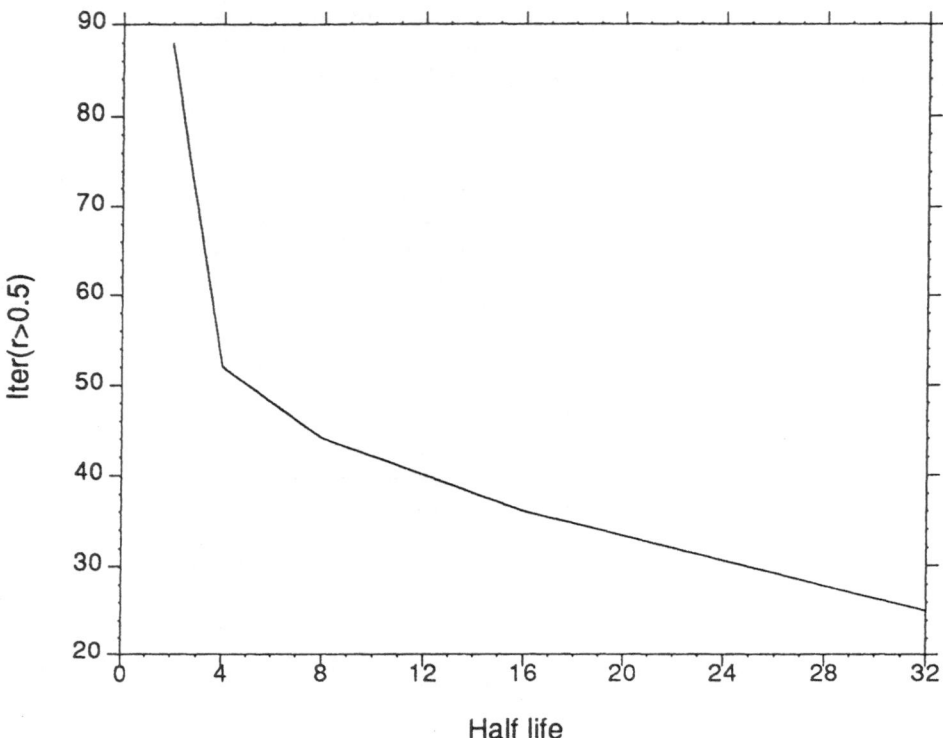

Figure 3: Graph of half-life h versus number of iterations k required to exceed $r = 0.5$. A graph of $k(r > 0.5)$ versus h^{-2} yields a linear fit with a correlation of 0.993 for $h = \{2, 4, 8, 16, 32\}$.

5   The Frustration of Learning

For small values of the half-life h, adjusting the model's weights so as to reduce the difference d_t between z_t and $\tilde{z}_t \approx z_{t-1}$ creates a form of *frustration* [6]. That is, the benefits of decreasing d_t are cancelled by the costs of *increasing* corresponding differences $d_\tau (\tau \neq t)$ of other times. The 'temporal myopia' associated with small h values obstructs the discovery of a set of weights which minimises d for all times, and which corresponds to a global maximum in F.

The temporal half-life parameter h acts somewhat like an *annealing parameter*, smoothing out local maxima in F at high values of h. As $h \to \infty$, so $U \to V$, and therefore $V/U \to 1$ (for any weight values). As in [5, 4, 10], at high 'temperatures' the energy function defined by F is convex, and there exists a single maximum. As the temperature (h) is reduced, the energy function becomes increasingly non-convex. Each of a series of decreasing temperatures is associated with an increasingly non-convex energy function. If consecutive temperatures are sufficiently similar then the maximum of an energy function associated with one temperature h_i can be used as the starting point for the search for the maximum of the next function (associated with the new, lower temperature h_{i+1}). This annealing method has not been empirically tested, and, within each simulation reported here, the value of h is constant.

6 Discussion

The model discovers high order invariances by computing a non-linear function of components of each input vector. Informally, this often amounts to evaluating *relations* between sets of components of each input image.

The stereo disparity task learned is a hyper-acuity task. That is, the amount of disparity is smaller than the width of any single receptor (pixel). The model discriminates disparities as small as one tenth of the width of an input receptor, which compares with human performance on stereo hyper-acuity tasks[13]. Specifically, 19 of the 21 disparities were less than one pixel. Members of a stereo pair which have a sub-pixel disparity differ in terms of the local slope and curvature of their intensity profiles, and not necessarily in terms of the positions of the peaks and troughs in these profiles. Thus, detecting disparities of less than one pixel requires more than the construction of a pixel-to-pixel correspondence between members of a stereo pair. It requires comparisons of relations-between-pixels in one image with relations-between-pixels in the other image. The resultant meta-relation that specifies the amount of disparity in each pair is, in statistical terms, of a high order. The only means available to the model to discover this high order parameter was the assumption of its temporal smoothness.

The assumption of temporal smoothness was implemented via a time decay constant λ. Choosing a value for λ implicitly specifies a temporal 'grain size' and therefore delimits which types of parameters can be learned. Perceptually salient events (such as motion) occur within a relatively small range of temporal windows. At rates of change which are either too high or too low, events cannot be detected. Between these two extremes, we hypothesize that different neurons have temporal tuning curves which ensure that the range of salient rates of perceptual change can be detected by a sub-population of neurons. The value chosen for λ was important (though not critical) for learning to succeed. However, for any 'reasonable' rate of change of disparity, some units (neurons) in a population tuned to different temporal frequencies (λ's) would learn disparity.

It is widely accepted that learning relies upon the temporal proximity of learned events. Classical conditioning only occurs if the conditioned stimulus is presented within a small interval before the unconditioned stimulus; reinforcement learning typically relies upon events which are temporally proximal. There is evidence that the 'body maps' in the sensory cortex can be modified by altering the temporal relations between inputs from adjacent sensory regions[3]. Given the importance of time in these different types of learning, it does not seem unreasonable to suggest that time also plays a critical role in the learning of perceptually salient parameters.

As has been demonstrated here, learning to extract perceptual parameters from continuously changing visual inputs relies upon the temporal continuity of parameter values. Given such a sequence of inputs, any learning system that did not take advantage of the temporal continuity of invariances would be discarding a powerful and general heuristic for discovering important properties of the physical world.

7 Conclusion

Conventional low-level computer vision techniques rely upon the assumption that a parameter value is invariant over some region of space(see [11]). The model described in this paper assumes that useful parameters vary relatively slowly over time. When presented with a sequence of images, the model discovers precisely those parameters which describe the behaviour of the imaged surface through time.

Whereas the particular algorithm used here is by no means ideal, the spatio-temporal assumptions upon which the method is based are quite general. In this regard, the method is consistent with Marr's approach:

> "The critical step in formulating the computational theory of stereopsis is the discovery of additional constraints on the process that are imposed naturally and that limit the result to allow a unique solution"
> Marr, [7], page 104.

Acknowledgements: Thanks to R Lister, S Isard, T Collett, A Bray, J Budd and C North for comments on drafts of this paper, and to Harry Barrow for useful discussions. This research was supported by a Joint Council Initiative grant awarded to J Stone, T Collett and D Willshaw.

References

[1] S Becker. Learning to categorize objects using temporal coherence. *Neural Information Processing Systems*, pages 361–368, 1992.

[2] S Becker and GE Hinton. Self-organizing neural network that discovers surfaces in random-dot stereograms. *Nature*, 335:161–163, 1992.

[3] SA Clark, A Allard, WM Jenkins, and MM Merzenich. Receptive fields in the body-surface map in adult cortex defined by temporally correlated inputs. *Nature*, 332:444–445, March 1988.

[4] R Durbin and D Willshaw. An analogue approach to the travelling salesman problem using an elastic net method. *Nature*, 326(6114):689–691, 1987.

[5] JJ Hopfield. Neurons with graded response have collective computational properties like those of two-state neurons. *Proc Nat Ac Sci*, 81:3088–3092, 1984.

[6] S Kirkpatrick, CD Gelat, and MP Vecchi. Optimization by simulated annealing. *Science*, 220(4598):671–680, May 1983.

[7] D Marr. *Vision*. Freeman, New York, 1982.

[8] GF Poggio. Cortical neural mechanisms of stereopsis studied with dynamic random-dot stereograms. *Cold Spring Harbour Symposia on Quantitative Biology*, LV:749–756, 1990.

[9] DE Rumelhart, GE Hinton, and RJ Williams. Learning representations by back-propagating errors. *Nature*, 323:533–536, 1986.

[10] JV Stone. The optimal elastic net: Finding solutions to the travelling salesman problem. *ICANN92*, pages 170–174, 1992.

[11] JV Stone. Shape from local and global analysis of texture. *Phil. Trans. Roy. Soc. Lond.(B)*, 339(1287):53–65, January 1992.

[12] JV Stone. Computer vision: What is the object? In *Prospects for AI, Proc. Artificial Intelligence and Simulation of Behaviour, Birmingham, England. IOS Press, Amsterdam.*, pages 199–208, April 1993.

[13] G Westheimer. The ferrier lecture, 1992. seeing depth with two eyes: Stereopsis. *Proc Royal Soc London, B*, 257:205–214, 1994.

[14] RS Zemel and GE Hinton. Discovering viewpoint invariant relationships that characterize objects. *Technical Report, Dept. of Computer Science, University of Toronto, Toronto, ONT MS5 1A4, 1991*, 1991.

Topographic Map Formation as Statistical Inference

Roland Baddeley

Department of Psychology

University of Oxford

England

Abstract

Neurons representing similar aspects of the world are often found close together in the cortex. It is proposed that this phenomenon can be modelled using a statistical approach. We start by using a neural network to find the "features" that were most likely to have generated the observed probability distribution of inputs. These features can be found using a Boltzmann machine architecture, but the results of this simple network are unsatisfactory. By adding two additional constraints (*priors*), that all representational units have the same probability of being true, and that nearby representational units are correlated, the network is shown to be capable of extracting distributed, spatially localised topographic representations based on an input of natural images. This is believed to be the first network capable of achieving this.

As a model of topographic map formation, this framework has a number of strengths: 1) The framework is a general one, in which winner-takes-all and distributed representations are special cases. 2) Though slow, the learning is simple and approximately Hebbian. 3) The network can extract topographic representations based on distributed input such as natural images.

1   Introduction

One of the most striking aspects of the visual cortex is that within a visual area, the receptive field properties possess topographic structure. Specifically, if two cells within a visual area are close together, then these cells will usually be tuned to similar characteristics of the world. The example considered here is that cells located close together in striate cortex tend to represent similar locations in visual space. It is of interest to know not only how this organisation could come to occur, but also why?

Pertinent to any theory of this phenomena is that this topographic structure is partly, but not entirely, based on input activity. In animals reared in the dark, under stroboscopic lighting conditions, or with input activity entirely blocked chemically, the representation in striate cortex has topographic organisation. Despite this, fine tuning of the representation requires input activity with the degree of topographic organisation in experimentally manipulated animals being less than that found in normally reared animals.

This makes sound engineering sense given that developmental processes may introduce errors. By passing a known signal through the system, the system can be checked for damage and errors by comparing the resulting signal to that expected if the system was undamaged. Any deviations found can then be used to direct efforts to compensate for this damage. If the system is to compensate for optical damage any calibration signal will have to be passed through the eye (consisting of, say, statistical regularities of the world (Baddeley, 1994)), and it is proposed that the visual system of a dark reared animal is analogous to a television that has not been exposed to television signals. Whilst the channels (receptive field locations) are tuned to approximately the correct place they have not been fine tuned and reception is not all it could be.

The problem of generating the relationship between the visual world and its representation in cortex is not new. Hebb (1949), proposed a framework for understanding these phenomena. Unfortunately, the process proposed was not sufficiently specified to tell if it would work. More recently, models specified in sufficient detail to allow computer implementations have been described, starting with the work of von der Malsburg and Willshaw (1977). Of these subsequent models, probably the most influential has been that of Kohonen (Kohonen, 1982). Specifically inspired by biological phenomena, its major influence has been in engineering, but it has also been applied to modelling detailed aspects of topographic map formation in cortex.

2 Kohonen's approach

Kohonen's proposal is based on classification. Given N representational units (neurons), and an input, the initial operation is to find the representational unit that best represents the input. The representational unit's weights are then changed, to make it better represent this input. By presenting many different inputs, this process results in each of the N units corresponding to classifications determined by the data. This classification process groups into the same category similar events, and places the category centres where inputs have previously been found. Both of these characteristics are useful, and if given no other information as to what are useful classifications, this process is a reasonable first step in processing high dimensional data.

This scheme on its own does not impose any topographic structure onto those classifications. To achieve this, topographic structure is associated with the representation units. After finding the "best" unit to classify a given input, as well as modifying this unit, its neighbours are also modified towards the input. This process is still, at heart, a classifier system but by training neighbouring units, this results in classifications where nearby units (in representational space) correspond to similar classifications.

Why then, given a simple model with a method of learning not wildly incompatible with the known physiology and one that results in representations that mirror a number of aspects of known physiology, do we need to look further for a model of topographic map formation? This stems from a number of problems associated not with the topographic mapping component of the system but from the identification of classification as the fundamental operation of the striate cortex.

In the Kohonen net a given input is represented by a classification. Whilst such a "grandmother cell" representation may be compatible with higher level vision, if proposed to operate at the level of the striate cortex, it severely reduces the number of communicable signals. It also fails to capture the factorial nature of the representations found in striate cortex where a given image appears to be represented by a large number of features (lines, edges ...) and not by one single global predicate. This aspect makes it incompatible with known physiology and potentially bad engineering for a front–end to general purpose visual system.

In the Kohonen network, like many competitive learning schemes, the units weights converge approximately to a within-class average. The standard demonstration of topographic mapping in the Kohonen network is to present the network with spatially localised Gaussian blobs. Here the average of all inputs that would be close to a given blob detector is also a blob, and so, not unsurprisingly, the system develops spatially localised "blob" detectors. If the input is made more complicated (eg elongated and oriented blobs), then the units will converge to elongated blob detectors that appear more "biological". Unfortunately, if the system is presented with natural images, as is required if it is to compensate for optical damage, then there is not a sensible "average" for the units to make. In this situation, the Kohonen network fails to converge to an interpretable solution.

To summarise, given that classification is the desired task, that only a single unit is required to signal a given input, and that the input is spatially localised, then the Kohonen network can be a very useful tool. When classification is an inappropriate form of computation, where each input should be coded by the activity of a number of units, and the input is not spatially localised, the Kohonen network is inappropriate. It is claimed that the task of calibrating topological representations in the brain is of this second type.

3   An alternative definition of "features"

Kohonen's proposal therefore has a number of problems and these stem from the choice of classification as its basis of operation. What then would be a more appropriate metaphor?

> It is proposed that the visual system is attempting to infer the "features" that generated the visual images it is presented with, and that, since this is an ill-defined problem, topographic structure is imposed in order to generate unique, repeatable, and usable solutions.

This requires further explanation: consider a simplified model of a world which is generated by the presence and absence of a number of features. This model can be thought of in terms of a conceptual jigsaw, where each image is constructed by selecting a subset of the available pieces and placing them down to construct an image. If the world is generated by such a method, then a reasonable representation of an image is in terms of the particular "features" or jig-saw pieces that were used to generate that image. This corresponds quite closely to Hubel and Wiesel's original proposal as to why the cells in striate cortex operate as they do: The world is represented in terms of "blobs", "bars", and "edges", because the visual images we meet in the world are generated by "blobs", "bars", and "edges".

Representational Units

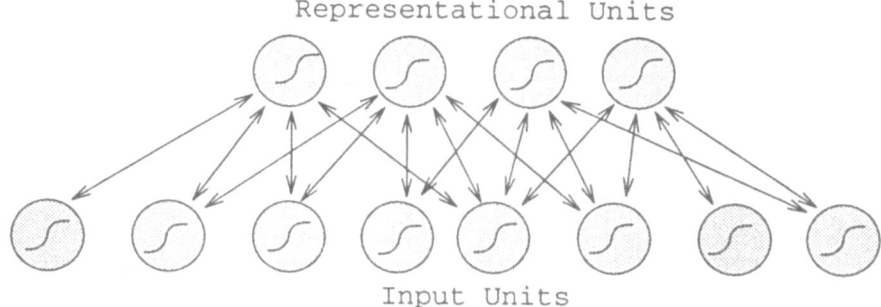

Input Units

Figure 1: A simple two layer network of input and representational units, with complete bi-directional connectivity between the input layer and the representational layer. The aim of learning in this network is to change the weights (and thresholds) of the system to minimise the difference between the probability distribution of the inputs observed in the world, and that "generated" by the representational units in the absence of the input. When learning is complete, the weights to the hidden units correspond to a (very simplistic) model of the image generation process. It is proposed that a representation in terms of these proposed "generators" is a useful representation of the images and a more useful metaphor than classification for understanding topographic map formation.

If we knew what was generating the our images of the world, then this proposal is (relatively) simple: We represent the world in terms of the objects that are generating the images we see. Unfortunately we only have access to example images and not the underlying image generators. It is proposed that the process of learning is to infer these probable image generators and then use these to represent the image. This framework of viewing learning as the inference of probable "image generators" is a more appropriate framework for understanding topographic map formation than the classification-based Kohonen approach.

Formalising the idea of inferring probable image generators requires some simplifications. Firstly, consider the input neurons $\mathbf{X}$. These represent measurements from the world and signal the probability that their associate measurement is true: $P(\mathbf{X}) = 1$. This step of representing the world in terms of probabilities seems an extreme simplification but consideration of the properties of real "input" neurons such as retinal ganglion cells, makes this approximation less unreasonable. To a first approximation, retinal ganglion cells can be approximated as a Poisson process and such processes can be entirely summarised by the probability that the neuron will fire within a given time interval. Estimates of the information transmission of visual neurons vary, but are usually small and of the order of 1-2 bits per second. In such a system, the output of each neuron is well captured by a simple probability associated with each input neuron. Given this simplification, all knowledge of the world can be captured in the observed probability distribution of input neurons: $P(\mathbf{X})$.

We then wish to infer a set of features $\mathbf{Y}$ that are likely to have generated $P(\mathbf{X})$. To do this we need to define the relationship between $\mathbf{Y}$ and $\mathbf{X}$. For simplicity, following (Hinton & Sejnowski, 1983), we use the Boltzmann machine dynamics:

$$P(x_i = 1) = 1 - P(x_i = -1) = \tanh\left(\sum y_j w_{ij} + \mu_i^x + I_i\right) \tag{1}$$

and

$$P(y_i = 1) = 1 - P(y_i = -1) = \tanh\left(\sum x_j w_{ij} + \mu_i^y\right) \tag{2}$$

where $P(x_i)$ is the probability that a given input is 1, $P(y_i)$ is the probability that representational feature y_i is present, w_{ij} is the symmetric weight between the input and representational units, the μ are the units thresholds, I_i is the external input from the world, and 1/-1 dynamics are chosen for computational efficiency. This constitutes an extremely simplified model of image generation! If a particular inferred representational feature is present then this simply changes the probability of input features being present. It cannot possibly capture anything of the subtleties of real image generation but noting that higher order regularities can be simply included in this framework it is enough to explore whether such a framework is sufficient to understand topographic map calibration.

We want now to find a set of features (weights) between the input and the representation units so that the representation units are "likely" to have generated the observed $P(\mathbf{X})$. Following (Hinton & Sejnowski, 1983), we define a cost function G, the Kullback-Leiber distance:

$$G = P(\mathbf{X}) \log \frac{P(\mathbf{X})}{P(\mathbf{X'})} \tag{3}$$

where $P(\mathbf{X'})$ is the probability distribution of input units "generated" by our model of the world when the system is not connected to the outside world. When G is minimised, we have the set of representational units that will generate a probability distribution of input units that is as close as possible to that observed in the outside world. To perform gradient descent in G, we change the weights by $\delta w_{ij} = K(P(x_i)P(y_i) - P'(x_i)P'(y_j))$, where $P'(x)$ and $P'(y)$ are the observed probabilities of the input and output variables when the system is run without external input. In other words, learning consists of measuring the world, observing what our model would predict, and then changing our model to become more like the observed world. We are now in a position to find out if, when trained with examples from real natural images, a system based on this principle of inferring the generating features, infers features (w_{ij}) that are at all sensible.

4   General Methods

To test the hypothesis that topographic map formation can be understood in terms of finding features likely to have generated the observed images, a collection of natural images was required. These images consisted of a collection of pictures of natural scenes. Pictures were taken on a 35mm camera with a 50mm lens (unless otherwise specified). The photographs were then digitised using a Hewlett Packard Scanjet Plus at the 75 dpi setting. The central 256 by 256 pixel region was then sampled and the grey levels normalised so that the lowest value was 1 and the largest was 256. This process was used to create the 81 images from urban, country, and the office environment. These images are considered to be representative of the images potentially used to calibrate a topographic representation. The network inputs consist of the probability of input neurons firing but the inputs are simple gray levels. As an approximate model of retinal ganglion cells, based on the work of Laughlin and van Hateran (Laughlin, 1981; Van Hateran, 1993), the following pre-processing steps were, therefore, performed on the images:

- The image intensities were logarithmically transformed.

- The transformed images were convolved with a centre surround filter. The parameters of this filter were found by maximising the mutual information between the log transformed image and the filtered outputs using methods described in van Hateren (1993).

- The filtered outputs were, in turn, passed through a tanh non-linearity, the parameters of which were chosen to best perform histogram equalisation as proposed by Laughlin (1981) based on work on fly retina.

This resulted in 81 processed images with values ranging between 1 and -1 which correspond to (2* probability of the cell firing)-1. To simplify and speed up computation, rather than work in two dimensional samples, one dimensional random samples of length 100 were taken from the 81 images. These constituted the input to the network.

5 Experiment one: the most "likely" generating features

The first experiment attempts to find what features would be the most likely to have generated the images given the pre-processed natural images as input. Ten representational units were used fully connected to 100 input units. The input-output correlations were estimated as in the standard Boltzmann machine learning algorithm except that in the unclamped phase, rather than unclamping all input units, 50% were randomly left clamped. On line learning was used and mean feiled update was used for the input units[1]. The presented results are the solutions after 50,000 iterations and are shown in Figure 2.

As can be seen, the "receptive fields" of the representational neurons are vaguely localised in space and given that they started with no information as to spatial localisation, this is something. The "receptive fields" overlap and on each simulation the weights were very different. These results provide little evidence for the proposed mechanism.

---

[1] In many situations, mean field annealing can lead to great problems, but in this situation, with no within layer connections, the approximation is exact (Galland, 1993).

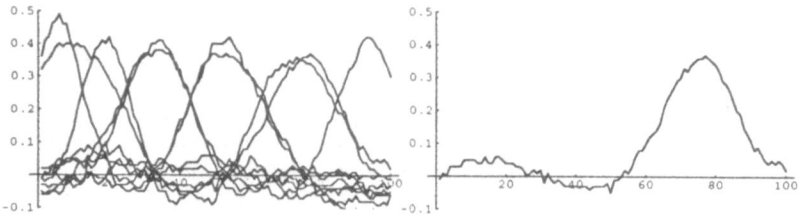

Figure 2: The results of one run of the proposed network operating on samples of natural images. The left diagram represents the weights from the input units to each of the ten representational units. B shows the weight profile of representation unit six. Each run resulted in a different set of weights, with this run being reasonably representative. As can be seen the results are not impressive.

6 Experiment two: A prior on feature probability

What is wrong? The fact that the solutions are different on every run indicates that the problem is (unsurprisingly) under-specified. This is an opportunity to place constraints on the system. These constraints can consist of characteristics of the system that would be desirable for a representation. One desirable characteristic is that all the representational units have the same probability of being true. By specifying such a constraint the task of interpreting the representation by subsequent levels will be made easier and will greatly reduce any potential redundancy. How then do we enforce a prior belief that all the representational units will have the same chance of firing?

In order to train the system to increase the probability of generating the observed inputs we train with examples of these inputs and iteratively update the weights. To increase the probability that each of the representational units will be true with a given probability C, we could generate a virtual training set where all other statistics in the network are random but where the probability of the representational units being on is C. For such a simple regularity and to a reasonable approximation we need not do this. Instead during the normal training in the clamped phase, we can combine the actually collected statistics with what they would be if the unit was firing with the correct probability. Here, for simplicity, we assume a Dirac prior and ignore the empirical statistics: the hidden unit threshold statistics are set to $2C - 1$, where C, the probability a given unit is the desired unit output probability set again for simplicity to 0.5. This forces all the representational units to have a probability of firing of 0.5.

The results of running the network, with the representational units constrained to be on 50% of the time are shown in Figure 3. As can be seen, these results are far more satisfactory, except that the system has no topographic ordering (since there is no constraint for it to have such ordering). This is the

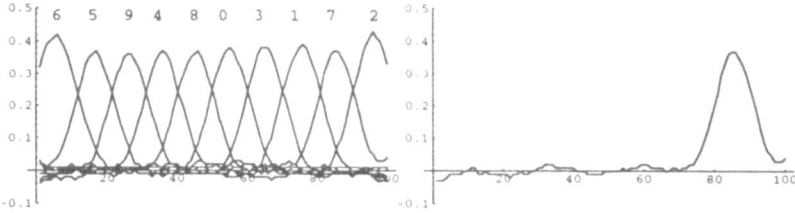

Figure 3: The results of the network trained on natural images but with a prior on the representational units all being on 50% of the time. The left diagram shows the weights to the ten representational units. The right diagram shows only the weights to unit 7. As can be seen the results are more convincing. Each unit is spatially localised and the input space is well partitioned into separate receptive fields producing a distributed representation of the input. There is no topographic ordering of these receptive fields since there is no constraint in the system to prefer such mappings.

next avenue to be explored.

7 Experiment three: A prior on inter-unit correlations

To create a topographic representation we need some term in the cost function that will encourage this. One way of doing this is to force nearby units to be correlated. Again this can naturally be done by allowing lateral connections between nearby units and in the clamped phase, rather than collect the actual statistics, supply statistics indicating that nearby units are correlated. Again, since the network tries to minimise the (Kullback-Leiber) distance between the observed (in this case, some of these observations have been "invented"), and the model statistics, the network will attempt to change the lateral weights until the between-neighbour correlations are at the desired level.

This was performed whith the desired statistics that each unit was correlated at the 0.5 level with its two nearest neighbours, 0.3 with both of its neighbours at distance two, and at the 0.15 level with its neighbours at distance three. The results are shown in Figure 4 and, as can be seen, this is not sufficient to force the network to find a topographic representation.

8 Experiment four: Non-random initial conditions

One possible reason for the failure of the network to converge is that the optimisation is too difficult. One way to approach this would be to, in some way,

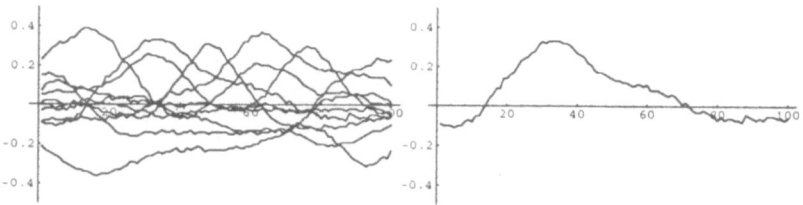

Figure 4: The neural network run on the collection of natural images but with the constraint that the hidden units will be true 50% of the time and that nearby units will be more highly correlated. As can be seen, in this case the network does not converge to a topographic representation. It is proposed that this problem has many local minima and though the system may sometimes converge to solutions with partial topographic ordering, this is the exception. One possible solution to this problem, inspired by the biology, is to start the system from an non-random initialisation point. This is explored in the next section.

"anneal" the area of local interaction as is done in the Kohonen network. Here we instead observe that in the biology, the input activity-based system starts with some gross topographic structure, and what the input activity does is to refine this structure. We therefore, explored the possibility of starting the network with approximate topographic structure. Instead of random initialisation, the weights from the input to the representational units were initialised to:

$$\|N(1,0) + 1\| \times \exp -\frac{(x - i)^2}{25^2} \tag{4}$$

where i is the centre location of the unit, x is the location of the input weight, $N(1,0)$ is a value drawn from a Gaussian distribution mean zero sd = 1, and $\|.\|$ is the absolute value. Additionally a random 5% of the weights had 0.2 added. This resulted in very rough topographic structure, but with considerable noise. One start state is shown in Figure 5 A). Given this initialisation, the same procedure of constraining the representational units to be on 50% of the time, and to be correlated with their neighbours reliably results in representations with topographic structure (Figure 5).

9 Conclusion

It has been argued that the Kohonen network is inadequate to model the refinement of topographic representations if the input is sampled natural images: it both produces winner-takes-all representations which are inappropriate for low level vision and has difficulty with input data where performing an average is not a sensible operation.

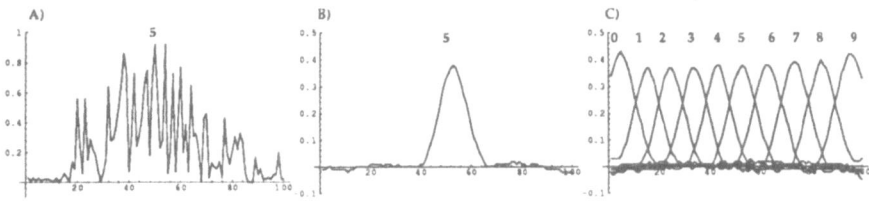

Figure 5: The representation resulting from non-random initial conditions. A) shows the initial weights going into a single unit. As can be seen there is limited topographic structure. B) The final "receptive field" for the same unit after training. C) The inputs of all ten units. As can be seen the "receptive fields" are topographically ordered, spatially localised, and the representation is distributed. These are all desirable characteristics for a topographic map calibration system.

An alternative model based on the Boltzmann machine learning algorithm is argued to produce a more natural metaphor for understanding these phenomena. With no constraints, this system results in unsatisfactory representations. With a constraint that all representational units signal with the same probability, the network produces spatially localised distributed representations of the images, but without topographic structure. When the network also has a constraint that the nearby units are correlated, and is set up with some initial structure, this system reliably results in distributed representations with a spatially localised topographic structure. It is believed that the network is the first demonstrated to be capable of performing topographic map learning based on an input of natural images.

References

Baddeley, R.J. 1994. *The Correlational Structure of Natural Images*. Submitted to Pyschological Review.

Galland, C.C. 1993. The Limitations of Deterministic Boltzmann Machine Learning. *Network*, 4, 355–380.

Hinton, G, & Sejnowski, T. 1983. Optimal Perceptual Inference. *Proceedings of the IEEE Computer Society Conference on Computer Vision and Patern Recognition*, 448–453.

Kohonen, T. 1982. Self-Organized Formation of Topologically Correct Feature Maps. *Biological Cybernetics*, **43**.

Laughlin, S. 1981. A Simple coding Procedure Enhances Information Capacity. *Zeitschrift fur Naturforschung, Section C-Biosciences*, **36**, 910–912.

Van Hateran, J.H. 1993. Spatiotemporal Contrast Sensitivity of Early Vision. *Vision Research*, **33(2)**, 257–267.

von der Malsburg, C, & Willshaw, D. 1977. How to label nerve cells so that they can interconnect in an ordered fashion. *Proceedings of the National Academy of Sciences, USA*, **74**, 5176–5178.

Edge Enhancement and Exploratory Projection Pursuit

Colin Fyfe

Dept. of Computer Science, University of Strathclyde.

Roland Baddeley

Dept. of Experimental Psychology, University of Oxford.

Abstract

We present a neural network algorithm based on simple Hebbian learning which allows the finding of higher order structure in data. The neural network uses negative feedback of activation to self-organise; such networks have previously been shown to be capable of performing Principal Component Analysis (PCA). In this paper, this is extended to Exploratory Projection Pursuit (EPP) which is a statistical method for investigating structure in high-dimensional data sets.

Recently, it has been proposed [3, 5] that one way of choosing an appropriate filter for processing a particular domain is to find the filter with the highest output kurtosis. We pursue this avenue further by using the developed neural network to find the filter with the highest output kurtosis when applied to a collection of natural images. The method does not appear to work but interesting lessons can be derived from our failure.

1 The Statistics of Natural Images

It has been proposed that the form of the initial visual processing (specifically that occurring in the retina and early cortical areas) can be understood in terms of filters extracting simple statistical regularities in the world they are used to process. Most previous approaches have characterised the statistics of the natural images processed using only the means and pair-wise correlations of measurement local image intensities. In this case, the "optimal" filters are often found to be related to the principal components of the images [12, 2] or are entirely defined by the spatial frequency content of the images [1]. More recently, a new approach to this problem has been suggested based on higher order statistics. Specifically, a good filter (projection onto the image) is one where the output distribution has high kurtosis [3, 5]. Kurtosis is the fourth moment of a distribution (the mean being the first and variance the second), and basically measures what proportion of the distribution is found in the tails of the distribution.

Barlow and Tolhurst [3] have shown that in whitened images (the images are preprocessed so that the amplitude at all frequencies is equal) there is an excess of kurtosis in an image when 9 pixels are sampled in a line compared to that when 9 random pixels or 9 pixels in a square are sampled. Field [5] also showed that, for a different collection of natural images, an orientated bar detecting filter gave a higher output kurtosis than a center surround cell, and in turn, a center surround filter gives a higher kurtosis than the representation in terms of the raw gray levels. Based on these results, it was argued that the filtering observed in cortex could be understood in terms generating a new representation which had higher kurtosis than the original input. If this is so, then one sensible way to proceed is to identify those filters (projections) that result in the representation with the highest kurtosis.

We have discovered a simple ANN method to find those directions in high-dimensional spaces which exhibit most kurtosis. We conjecture that such a direction might lead to the enhancement of edges in an image. Instead of whitening our images (as Barlow and Tolhurst did) we performed a sphering operation on them which projects the image onto the Principal Components of the set of images and equalises the variance in each direction. This process also ensures that all measurements are uncorrelated.

2 Exploratory Projection Pursuit

Exploratory Projection Pursuit(for reviews see [9, 10]) is based on one central idea: rather than solving the difficult problem of identifying structure in high dimensional data, project the data onto a low dimensional subspace and look for structure in the projection. But to look for structure in randomly-generated directions would lead to a long search; thus we require a method which will tell us whether there is structure in the data projection. Therefore we define an index that measures how "interesting" a given projection is, and then represent the data in terms of the projections that maximise the index and are therefore maximally "interesting".

2.1 Interesting Directions

Friedman [6] notes that what constitutes an interesting direction is more difficult to define than what constitutes an uninteresting direction. Diaconis and Freedman[4] note that most projections of high-dimensional data onto arbitrary lines through most multi-dimensional data give almost Gaussian distributions. This would suggest that if we wish to identify "interesting" features in data, we should look for those directions α, projections onto which are as non-Gaussian as possible.

Two common measures of deviation from a Gaussian distribution are based on the higher order moments of the distribution (see Figure 1). Skewness is based on the normalised third moment of the distribution and basically measures if the distribution is symmetrical. Kurtosis is based on the normalised fourth moment of the distribution and measures the heaviness of the tails of a distribution.

3 The Data and Sphering

Because a Gaussian distribution with mean a and variance x is neither more nor less interesting (on the above definition of interesting) than a Gaussian distribution with mean b and variance y - indeed this second order structure can obscure higher order and more interesting structure - we remove such information from the data. This is known as "sphering". That is, the raw data is

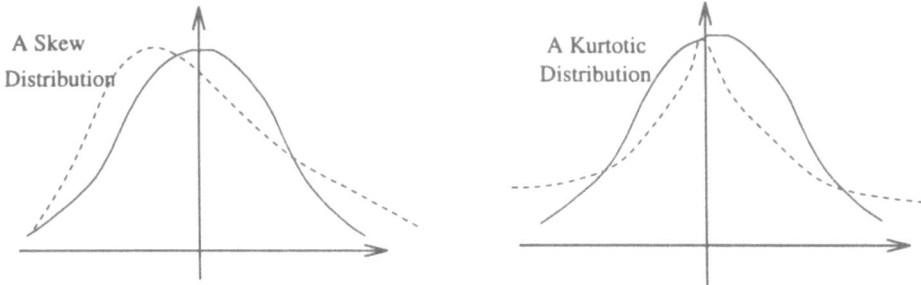

Figure 1: Deviations from Gaussian distributions: the dotted line on the left represents a negatively skewed distribution; that on the right represents a positively kurtotic distribution; in each case, the solid line represents a Gaussian distribution

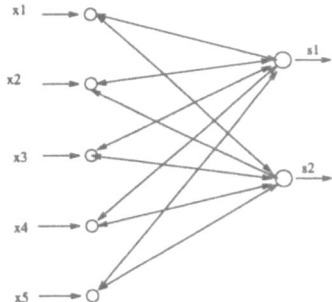

Figure 2: The negative feedback network. Initially there is no activation in the network; then the x-values are fed forward through weights and summed at the output neurons. The output neuron activation is fed back through the same weights to the initial neurons and subtracted. A non-linear function of the output neuron activations is calculated and the weights are adjusted through simple Hebbian learning

translated till its mean is zero, projected onto the principal component directions and multiplied by the inverse of the square root of its eigenvalue to give data in all directions which has mean zero and is of unit variance. This removes all potential differences due to first and second order statistics from the data. Typically this greatly reduces the dimension of the data and so this operation makes high-dimensional data more manageable. It is important to note that any linear combinations of the sphered data also retains these properties of the mean and variance e.g. see [13], Corollary 3.2.1.3.

4 The Projection Pursuit Network

Figure 2 shows the network which we will use to perform Exploratory Projection Pursuit: (the sphered) data is fedforward from the input neurons (the x-values) to the output neurons. Here a linear summation is calculated to give the activation of the output neurons and this activation is fed back to and subtracted from the input neurons. A function of the output activations is calculated and used in the simple Hebbian learning procedure. We have for N dimensional input data and M output neurons

$$s_i \;=\; \sum_{j=1}^{N} w_{ji} x_j \tag{1}$$

$$x_j(t+1) \;\leftarrow\; x_j(t) - \sum_{k=1}^{M} w_{jk} s_k \tag{2}$$

$$r_i \;=\; f(\sum_{j=1}^{N} w_{ji} x_j(t)) = f(s_i) \tag{3}$$

$$\Delta w_{ji} \;=\; \eta_t r_i x_j(t+1) \tag{4}$$

$$=\; \eta_t f(\sum_{k=1}^{N} w_{ki} x_k(t)) \{ x_j(t) - \sum_{l=1}^{M} w_{jl} \sum_{p=1}^{N} w_{pl} x_p(t) \} \tag{5}$$

where η_t is a learning rate at time t, w_{ji} is the weight between the jth input with value x_j and the ith output with value s_i, r_i is the value of the function f() on the ith output neuron and Δw_{ji} is the change in weights w_{ji}. Note that (5) may be written in matrix form as

$$\Delta \mathbf{W}(t) \;=\; \eta(t)[\mathbf{I} - \mathbf{W}(t)\mathbf{W}^T(t)]\mathbf{x}(t) f(\mathbf{x}^T(t)\mathbf{W}(t)) \tag{6}$$

where t is an index of time and I is the identity matrix.

The network is a generalisation of that which has previously [7, 8] been shown to perform a PCA. For this reason we feel able to link the Exploratory Projection Pursuit network to current work on Non-linear PCA.

Recently, the topic of "non-linear PCA" has been receiving a great deal of attention from the neural net community e.g. [11]. The impetus for such a development is the recognition that neural networks are ideally suited to non-linear adaption because of their incremental methods of learning: while closed form solutions may exist for linear processes such as PCA, such methods are simply not possible for non-linear algorithms.

Following [11], we can derive (6) as an approximation to the maximisation of a function, J, of the weights $J(\mathbf{W}) = \sum_{i=1}^{M} E(g[\mathbf{x}^T \mathbf{w}_i]|\mathbf{w}_i)$, where g() is some function of the weighted inputs.

We must ensure that the optimal solution is kept bounded; otherwise there is nothing to stop the weights from growing without bound. Formally,

$$\text{Let } J(\mathbf{W}) = \sum_{i=1}^{M} E(g[\mathbf{x}^T \mathbf{w}_i]|\mathbf{w}_i) + \frac{1}{2} \sum_{i=1}^{M} \sum_{j=1}^{M} \lambda_{ij} [\mathbf{w}_i^T \mathbf{w}_j - a_{ij}] \tag{7}$$

where the last term enforces the constraints $\mathbf{w}_i^T \mathbf{w}_j - a_{ij}$ using the Lagrange multipliers λ_{ij}. As usual, we differentiate this equation with respect to the weights and with respect to the Lagrange multipliers. This yields respectively, at a stationary point,

$$\frac{\partial J(\mathbf{W})}{\partial \mathbf{W}} = E\{\mathbf{x}g'(\mathbf{x}^T\mathbf{W})|\mathbf{W}\} + \mathbf{W}\Lambda = 0 \text{ and} \qquad (8)$$

$$\mathbf{W}^T\mathbf{W} = \mathbf{A} \qquad (9)$$

where $g'(\mathbf{x}^T\mathbf{W})$ is the elementwise derivative of $g(\mathbf{x}^T\mathbf{W})$ with respect to $\mathbf{W}$, A is the matrix of parameters a_{ij} (often the identity matrix) and Λ is the matrix of Lagrange multipliers. Equations (8) and (9) define the optimal points of the process. Pre-multiplying (8) by $\mathbf{W}^T$ and inserting (9), we get

$$\Lambda = -\mathbf{A}^{-1}\mathbf{W}^T E[\mathbf{x}g'(\mathbf{x}^T\mathbf{W})|\mathbf{W}]$$

and using this value and reinserting this optimal value of Λ into (8) yields the equation,

$$\frac{\partial J(\mathbf{W})}{\partial \mathbf{W}} = [\mathbf{I} - \mathbf{W}\mathbf{A}^{-1}\mathbf{W}^T]E[\mathbf{x}g'(\mathbf{x}^T\mathbf{W})|\mathbf{W}] \qquad (10)$$

We wish to use an instantaneous version of this in the gradient ascent algorithm

$$\Delta \mathbf{W} \propto \frac{\partial J(\mathbf{W})}{\partial \mathbf{W}}$$

to yield

$$\Delta \mathbf{W} = \mu[\mathbf{I} - \mathbf{W}\mathbf{A}^{-1}\mathbf{W}^T]\mathbf{x}g'(\mathbf{x}^T\mathbf{W}) \qquad (11)$$

which is the algorithm we wished to derive. We will be interested in the special case where the W values form an orthonormal basis of the data space and so $\mathbf{A} = \mathbf{I}$, the identity matrix.

4.1 The Projection Pursuit Index

Now for projection pursuit we wish to maximise a specific index. But note that from the derivation in the last section, when we wish to maximise an index function we must use its derivative in the learning algorithm: the function $f()$ in (5) is equivalent to the function $g'()$ in (11). Thus to maximise a projection pursuit index, we could use a learning process like that described in (11) noting that to maximise the index we must use the derivative of the index in the learning process.

The index which we use here measures deviation from Normality usgin kurtosis(see Figure 1): to measure kurtosis in a Normal distribution, $N(\mu, \sigma)$ we use

$$g(s) = \frac{E(s - \mu)^4}{\sigma^4}$$

where s is a random variable drawn from the distribution with mean μ and standard deviation σ and E() is the expectation operator. Now our data-distributions have all been sphered i.e. $E(x) = 0; E(x - E(x))^2 = 1$ and our weights, $\mathbf{w}_i$ are normalised and therefore every direction s_i has the same first and second moments. Thus $g(s) = s^4$ is a measure of the kurtosis of the distribution. Therefore in the algorithm, (6) we use

$$f(s) = k * s^3 \propto \frac{d}{ds} s^4$$

Now in all Normal directions, this measure will be approximately 3 but in a direction with a kurtotic distribution, there will be a kurtosis measurement in excess of this value.

Traditional statistical methods require a computationally-intensive recalculation of the distribution's moments from a reasonable sample of data points from the distribution each time a measure must be recalculated. However, it will be shown that a Hebbian learning rule for neural networks based on a measure of the instantaneous moments does in fact find that direction of maximum interest in the sense of Section 2.1. This very simple measure of deviation from Normality is not, in general, used in the statistics community due to its susceptibility to outliers. However the incremental nature of neural network learning allows us maintain stability even when occasional extreme inputs are encountered.

5   Experiment 1 - Synthetic Data

To prove the network's capabilities, we initially perform a simulation with artificial data.

5.1   Method

The neural network shown in Figure 2 was set up with 10 inputs, 10 interneurons and (initially) 1 output neuron. Input data was drawn from 9 independent zero-mean Gaussians while in the tenth direction data was also drawn from a Gaussian distribution but was modified in some way to make it interesting.

The modifications were designed to be simple yet ensure that there existed differences in the high order statistics between this interesting direction and all other directions. Therefore to create a distribution showing positive kurtosis (leptokurtic data) which appears as a value greater than the Normal distribution's value of 3 in our tables, we randomly selected samples (typically 20% of the total available) and substituted small random numbers in the range -0.25 to 0.25. This gives a narrowly peaked distribution. This distribution is generally one of the most difficult to find as it is only visible in one very tightly defined direction.

5.2   Results

The network consistently finds the leptokurtic direction i.e. that with kurtosis greater than the Gaussian's.

Statistics from the data to which this network is responding are shown in Table 1. Note that since the data is first sphered, it is not possible to base learning on first or second order statistics which are respectively 0 and 1 in each direction. In summary, the network consistently finds the direction of highest kurtosis at least for the synthetic data. Therefore, we feel confident in using the network on real image data

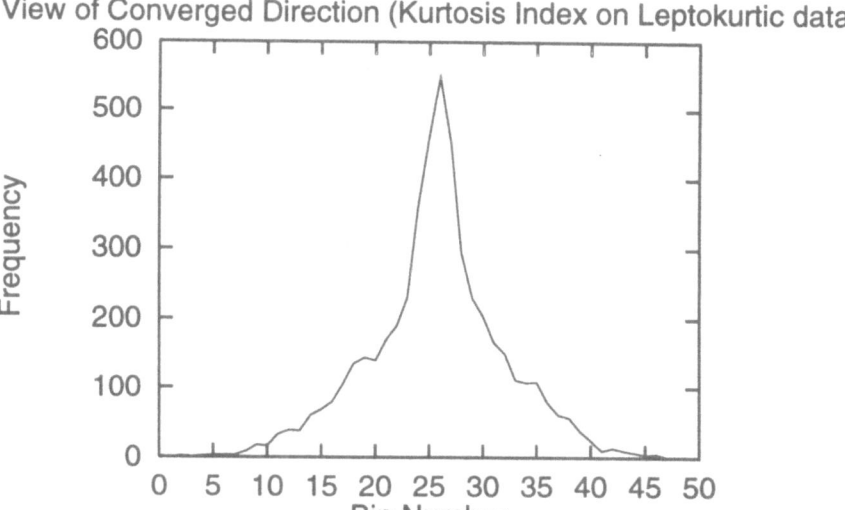

Figure 3: The input data were projected onto the direction in which the net converged and categorised into equal sized bins. Thus the view here shows the distribution as it would be seen by an observer looking at the projection of the data in the "interesting" direction

Direction	Mean	Variance	Cube	Fourth Power
1	0.000	1.015	0.055	3.082
2	-0.019	0.968	-0.045	2.761
3	0.007	0.987	0.015	2.890
4	0.004	0.981	0.024	2.893
5	-0.006	0.990	-0.022	2.949
6	-0.006	0.998	-0.017	3.016
7	-0.017	1.017	-0.037	3.103
8	0.011	0.992	0.058	2.889
9	-0.013	1.023	-0.087	**4.001**
10	-0.010	0.988	-0.000	2.960

Table 1: Statistics of the first set of 10-dimensional data: only one direction(9) has been modified to create a positively kurtotic distribution. Note that the sphering has produced a distribution with zero mean and unit variance in every direction

Direction	First	Second	Third	Fourth
1	0.020	0.961	-0.841	4.408
2	-0.012	1.032	-0.052	6.524
3	-0.018	1.053	-0.201	7.026
4	-0.002	1.040	-0.130	5.372
5	-0.008	0.968	-0.077	4.258
6	0.011	1.012	0.055	4.425
7	0.006	0.996	0.095	4.696
8	-0.011	1.046	-0.047	4.357
9	-0.022	1.025	-0.046	3.953
10	-0.004	1.022	-0.031	4.410
11	0.007	1.048	0.019	4.274
12	-0.008	1.015	0.340	15.136
13	0.000	0.987	0.007	3.844
14	0.001	0.990	-0.031	5.139
15	0.000	1.042	-0.103	4.953
16	-0.023	1.042	-0.188	5.962
17	0.023	0.984	0.042	4.277
18	-0.003	0.966	-0.123	4.107
19	-0.001	1.039	-0.052	6.574
20	0.001	0.987	-0.041	4.162

Table 2: The first four moments of the sphered image statistics as seen by the EPP network

6 The Statistics of Real Images

We are now ready to test our conjecture that our EPP network would, in finding those directions with greatest kurtosis, find those directions which would enhance the projection of lines.

We used 12 images of typical street scenes. Each image was 256 by 256 pixels and was converted so that each pixel was represented by an integer in the range 0-255. The principal component network was used to extract the first 20 principal components from a randomly selected selection of 32 by 32 squares from this set of images. The statistics of the sphered data are given in Table 2.

The statistics of the directions to which the EPP network converged in 12 simulations are given in Table 3. The EPP network was allowed 200000 iterations in order to converge. The statistics were taken thereafter from a sample of 10000 presentations of the 32*32 partial images.

Note first that the statistics of the images are far less Gaussian than the artificial data used previously: almost every direction shows both kurtosis and skewness; note also that every direction shows positive kurtosis ; this confirms the findings of Barlow and Tolhurst and shows that it was not their method of sphering which created the kurtosis in the data.

For the directions found by the network, note that the sphering has been preserved under the transformation. We see that the network is converging to a direction with high kurtosis each time.

However, while the network does have preferred directions to which it converges, e.g. simulations 1 and 3 converged to almost the same direction , the

Simulation	First	Second	Third	Fourth
1	-0.021	1.053	-0.117	17.295
2	0.023	1.154	0.355	18.621
3	0.026	1.081	0.502	16.911
4	-0.009	1.057	-0.185	7.000
5	0.006	1.044	0.924	17.531
6	-0.008	0.956	0.189	15.489
7	0.009	1.005	-0.208	15.653
8	0.003	1.022	-0.017	15.582
9	0.005	1.093	-0.008	8.422
10	-0.005	1.076	-0.244	9.522
11	0.007	1.067	0.486	19.905
12	-0.005	0.969	0.499	16.735

Table 3: First four moments of the distribution to which the EPP network converged

direction to which simulation 2 converged is virtually orthogonal ($\approx 87°$) to these two. A visual inspection of the projections of images onto these directions does not confirm our conjecture: we see no evidence that lines are more strongly projected on one direction than another.

However, we have gained insight into the statistics from street scenes from the study: we note that nearly every direction has a strongly kurtotic distribution. Note also that it is not a simple matter to disentangle the third and fourth moments of a distribution - nearly every direction exhibits both skewness (in the third moment) and kurtosis (in the fourth); further, it is noteworthy that nearly every principal component of these images is strongly kurtotic and the kurtosis is even more pronounced across Principal Components. Clearly, the method of sphering visual data before performing more advanced data investigation seems to be worthy of more study.

7 Conclusion

We have introduced a neural network architecture which, using an extremely simple architecture and learning rule, has been shown to be capable of performing sophisticated statistical functions.

In particular the network was used to investigate the properties of images of street scenes. While the final result was inconclusive in terms of attempting to find directions in which the edges of images are enhanced, we feel that the attempt to do so has provided insight into the statistical composition of images of man-made constructions. We see that the statistics of such images are strongly kurtotic suggesting that detectors which respond to directions of maximum kurtosis might be useful in such an environment. We also note that it is not possible to separate the kurtosis from the skewness of such real data; our experiments on artificial data were unrealistic in that we were able to do precisely this.

Finally, the fact that different convergence points were found when we started from different initial conditions seems to suggest that the error descent surface is very rugged. We know that when back propagation is used on a network which has linear activation functions there is only one (global) minimum while when such a network uses non-linear functions, we find a great number of minima. We view the situation which we have found as the direct counterpart of this.

References

[1] J.J. Atick and A. N. Redlich. Towards a theory of early visual processing. *Neural Computation*, 4:196–210, 1990.

[2] R. J. Baddeley and P. J. Hancock. A statistical analysis of natural images matches psychophysically derived orientation tuning curves. *Proceedings of the Royal Society, London B*, 246:219–223, 1991.

[3] H. Barlow and D. Tolhurst. Why do you have edge detectors. JOSA Meeting, Albuquerque, 1992.

[4] Persi Diaconis and David Freedman. Asymptotics of graphical projections. *The Annals of Statistics*, 12(3):793–815, 1984.

[5] David J. Field. What is the goal of sensory coding. *Neural Computation*, 6:559–601, 1994.

[6] Jerome H Friedman. Exploratory projection pursuit. *Journal of the American Statistical Association*, 82(397):249–266, March 1987.

[7] C. Fyfe. Interneurons which identify principal components. In *Recent Advances in Neural Networks, BNNS93*, 1993.

[8] C. Fyfe. Pca properties of interneurons. In *From Neurobiology to Real World Computing, ICANN 93*, 1993.

[9] Peter J Huber. Projection pursuit. *Annals of Statistics*, 13:435–475, 1985.

[10] M. C. Jones and Robin Sibson. What is projection pursuit. *The Royal Statistical Society*, 1987.

[11] Juha Karhunen and Jyrki Joutsensalo. Representation and separation of signals using nonlinear pca type learning. *Neural Networks*, 7(1):113–127, 1994.

[12] R. Linsker. From basic network principles to neural architecture. In *Proceedings of National Academy of Sciences*, 1986.

[13] K. V. Mardia, J.T. Kent, and J.M. Bibby. *Multivariate Analysis*. Academic Press, 1979.

The "Perceptual Magnet" Effect: A Model Based on Self–Organizing Feature Maps

M. Herrmann

NORDITA

DK–2200 Copenhagen, Denmark

H.–U. Bauer

Institut für theor. Physik, Universität Frankfurt

D–60054 Frankfurt, Germany

R. Der

Institut für Informatik, Universität Leipzig

D–04009 Leipzig, Germany

Abstract

The perceptual magnet effect describes an increased generalization capability for the perception of vowels, if the perceived vowels are prototypical. We here propose an unsupervised, adaptive neural network model which allows to control the relation between stimulus density and generalization capability, and which can account for the perceptual magnet effect. Our model is based on a modification of the self–organizing feature map algorithm, and includes local variations of the adaptability. Numerical and analytical results for the model are given, together with a brief discussion of possible other domains of application for the model.

1 "Perceptual magnet" effect

In human adults and infants the discriminability of vowels has been found to depend on the degree of typicality of the vowels within their respective phonetic category (*perceptual magnet effect*, [1]). In experiments by P. Kuhl it was shown first, that adults identify in a group of 64 different versions of the vowel /i/ a particular region of vowel space as prototypical. The perceived "goodness" of /i/ vowels declined with distance from the prototype. Second, discriminability between two vowels was found to be better for non–prototypical vowels as compared to prototypical vowels. Formulated the other way round, generalization was found to be better for prototypes; an observation which gave rise to the notion of "perceptual magnets". In a different experiment Kuhl et al. were able to show, that the perceptual magnet effect depends on the linguistic experience of infants [2]. The innate pattern of phonetic perception being language universal, already at the age of 6 months, well before the acquisition of language, the position of perceptual magnets was found to differ between infants which were raised in countries with differing languages.

In this contribution we propose to discuss the perceptual magnet effect and its development in the realm of adaptive map formation algorithms. Kuhl et al. parametrized their stimuli in the two–dimensional space spanned by the first two formants of the vowel [1]. Similar versions of a vowel were represented by neighboring positions in this space, a typical feature of computational maps. The adaptability of the vowel representation can not only be assumed on the basis of the infant experiment [2], but can also be expected by analogy to other auditory maps in the brain [3]. Finally the absence of language influences on the formation of perceptual magnets in the young infants suggests, that this developmental phenomenon is based predominantly on external stimulation.

If we assume for these reasons that the vowels are represented by a topo-graphic map in a low–dimensional, e.g. two–dimensional, feature space, and that the map is adapted by a self–organization process like, e.g., the self–organizing feature map (SOFM, [4]), a challenging problem arises. Such pro-cesses typically produce maps where regions of frequent stimulation are repre-sented with high resolution, whereas regions of rare stimulation are represented with low resolution. Assuming that the vowels identified as prototypical are also preeminent in the stimulus ensemble, these vowels and their neighborhood should be represented with high resolution in the map, as opposed to the non-prototypical vowels. Such a representation would allow high discriminability close to the category centers, and low discriminability at the boundary of the category, just opposite to the observed magnet effect. Therefore, what is needed is a modification of map formation algorithms which allows to control the re-lation between stimulus density and resolution of the map. In the remainder of this paper, we will present such a modification, based upon an extension of the widely applied SOFM–algorithm.

2 Self–organizing feature maps with node–dependent adaptability

Kohonen's self–organizing feature map [4] maps stimuli $\mathbf{v}$ in an input space V onto neurons at positions $\mathbf{r}$ in an output space A. The neuron positions $\mathbf{r}$ are located at the vertices of a one–, two– or higher–dimensional lattice in A. Each neuron in the output space has associated to it a receptive field in the input space which is defined by a prototypical stimulus $\mathbf{w_r} \in V$ in the following manner: A stimulus $\mathbf{v} \in V$ is mapped onto that neuron $\mathbf{s} \in A$ the receptive field center $\mathbf{w_s}$ of which lies closest to $\mathbf{v}$,

$$\mathbf{v} \to \mathbf{s}, \quad \text{if} \quad ||\mathbf{w_s} - \mathbf{v}|| = \min_{\mathbf{r} \in A} ||\mathbf{w_r} - \mathbf{v}||. \tag{1}$$

During an adaptation phase, the receptive field center positions are adjusted such that the resulting map spans the input space in a topographic fashion [5], i.e. neighboring nodes $\mathbf{r}, \mathbf{r}'$ in the output space have neighboring receptive field centers in the input space. To achieve this adaptation, a sequence of random stimuli is applied to the map. For each stimulus, the best–matching neuron $\mathbf{s}$ is determined, and its receptive field center $\mathbf{w_s}$ is shifted towards the stimulus. In addition, all receptive field centers of neurons in the neighborhood of $\mathbf{s}$ are — to a lesser extent — also shifted, in this way inducing the topography of the map. In mathematical terms a single adaptation step leads to changes

$$\Delta w_{\mathbf{r}} = -\epsilon h_{\mathbf{rs}}(\mathbf{w_r} - \mathbf{v}) \qquad (2)$$

where $h_{\mathbf{rs}}$ denotes the neighborhood function, usually chosen to be a Gaussian of width σ,

$$h_{\mathbf{rs}} = \exp(-\frac{\|\mathbf{r} - \mathbf{s}\|^2}{2\sigma^2}). \qquad (3)$$

Two common refinements of the SOFM are to gradually decrease the learning step size ϵ (in order to converge to an equilibrium state of the map) and the neighborhood width σ (in order to resolve finer details of the input space). A comprehensive treatment of these issues can be found in [4, 6]. SOFMs have successfully applied to many self–organization phenomena in sensory processing, including the ocular–dominance and orientation columns systems in primary visual cortex [7, 8], deviations from retinotopy in extrastriate visual areas [9], and the organization of tonotopy in the auditory cortex of bats [10]. The issue of the physiological relevance of SOFMs has been addressed in Ref. [11], where evidence has been presented for an implementation in biological neural networks mediated by extrasynaptical chemical diffusion processes.

A typical feature of many sensory maps is an increase of the areal magnification factor (originally defined for visual maps as mm of cortex per degree of visual space [12]) in areas of intense stimulation. The relation between the areal magnification factor of the map (given by the receptive field center density $P(\mathbf{w})$) and the stimulus density $P(\mathbf{v})$ can be characterized by an exponent M,

$$P(\mathbf{w}) \sim P(\mathbf{v})^M. \qquad (4)$$

For one–dimensional SOFMs an exponent $M = 2/3$ has been analytically derived [13]. For higher–dimensions only a few special cases could be solved [14].

As was pointed out in the introductory section, modeling of the perceptual magnet effect requires maps with a negative exponent, such that areas of low intensity of stimulation are are magnified to a high degree (corresponding to lesser generalization capability), and vice versa. Such negative exponents do not occur in maps which are generated by an unmodified SOFM–algorithm. Here we propose to gain control over M by replacing the uniform learning step size ϵ by neuron–dependent, local adaptabilities $\epsilon_{\mathbf{r}}$, resulting in a modified learning rule

$$\Delta \mathbf{w_r} = -\epsilon_s h_{\mathbf{rs}}(\mathbf{w_r} - \mathbf{v}). \qquad (5)$$

Chosing local adaptabilities $\epsilon_{\mathbf{r}}$ such that

$$\langle \epsilon_{\mathbf{r}} \rangle = \epsilon_0 P(\mathbf{v})^m, \qquad (6)$$

the stimulus distribution $P(\mathbf{v})$ now enters the learning procedure explicitly. Selecting particular values for m, we can now modify or cancel out the effects of heterogeneities of the stimulus distribution.

Since $P(\mathbf{v})$ is not explicitly known during learning, we cannot impose Eq. (6) directly, but have to determine the local adaptabilities in an indirect way. To this purpose we exploit the relation

$$P(\mathbf{v}) \propto P(\mathbf{w_s})P(\mathbf{s}) \qquad (7)$$

where $P(\mathbf{s})$ is the probability of neuron $\mathbf{s}$ being the best–matching unit. For slow changes in the receptive field centers $\mathbf{w_r}$, $P(\mathbf{s})$ and $P(\mathbf{w_s})$ can be approximated by accumulating temporal means of the excitation frequency and of the deviations between stimulus and receptive field center in each bestmatching unit, resp. The latter quantity is inversely proportional to the local receptive field center density. In simulations of this learning rule it turned out, that no long time local averaging is necessary to approximate $P(\mathbf{w_s})$ and $P(\mathbf{s})$. Instead, at each learning step the present deviation between stimulus and receptive field center, plus the time interval $\Delta t_\mathbf{s}$ elapsed since the present bestmatching neuron was bestmatching neuron for the last time, can be exploited. For a two–dimensional output space this scheme yields

$$\epsilon_\mathbf{s}(t) = \epsilon_0 \left(\frac{1}{\Delta t_\mathbf{s}} \left(\frac{1}{4\|\mathbf{v} - \mathbf{w_s}\|^2} \right) \right)^m . \tag{8}$$

To avoid large, destabilizing learning step sizes, we bounded $\epsilon_\mathbf{s}(t)$ with an upper bound $\epsilon_{max} = 0.9$.

3 Results for one–dimensional maps

We first apply this modified algorithm to the mapping of stimuli in a one–dimensional input space onto a chain of neurons. This test application is very useful, because the maps resulting from our modified algorithm can be compared to analytical results. As was mentioned above, stimulus density $P(\mathbf{v})$ and receptive field center density $P(\mathbf{w})$ of one–dimensional maps generated by the unmodified SOFM–algorithm are related by

$$P(\mathbf{w}) = P(\mathbf{v})^{2/3} . \tag{9}$$

Having neuron–dependent adaptabilities according to Eq. (6), Eq. (9) does no longer hold. Including Eq. (6) into the derivation of the exponent, we find instead

$$P(\mathbf{w}) = P(\mathbf{v})^{M'} \tag{10}$$

with a modified exponent

$$M' = \frac{2}{3}(1 + m). \tag{11}$$

$m = 0$, the choice of constant ϵ as in the regular SOFM, reproduces the known $M' = M = 2/3$. Adapting units in densely stimulated regions more often by chosing $m = 1/2$ can even result in a faithful map with $M' = 1$, whereas decreasing the adaptability by chosing $m = -1$ yields a map with uniform resolution in the input space ($M' = 0$). Finally, a choice of $m < -1$ yields maps with $M' < 0$. In such maps sparsely stimulated regions acquire a fine resolution, whereas often stimulated regions are coarsely resolved: the perceptual magnet effect in its one–dimensional variant.

We can now evaluate the quality of our approximation scheme (8) with regard to the reproduction of Eq. (6) and, consequently, of Eq. (11). To this purpose we trained maps with our modified algorithm for various stimulus densities $P(\mathbf{v}) = \mathbf{v}^\nu$, $\nu = 1/2, 1, 2$ and $0 < \mathbf{v} < 1$. Some of the resulting maps are displayed in Fig. 1.

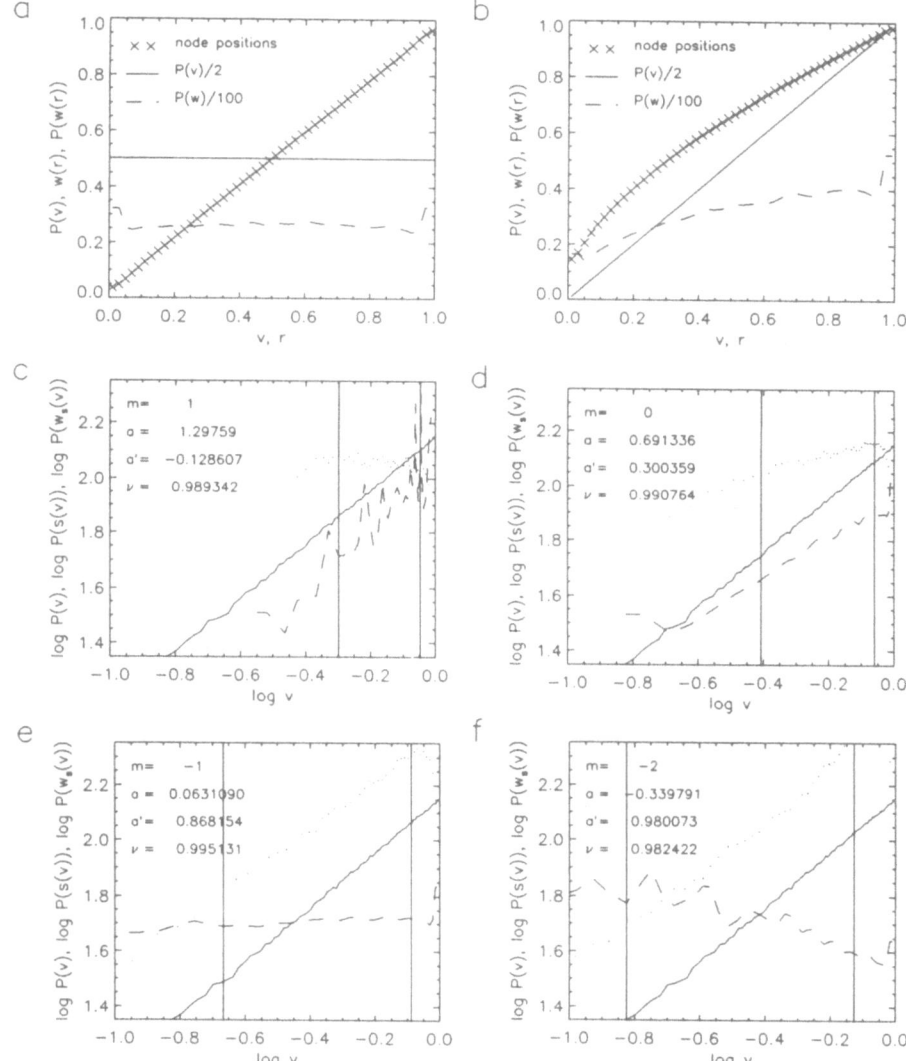

Fig. 1: Maps of the interval $[0, 1]$ onto chains of $N = 50$ neurons. For illustrative purposes, **a** and **b** show maps generated by the unmodified algorithm ($m = 0$). $P(\mathbf{v})$, $P(\mathbf{w})$ and $\mathbf{w}(\mathbf{r})$ are plotted in linear scale for $\nu = 0$, i.e. $P(\mathbf{v}) = const.$ (**a**) and for $\nu = 1$, i.e. $P(\mathbf{v}) = \mathbf{v}$ (**b**). **c** - **f** show maps generated by the modified algorithm for $\nu = 1, m = 1$ (**c**), $\nu = 1, m = 0$ (**d**, identical to **b**), $\nu = 1, m = -1$ (**e**), $\nu = 1, m = -2$ (**f**). In **c-f** the receptive field center density $P(\mathbf{w})$ (dashed), the excitation probability $P(\mathbf{s})$ of each output neuron (dotted), and the stimulus density $P(\mathbf{v})$ (solid) are plotted in logarithmic scale such that the resp. exponents a, a' and ν are easier to evaluate. The vertical lines indicate the intervals of the resp. maps, which were used to evaluate the exponents.

ν	m	M'_{ana}	a	M'_{num}
1	1	1.33	1.27	1.27
1	1/2	1.00	0.99	0.99
1	0	0.67	0.66	0.66
1	-1/2	0.33	0.34	0.34
1	-1	0.00	0.02	0.02
1	-2	-0.67	-0.42	-0.42
1/2	1	1.33	0.54	1.08
1/2	0	0.67	0.33	0.66
1/2	-1	0.00	0.01	0.02
1/2	-2	-0.67	-0.26	-0.54
2	1	1.33	2.22	1.11
2	0	0.67	1.31	0.61
2	-1	0.00	0.08	0.04
2	-2	-0.67	-0.68	-0.34

Tab. 1: Analytical exponents $M'_{ana}(\nu, m)$ and numerical exponents $M'_{num}(\nu, m)$, the latter averaged over three maps each. The maps ($N = 50$ neurons) were trained according to Eqs. (5) and (8) with σ decreasing from $\sigma_{init} = 10$ to $\sigma_{final} = 1$, ϵ_0 decreasing from $\epsilon_{0,init} = 0.5$ to $\epsilon_{0,final} = 0.0001$, 10^6 steps per map.

In the final maps, we obtain $P(\mathbf{w})$ by evaluating the local distances between receptive field centers. Fitting a linear function to the center part of $\log(P(w))$ yields the exponent a of the maps ($P(w) \approx v^a$), which is then transformed back into M'. The linear fit is restricted to the center part of the map in order to avoid deviations due to the open boundary conditions. Training three maps for each exponent combination ν and m, we obtain the averaged values $M'(\nu, m)$ shown in Tab. 1. The values for M' from the simulations correspond quite well to the values which are analytically expected. In particular, we indeed obtained a regime with negative M' for $m < -1$.

4 Results for two–dimensional maps

We now proceed to apply our modified algorithm to a two–dimensional mapping problem. In order to highlight the relation between maps adapted with $m < -1$ and the perceptual magnet effect, we chose as stimuli points $\mathbf{v} = (v_x, v_y)$ in the unit square, i.e. with $0 < v_x, v_y < 1$, which were draw according to the probability distribution

$$p(v_x) \propto 1/2 \left(1 + \exp\left(-\frac{(v_x - v_{x,0})^2}{2\sigma_v^2}\right)\right), \qquad (12)$$

$$p(v_y) \propto 1/2 \left(1 + \exp\left(-\frac{(v_y - v_{y,0})^2}{2\sigma_v^2}\right)\right), \qquad (13)$$

with $v_{x,0} = v_{y,0} = 1/3$, $\sigma_{\mathbf{v}} = 8$. So the stimulus density was a Gaussian, located in the left lower center of the unit square, in front of a constant background

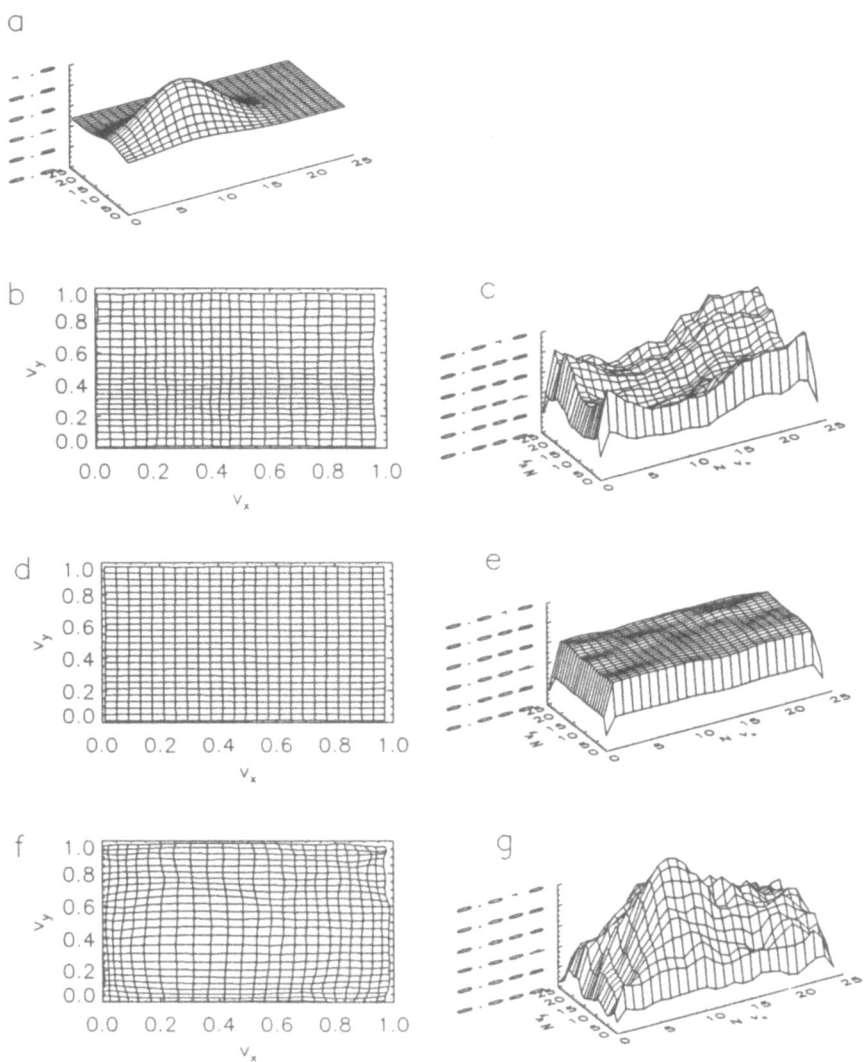

Fig. 2 Maps from a two-dimensional input space with a stimulus distribution exhibiting a peak in front of a background (**a**) onto a grid of 50 × 50 neurons. (**b, d, f**) show the maps themselves for $m = 0, -1, -2$, (**c, e, g**) show the corresponding local generalization capabilities, as given by the size of the input space regions, which map onto the respective neuron (in technical terms: the size of its Voronoi polygon).

(see Fig. 2a). This input space was mapped onto quadratic output spaces, with $N \times N = 50 \times 50$ neurons. Depending on the exponent m of the local adaptability, the resulting maps provided a higher resolution of the Gaussian peak (Fig. 2b,c), they equilibrated the resolution over the whole input space (Fig. 2d,e), or they decreased the resolution in the region of the peak (Fig. 2f,g). The latter case corresponds to an increased generalization capability in the region of the peak.

5 Discussion

By means of the simulations presented in sections 3 and 4 an idealized model of an interesting stage in phonetic perception is investigated numerically. The results for the one-dimensional case confirm analytic expectations for the model. The two-dimensional case also complies very well with theoretical results available for it.

The present network is intimately related to the usual self-organizing feature map model, which is able to account for many phenomena of adaptive map formation in the brain. To yield a magnification behaviour as observed in the perceptual magnet effect, and as opposed to, say, the magnification behaviour observed in the somatosensoric cortex (regions of frequent stimulation like the digits are highly magnified, with a small "generalization capability"), the SOFM-algorithm has to be modified only slightly. Learning steps have to become larger with increasing time since the last learning step for the particular neuron, and learning steps have to become larger if there is less competition to become winner. These modifications are neither drastic nor unplausible. Therefore, one can regard the present model as another example which underlines the universality of a single self-organization rule with regard to pattern (i.e. map) formation in the brain. The hypothetical danger of a diverging magnification, which might be suggested by the form of Eq. (10) and (11) for $m < -1$ and which would correspond to all units located in never-stimulated regions of input space, does not occur in our model for two reasons. First, the finite number of nodes in the model as well as the finite amount of learning time avoid infinite receptive field center densities and a positioning of nodes in empty parts of stimulus space. In addition, the bounding of the learning step sizes at values of $\epsilon < \epsilon_{max}$, which is necessary to prohibit an unplausible overshooting also prohibits diverging magnifications.

The modifications of the present model as compared to the usual SOFM can also be interpreted as incorporating an attentional control of feature maps which is to be understood as emergent from an interaction among several levels of the auditory system. Rare as well as hardly classifiable stimuli, i.e. stimuli that do not relate easily to an item known by the system, will receive a novelty bonus, which in turn increases the respective learning rate.

In future work the process of discrimination between two stimuli, which is in fact a temporal problem, will be dealt with in a way which we sketch here only briefly. In the usual version of the SOFM-algorithm only a single unit is activated as a result of the winner-take-all principle. In this way there is no overlap between neighboring receptive fields. Only due to lateral connections among the neural units, which are effectively incorporated in the neighborhood function, the neurons share single inputs. In this way a discrimination between any two neurons is possible. More realistically, if overlapping receptive fields are included the activation spreads over a group of neurons. The activation is now related to the probability of being the winning unit, such that crosstalk among the neurons occurs. Thus discrimination rates will be different from zero or one, but will vary continuously in accordance with the figures given in [2].

The proposed model was shown to reproduce the perceptual magnet effect due to its ability of adjusting the *resolution* of the evolving feature map. We have motivated the choice in the introduction, but it is worthwhile to compare the present approach to other connectionist models. A very simple alternative model could consist in a single unit per vowel with maximal output for the prototypical stimulus and stimuli close to it and rapidly decaying flanks as it is the case in e.g. a Gaussian radial basis function unit. [15] The discriminability measured as output difference between two stimuli, clearly will be lower at the plateau near the prototype, and higher at the flanks. Since the storage by a single unit ("grandmother cell") per memory item is not likely to occur in the cortex a model of this type would refer to a very abstract level of cognitive processing.

Several modeling schemes were presented in Ref. [16], where it was concluded that attractor-like structures in a deterministic Boltzmann machine or in a competitive learning network are essential to produce a perceptual magnet effect. An attractor generally is surrounded by a basin from where all inputs are mapped to an attractor state which is considered to be the output of the system. By repeated stimulation the basins of attraction of the prototypical sounds enlarge, whereas rarely presented stimuli will not create such basins. Although the idea of processing by attractors is clearly relevant in understanding of higher level cognition, it leaves out completely the presence of the topological arrangement of cortical structures which is essentially taken into account by the topographic map approach. The fact that vowels form clusters in the space spanned by their first two formants, and can be distinguished quite successfully on the basis of these two parameters [17], means that a map which extends in two dimensions as in the present paper is a very plausible representation for phonological information which is used for subsequent speech recognition and understanding.

The question whether a mechanism analogous to the perceptual magnet effect is desirable in technical applications of SOFMs to vector quantization and classification in information processing tasks is addressed in a forthcoming paper.

Acknowledgement

We would like to thank Z. Li, who brought the perceptual magnet effect to our attention.

The reported results are partially based on work done in the LADY project sponsored by the German Federal Ministry of Research and Technology under grant 01 IN 106B/3. HUB gratefully acknowledges support from the DFG through Sonderforschungsbereich 185 Nichtlineare Dynamik, TP E3. MH received support from the EC HCM network *Principles of Cortical Computation*.

References

[1] P. K. Kuhl, Human adults and human infants show a "perceptual magnet" effect for the prototypes of speech categories, monkeys do not. *Perception & Psychophysics* **50** (2), 93-107 (1991).

[2] P. K. Kuhl, K. A. Williams, F. Lacerda, K. N. Stevens, B. Lindblom, Linguistic experience alters phonetic perception in infants by 6 months of age. *Science* **255**, 606-608 (1992).

[3] A. J. King, D. R. Moore, Plasticity of auditory maps in the brain. *TINS* **14**, 31-37 (1991).

[4] T. Kohonen, Self–organization and associative memory. Springer (1984).

[5] Th. Villmann, R. Der, M. Herrmann, Th. Martinetz, Topology preservation in self–organizing feature maps: Exact definition and measurement. Submitted to *IEEE Transact. Neural Networks* (1994).

[6] H. Ritter, T. Martinetz, K. Schulten, Neural computation and self–organizing maps. Addison Wesley, Reading, Mass (1992).

[7] K. Obermayer, G.G. Blasdel, K. Schulten, Statistical–mechanical analysis of self–organisation and pattern formation during the development of visual maps, *Phys. Rev. A* **45**, 7568-7589 (1992).

[8] H.–U. Bauer, Development of oriented ocular dominance bands as a consequence of areal geometry, *Neural Computation*, in print (1994).

[9] F. Wolf, H.–U. Bauer, T. Geisel, Formation of field discontinuities and islands in visual cortical maps, *Biol. Cyb.* **70**, 525-531 (1994).

[10] T.M. Martinetz, H. Ritter, K. Schulten, Kohonen's self–organizing map for modeling the formation of the auditory cortex of a bat, *SGAICO–Proc. "Connectionism in Perspective"*, (Zürich), 403-412 (1988).

[11] T. Kohonen, Physiological interpretation of the self–organizing map algorithm. *Neural Networks* **6**, 895-905 (1993).

[12] P.M. Daniel, D. Whitteridge, The representation of the visual field on the cerebral cortex in Monkeys, *J. Physiol.* **159**, 203-221 (1961).

[13] H. Ritter, K. Schulten, On the stationary state of Kohonen's self–organizing sensory mapping. *Biol. Cybern.* **54**, 99-106 (1986).

[14] M. Cottrell, J. C. Fort, G. Pagès, Two or three things that we know about the Kohonen algorithm. Proc. ESANN'94, Brussels (1994).

[15] R. Baddeley, personal communication.

[16] P. Gupta, Investigating phonological representations: A modeling agenda. In: M. C. Mozer e.a. (eds.) Proceedings of the 1993 Connectionist Models Summer School, Hillsdale, NJ; Lawrence Erlbaum (1993).

[17] D.P. Morgan, C.L. Scofield, Neural Networks and Speech Recognition, Kluwer Academic, Boston, see p. 198 (1991).

How Local Cortical Processors that Maximize Coherent Variation could lay Foundations for Representation Proper

W A Phillips
Centre for Cognitive and Computational Neuroscience
University of Stirling
Stirling FK 9 4LA UK

Jim Kay
Scottish Agricultural Statistics Service
Macaulay Land Use Research Institute
Craigiebuckler
Aberdeen AB9 2QJ UK

D M Smyth
Institute for Informatics
University of Leipzig,
Postfach 920, D-0-7010 Leipzig Germany

Abstract

This paper discusses computational capabilities that might be common to local processors in many different cortical regions. It examines the possibility that cortical processors may perform a kind of statistical latent structure analysis that discovers predictive relationships between large and diverse data sets. Information theory is used to show that this goal is formally coherent, and its computational feasibility is investigated by simulating multi-stream networks built from local processors with properties that this goal requires. The hypotheses developed emphasize cooperative population codes and the contextual guidance of learning and processing. Neurobiological and neuro-psychological evidence for contextual guidance and cooperative population codes is outlined. The possible relevance of these ideas to the concept of representation proper is discussed.

Acknowledgements: This work is supported by a Network grant from the Human Capital and Mobility Program of the European Community. We thank Peter Hancock for expert assistance in developing the simulation software, and for valuable discussions of these issues we thank Moshe Abeles, Vicki Bruce, Mike Burton, Peter Cahusac, David Cairns, Robin Campbell, Ralf Der, Dario Floreano, Will Goodall, John Hertz, Ralph Linsker, Wolf Singer, Leslie Smith, Paul Toombs, Tom Troscianko, Christoph von der Malsburg, and Roger Watt.

1 Introduction

How do we know things, and what things do we know? We assume that answers to these questions will include an understanding of how those parts of the brain that are concerned with cognition work. We do not see how such answers could be possible without a clear understanding of what work it is that they do. Different functions are of course performed by different cortical regions and at different levels of organization, but the hypotheses discussed here are based upon the assumption that some fundamental computational capabilities are common to local processors in many different cortical regions. The central concern of this paper is with what those capabilities might be.

Section 2 gives an informal outline of possible goals for cortical computation, focussing on the hypothesis that local processors perform a sophisticated kind of statistical latent structure analysis that discovers predictive relationships between large and diverse data sets. Section 3 shows that this goal is formally coherent and outlines studies of its computational feasibility. The hypotheses developed emphasize cooperative population codes and the contextual guidance of learning and processing. Section 4 therefore outlines evidence for these drawn from neurobiology and neuropsychology. Section 5 discusses the relevance of these ideas to the concept of representation proper.

2 The Maximization of Coherent Variation as a Local Goal for Cortical Computation

The cerebral cortex is central to human mental life through its role in language, thought, and other higher mental processes. Our concern here is with other, more basic, computational functions that are common to many different regions of the cortex and to mammals in general. One well known hypothesis is that a major local goal of cortical processing is recoding to reduce redundancy (Barlow, 1961, 1989; Barlow & Foldiak, 89; Baddeley & Hancock, 1991; Foldiak, 1990; Atick & Redlich, 1993; Redlich, 1993; Li & Atick, 1994). The basic idea is that the flood of data to be processed can be reduced to more manageable amounts by using the statistical structure within the data to recode the information that it contains into a more efficient form. Thus patterns, features, or objects that frequently recur in the raw data can be translated into codes that contain many less elements than the patterns themselves. We will refer to the general task of recoding to reduce redundancy as 'feature discovery'. This goal provides a valuable perspective from which to view sensory processing. It is clear and simple, and can be fully specified formally at the local level, for example as that of maximizing the mutual information between output and input under a constraint that ensures data reduction (Linsker, 1988).

An important limitation of this goal is that it is ultimately sub-ordinate to the goal of associative learning. There would be no point recoding information about some variable if that variable bore no relation to anything else known to the system. Proponents of the goal of feature discovery therefore usually see it as preparatory to associative learning. From that perspective feature discovery and associative learning are seen as two quite separate, and usually successive, goals. The possibility to be discussed here is that feature discovery and associative learning can be combined into a single common algorithm that can be used throughout the various stages of cortical processing. Information theory will be used to specify the goals of this algorithm in a way that is close to that used for feature discovery and which includes it as a special case. In relation to learning the goal of this algorithm is to combine feature discovery and associative learning so that they are mutually supportive. In relation to processing its goal is to maximize the transmission of information that is coherently related to the current context. In other words, the consequence of local processors operating in accordance with such a goal is a system that seeks change or variation in the activity of its local processors, provided that this produces patterns of activity that are coherently related across sub-sets of processors, i.e. it seeks "meaningful" information.

From a statistical point of view this task is an extension of some form of latent structure analysis, such as canonical correlation (Hotelling, 1936; Giffins, 1985; Kay, 1992). It seeks features defined upon separate data sets that maximize the amount of variance in each feature that is predictably related to variance in the others. It therefore combines the recoding role of principal component or factor analysis with the predictive role of multiple regression.

To contribute to such a task local processors must receive inputs from the data to be described and from the data sets to which any such descriptions may be related. This second form of input provides the context within which the primary input data is to be analyzed. In cortex these contextual inputs could be specific to the local role of the processor within the system as a whole, just as are the receptive field inputs. For example, at some stages of the analysis of a visual scene other parts of the scene might provide a useful context, whereas at later stages of processing information about reinforcement might provide a more appropriate context. The role of any contextual input is quite different from that of receptive field input from the data to be described. The receptive field input determines whether some description is applicable, whereas the context is concerned with whether it is relevant. If any such role is played out in cortex then we would expect input from the receptive field to provide the primary drive, and context to modulate the effects of that input.

Linsker (1988) calls the organizing principle underlying recoding so as to maximize information transmission within streams the "Infomax" principle. For brevity we will refer to the hypothesis developed here as the "Coherent Infomax" hypothesis because it emphasizes transmission of that information within streams that is coherently related across streams. A skeletal outline of the receptive field (RF) and contextual field (CF) organization hypothesized is illustrated in Figure 1, which suggests that one likely source of contextual input is from parallel processing streams, and that another is from later stages of processing. It is assumed that the parallel streams that provide contextual guidance to each other have distinct RFs. The feedback context might help adapt the information selected by the local processor to the use to which it is to be put. There is plenty of anatomical, physiological, and psychological evidence for horizontal and descending pathways, and also that their effects differ from those of the primary ascending inputs. To make the terminology more exact we could distinguish between proximal and distal RFs and CFs. The proximal fields are those providing the immediate inputs to the local processors. The distal fields are the more distant origins of those proximal fields.

In discussing the extent to which basic goals of perception and associative learning can be met by local processors with a set of common properties four controversial hypotheses will arise. First, in relation to learning, we will discuss the hypothesis that the entities that are discovered in the data are preferentially those that are predictably related to the context within which they occur. This contrasts with the common assumption that feature discovery and associative learning are separate goals. Second, in relation to the short-term dynamics we will discuss the hypothesis that local processors can use predictions to guide processing but without confusing them with the data. This contrasts with the common assumption that local

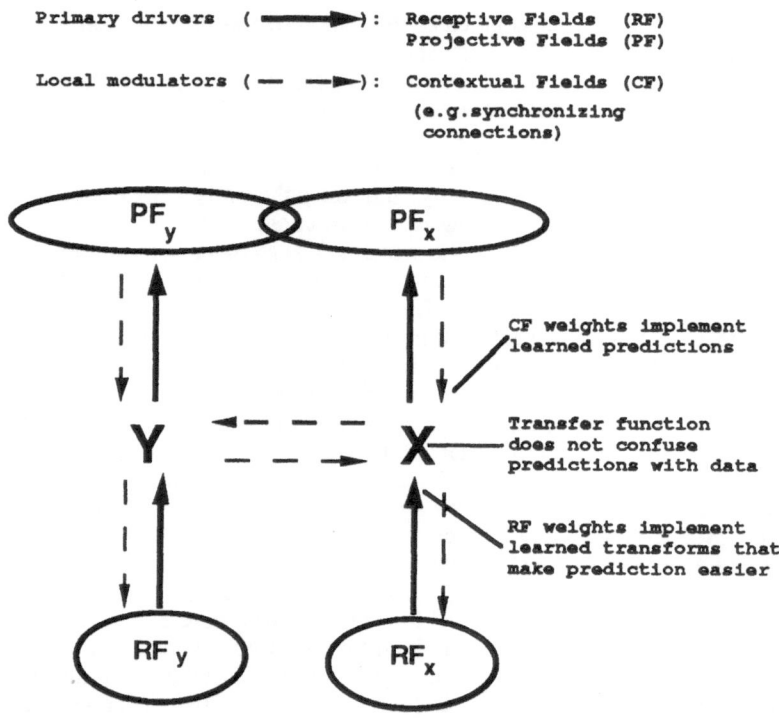

Figure 1. Two local processors, X and Y, with receptive field (RF) and contextual field (CF) inputs. They are assumed to operate within architectures consisting of very many streams of processing that converge and diverge in various ways over a few stages of processing.

processors treat all of their specific informative inputs in essentially the same kind of way. Third, in relation to coding, we will discuss the possibility of cooperative population coding. This is a special kind of population coding in which interactions between the elements ensure that they form a more effective cooperative whole if they are coherently related. Temporal synchronization is one obvious way in which this more effective cooperation could be achieved. Such codes contrast with single-cell codes in that they convey information about internal structure, and they contrast with the more usual form of distributed code in that processing involves internal knowledge that groups the elements into distinct cooperating subsets (von der Malsburg & Schneider, 1986). Finally, in relation to epistemology, we will suggest that by discovering latent variables that are predictably related to context the local processors are in effect discovering things and causes in the distal environment. As a consequence they lay foundations for representation. Nevertheless, we will argue that this does not constitute representation proper because such processors do not distinguish between the signals that they receive and the distal causes from which they arise.

3 A Formal Job Specification for Local Processors with Contextual Guidance and Studies of its Computational Feasibility

Formal specification of possible computational goals for cortical computation (Marr, 1982) is worth the effort for at least three reasons. First, if there is a cortical style of computation that is applicable to information about many different things, then it must be possible to specify what it achieves in some general abstract way that is free of reference to any specific content. Second, as we are concerned with the capabilities of local processors then it is essential that we view the task from such a viewpoint, i.e. we must specify the task in terms of just the information that is available to the local processors. Formal studies help ensure that we do this. Third, a clear and precise specification of what needs to be done may suggest ways in which it could be done. Giving a well specified goal does not constrain us to consider only optimal or analytically tractable algorithms for approaching that goal. Any algorithms that are proposed, however, should be computationally feasible, given relevant constraints upon things such as the amount of data to be analyzed by the local processor, its storage capacity, and processing speed.

3.1 Transfer Functions for Local Processors with Contextual Guidance

The hypothesis being considered here is that local processors produce succinct descriptions of the relevant information in their RF input. Contextual input is assumed to provide information that helps decide what is relevant. Information is relevant if it is predictably related to the context within which it occurs. This requires a transfer function that uses CF inputs to emphasize relevant descriptions without harming their ability to produce true descriptions.

Assuming processors with probabilistic binary outputs this requires a transfer function with the following properties. If there is no RF input then there should be no output; if there is no CF input then the output should be monotonically related to RF input in some nonlinear way, such as that specified by the commonly used and biologically plausible logistic function; if RF and CF inputs agree then the gain of the function relating output to RF input should be increased; if RF and CF inputs disagree then the gain of the function relating output to RF input should be decreased; only the RF input should determine which of the two possible outputs is more likely. To meet these requirements Kay and Phillips (1994) have specified the internal activation, A, of the local processor as follows

$$2A = r \, (1 + \exp(2rc))$$

where r = summed weighted RF inputs including bias input, and where c = summed weighted CF inputs including bias input. The internal activation is then entered into a standard logistic function to give the output probability. As Figure 2 shows output specified by this transfer function depends upon the RF input no matter what the CF input. When there is no CF input it becomes the standard logistic transfer function. CF input has no effect when there is no RF input. CF input cannot change an output of less than 0.5 to one of greater than 0.5, nor vice versa. The rate at which the output approaches saturation as a function of RF input is greater if it

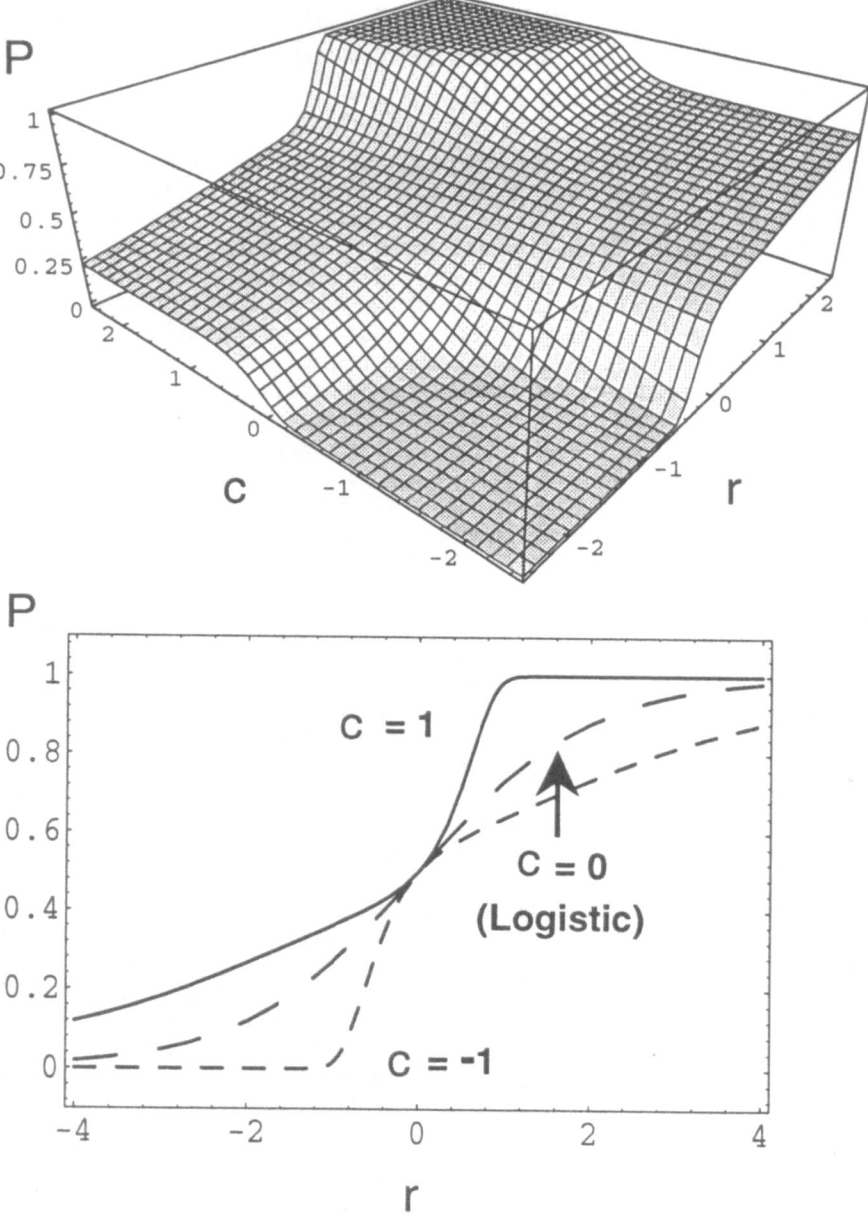

Figure 2. A transfer function for local processors with contextual guidance. The output probability, P, is shown as a function of the primary drive, r, and the contextual guidance, c. The lower panel shows P as a function of r for just three different values of c. It is included to make it clear that the context, c, does not simply change the slope of the logistic function, but increases the slope for outputs that agree with the context, and decreases the slope for those that disagree.

agrees with the CF input and slower if it disagrees. Furthermore, a context that agrees with the RF input has a greater effect than one that disagrees with it. This function therefore meets our requirements.

Note that inhibitory effects are implied by the transfer function shown in Figure 2. We assume that any thorough attempt to relate it to physiology must make the role of the ubiquitous local inhibitory circuitry explicit. Note also how the effects of the CFs hypothesized here differ from the more general modulatory effects of cholinergic and dopaminergic systems (Hobson, 1990; Cohen & Servan-Schreiber, 1992). These affect the ease with which output can be driven away from neutral in either direction. Modulation by the CFs is more specific. It makes it easier for output to be driven in the contextually predicted direction, but harder to drive it in the opposite direction. Together these various forms of modulation suggest that many cognitive phenomena may involve control of the transfer function of local processors.

3.2 Objective Functions for Contextual Guidance

The use of context to guide RF processing can be made precise by using information theory (Kay & Phillips, 1994, 1995), and it can be given an epistemological justification. Consider a processor to have input vectors R and C constituting the RF and CF inputs, and to produce an output vector X. The Shannon entropy in X can be decomposed as follows

$$H(X) = I(X; R; C) + I(X; R \mid C) + I(X; C \mid R) + H(X \mid R, C)$$

where the first term on the right is a measure of the information that is common to X, R and C; the second is that common to X and R but not to C; the third is that common to X and C but not to R; and the fourth is information in X that is in neither R nor C. Figure 3 illustrates this decomposition.

A goal for the local processor, X, can now be specified in terms of these four components. Each processor must adapt on the basis of just the information that is accessible to it. We therefore specify how X should adapt taking R and C as givens, but allowing for R and C to be themselves adapting in the same way. We require X to convey information about major sources of variation in R, and in particular those that are predictably related to C. Data compression and hence increased accessibility is ensured by the constraint that the information carrying capacity of X be much less than that of R.

Discovering major sources of variation in R requires the maximization of I(X; R), i.e. I(X; R; C) + I(X; R | C). Consider first the information that is common to the RFs and CFs, i.e. I(X; R; C). If the RFs and CFs arise from separate data-sets then any information that they share must reflect distal causes that are common to those data-sets. This information is therefore meaningful in the sense that it is part of a network of mutually predictable relationships with a distal origin. Such information is therefore likely to be of use and we require the local processor to transmit as much of it as possible. Succint descriptions of RF activity that are not contextually predictable, i.e. I(X; R | C), may also be useful at some later stage of processing or learning, however, so it may also be useful to increase this, though with a lower priority than predictability across streams. Information in X and C but not in R, i.e. I(X; C | R), should not be increased because the role of X is to transmit information about R, not about C. Finally, H(X | R, C) denotes variation in X that is due to neither R nor C. From the current perspective we would not

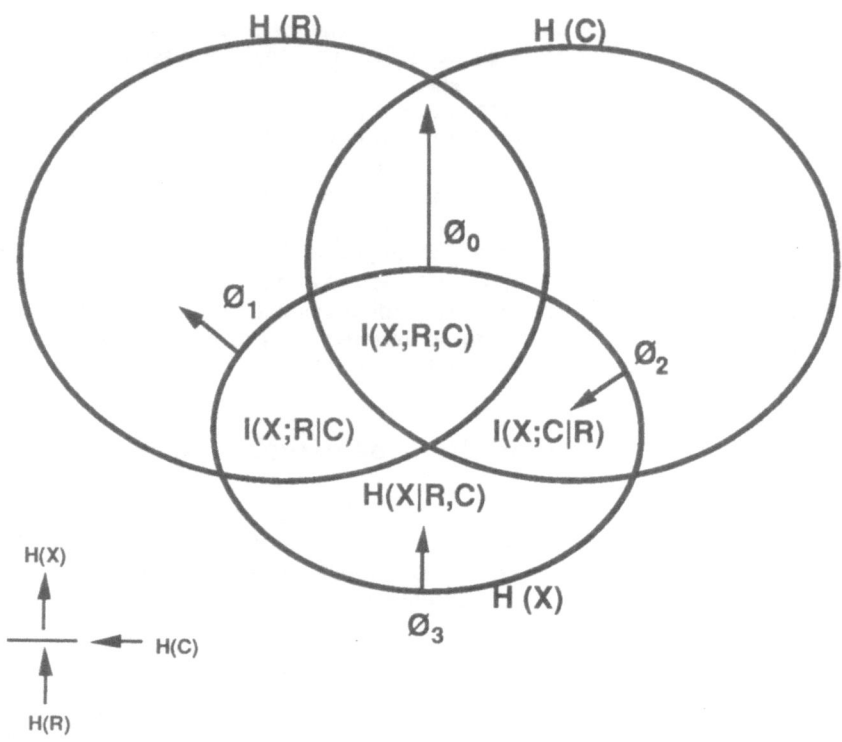

Figure 3. A Venn diagram illustrating the decomposition of the information in the output of a local processor, X, into four disjoint components. A goal for processing can be specified as the relative importance attached to increasing or decreasing each component, given by the $\varnothing_i$ parameters. H(X) is the total information (Shannon entropy) in X, etc. The length and directions of the arrows indicate a goal of reducing one component as much as possible, increasing another but with lower priority, and reducing the other two. The information flow is shown by the icon bottom left.

normally wish this to be increased, but note that the general neuromodulators provide a way of increasing it, thereby leading to unpredictable outputs such as those that occur in dreams or in schizophrenic disturbances.

Given these requirements we can formulate the following class of objective functions

$$F = \varnothing_0 I(X; R; C) + \varnothing_1 I(X; R \mid C) + \varnothing_2 I(X; C \mid R) + \varnothing_3 H(X \mid R, C)$$

where F is the objective to be maximized, and $\varnothing_0$, $\varnothing_1$, $\varnothing_2$ and $\varnothing_3$ are parameters in the range 1 to -1. The sub-class of objectives on which we focus assumes $\varnothing_0 = 1$, and $\varnothing_2 = \varnothing_3 = 0$. Different values for $\varnothing_1$ are then used to specify the relative importance to be given to increasing information transmission within streams and to increasing predictability across streams. The goals studied by Linsker (1988) and by Becker and Hinton (1992) are special cases of this sub-class of objective functions. Linsker (1988) seeks to maximize the information about R that is transmitted by X without distinguishing between that which is related to the context and that which is not. This requires $\emptyset_1 = 1$. Becker and Hinton (1992) seek to transmit only that information about R that is related to C. This requires $\emptyset_1 = 0$. Intermediate values specify the relative importance of these two goals, which might vary with the stage of processing and with the stage of learning.

3.3 Learning Rules for Processors with Contextual Guidance

The existence of a well specified objective, does not imply that it can be met, but one message of many previous studies of neural computation is that hill climbing methods are often effective, so we derived learning rules from this objective function by gradient ascent (Kay & Phillips, 1994; Phillips, Kay, and Smyth, 1995). The learning rules for the RF and CF weights both have the same general form. The change in synaptic strength that is specified by these rules is proportional to pre-synaptic activity, but it is non-monotonically related to post-synaptic activity. The rules are complex, but we take encouragement from the observation that the non-monotonicity required is similar to the computationally powerful learning rule proposed by Bienenstock, Cooper, and Munro (1982), and to a simpler version of this rule that has been shown to have useful computational properties (Hancock, Smith, & Phillips, 1991), and which was based upon a form of synaptic plasticity shown to occur in adult rat visual cortex (Artola, Brocher, and Singer, 1990).

3.4 Simulations

Simulations of a single processor with just two RF inputs and two CF inputs, plus adaptable RF and CF biasses, show that the local processor has the properties required (Kay and Phillips, 1994). For example, when the goal is to maximize the RF input that is predictably related to the context then this is done irrespective of whether that maximises transmission of information about the RF. When the goal is to maximize transmission of information about the RF then that is achieved irrespective of contextual predictability. Transition between these two goals can be achieved by varying $\emptyset_1$ between 0 and 1. When it is the most informative RF feature that is predictably related to the context then that can be found without contextual guidance, but it is found less rapidly. The simulations confirm that the learning rules can find non-zero values for the CF weights that allow the context to modulate processing, but without transmitting any information about the CF other than that which it shares with the RF.

Many simulations of multi-stream and multi-stage networks built from such processors have been run (e.g. Smyth, 1994), and will be reported in detail elsewhere (Phillips, Kay, and Smyth, 1995; Kay and Phillips, 1995). Here we provide just a brief summary. Multi-stream nets with mutual contextual guidance between streams can discover those linear features of their RF inputs that are predictably related across streams. Discovery is faster when these are the most informative features within streams, but it still occurs even when there is no evidence as to the existence of these features within streams. Performance improves as the number of streams increases and this encourages the view that the approach may have biological relevance. Two-stage multi-stream nets can discover linear features that are predictably related across streams, and under some conditions they can also discover non-linear features. Under other conditions they cannot, however, and this issue is still under investigation. Further work is required to determine whether the discovery of non-linear features is computationally feasible for these nets given realistic biological requirements and constraints.

However this turns out, the results already obtained show that feature discovery and associative learning can interact cooperatively. Thus it is not necessary to assume that features of the input must first be discovered by some form of unsupervised learning, and that a subsequent and quite separate process of supervised learning then searches for associations between those features. Furthermore, the results also show that it is possible for inputs to modulate the output of a processor even though the processor transmits no unconditional information about that class of inputs. The processors do transmit unconditional information about the RFs, however. This formalizes the claim that the CFs emphasize relevant outputs, and that the RFs determine what those outputs mean.

4 Evidence for Cooperative Population Coding and for Contextual Guidance

Evidence for the view that a major function of sensory systems is to reduce redundancy is already well known. The focus here is on neuropsychological evidence for cooperative population codes and contextual guidance. Evidence from neuroanatomy and neurophysiology will be reviewed in detail elsewhere, but, in brief: 1) voltage-dependent synaptic receptor channels are common throughout cortex and could provide a mechanism for gain control (e.g. Fox, Sato, & Daw, 1990); 2) long-range horizontal collaterals are also common (Gilbert, 1992) and could provide contextual input to the gain-control channels; 3) synchronization of the activity of cells with non-overlapping RFs (Singer, 1993) may reflect the formation of cooperative population codes resulting from contextual guidance; 4) activity-dependent plasticity of the synapses mediating the response to receptive field stimulation is well established (Singer, 1990); 5) there is now also evidence that the long-range horizontal connections undergo activity-dependent changes in synaptic strength (Hirsch & Gilbert, 1993; Lowel & Singer, 1992); 6) finally, as predicted by our hypotheses, the long-range horizontal collaterals in V1 have a voltage-dependent rather than a driving summative synaptic physiology (Hirsch & Gilbert, 1991).

4.1 Neuropsychological Evidence for Cooperative Population Codes

A major function hypothesized for the contextual connections is that they help form cooperative population codes. Neuropsychological evidence that some such code may be needed comes from recent studies of two patients who have difficulties in reading and writing (Goodall & Phillips 1995; Phillips & Goodall, 1995; Goodall, 1995). Their specific deficits are such that they are very poor at reading and writing phonically, i.e. by using the relations that hold between letters and phonemes. As a result they have particularly great difficulty reading unfamiliar nonwords, such as HELI for example. They are much better at reading and writing words as familiar wholes, however, and have no difficulties reading familiar concrete words such as HELICOPTER. Such neurological disorders are called phonological dyslexia and phonological dysgraphia.

The two patients studied (AN & AM) can read and write concrete words better than abstract words, spelling regularity has little or no effect, and performance with non-words is very poor, breaking down entirely for nonwords of six letters or more. As the ability of these patients to read and write depends so strongly upon familiarity with the particular whole item concerned they present a valuable opportunity for studying the effects of such familiarity. Goodall and Phillips (paper in preparation) therefore used this opportunity to ask whether or not familiarity with particular items produces population codes for those items. The patients were given visual experience of novel meaningless nonwords, ensuring that they neither heard nor wrote them. They were then later read various items for writing to dictation, including the visually familiar nonwords and unfamiliar nonwords of similar complexity. If the result of visual familiarity is just a process of recognition that attaches a new arbitrary label, or local unstructured code, to those items then this would not support writing to dictation because such codes convey no information about the internal structure of the items to which they are attached. If as a result of visual familiarity a description of the essential inner structure of those items can be maintained, can be matched with descriptions from other modalities, and can be transmitted all the way from input to output then this might support writing to dictation.

The effects of familiarity were studied by first giving just visual discrimination training on a set of nonwords, and then studying the effects of that on writing to dictation. Five new 4-letter nonwords were created and printed on a sheet that was placed in front of the patient, who had to say whether each of a number of separately presented test items was on the sheet or not. These test items included nonwords differing from the training items by just one letter to enforce accurate discrimination. This training proceeded until performance was accurate, which took about ten minutes. At no time did either the patient or the experimenter speak or write the nonwords, and indeed the patients could not accurately read them aloud, either before or after training. After a break of about 5 minutes, in this particular experiment, the 5 familiar nonwords and 5 unfamiliar nonwords were read for writing to dictation. All five familiar nonwords were written correctly and fluently. None of the unfamiliar nonwords were written either correctly or fluently. To confirm that the patients must have been using knowledge obtained from the visual discrimination training we read the familiar non-words to 42 normal subjects for writing to dictation. The spellings of these nonwords that were produced by the subjects who had never seen them were quite different from those given by our two patients. This is because in selecting the stimuli to be used with the patients we deliberately choose unlikely but plausible spellings.

These results therefore show that the patients must have been using their visual knowledge of these nonwords in writing to dictation, and that this must have enabled descriptions of their spelling patterns to be maintained, to be matched with a phonological description, and to be transmitted all the way from input to output. This implies that some form of population code must have been used throughout all stages of processing because if at any stage the code had been reduced to a local code, or to any other form of arbitrary label, then all information about inner structure would have been lost. The results further suggest that population codes are used because it is advantageous to deal with descriptions rather than just with arbitrary labels, even after an item has been recognised. As recognition is so commonly thought of as attaching a label to the thing recognized, an alternative way of looking at this is that it might be some form of description that serves as the label. This description could be a succinct one provided that it preserves information about essential inner structure. What is essential will depend upon the role of that stage of processing, and upon the set of items to be distinguished.

There is also another aspect of the results obtained from patient AN on which the hypotheses of contextual guidance and cooperative population codes might throw some light. This is the finding that she can copy whole familiar items better than novel combinations of their familiar parts. She was trained to copy bi-syllabic nonwords such as BONSED and MUNIZE, and then tested for transfer to the copying of BONIZE and MUNSED (Phillips and Goodall, 1995). The task used was immediate copying from memory. Twelve 6-letter nonwords were randomly divided into two sets of six, one set being used for training, and the other being reserved for later use as a control. Prior to training AN copied two of the six correctly. She was then given training by presenting one at a time for copying and telling her whether she was correct. She copied them all correctly after 11 runs through the whole set. These six familiar nonwords were then combined with the control nonwords that she had not seen before, and with six new nonwords formed by recombining the first and last halves of the familiar nonwords to make novel combinations but with the parts maintaining their position relative to the nonword as a whole. These 18 items were then presented for copying from memory. The six familiar nonwords were all copied correctly but only one was copied correctly from each of the other two sets.

These results show that the ability to copy familiar nonwords does not necessarily transfer to novel combinations of their parts. This is not how the distributed representations used in most neural network theories behave, because they support transfer to the sub-space within which familiar items lie in both feedforward networks (e.g. Baldi & Hornik, 1989; Brousse & Smolensky, 1989; Phillips, Hay, & Smith, 1993) and in recurrent architectures with attractors (e.g. Plaut and McClelland, 1993). The above results are therefore evidence for a special kind of population code; i.e. one in which patterns of activity are processed more effectively when they form a familiar cooperative whole. Because of this wholistic aspect it has some of the properties of a local code.

This suggests that in trying to understand cognition in neural terms we should not feel constrained to choose between local codes and distributed representations of the usual sort. We should also consider the possibilities of cooperative population codes that combine some of the properties of both local and distributed codes. Some such form of coding might arise because elements within a familiar context are supported by and synchronized with that context, with the result that the effects produced by the whole population is more than the sum of the effects that are produced by the elements of that population operating independently. Synchronized population codes operate in this latter, more wholistic way, so it may be worth studying simulated nets that use synchronization for dynamic grouping (e.g. von der Malsburg & Schneider, 1986; Wang, Buhmann & von der Malsburg, 1990) to see whether they generalize to novel patterns in a way that predicts the neuropsychological results reported above.

4.2 Neuropsychological Evidence for Contextual Guidance

Effects of context on the responses of single cortical cells to RF input are well established (e.g. Moran & Desimone, 1985; Gilbert and Wiesel, 1990). Psychophysical studies show that attention and imagery can enhance (Sagi & Julesz, 1986) or impair (Craver-Lemley & Reeves, 1987) discrimination, and that a familiar local context can enhance perception (e.g. Phillips, 1971; Biederman, 1972; Weisstein & Harris, 1974; McClelland, 1978). In some circumstances context can also impair perception (e.g. Gibson & Radner, 1937). Such effects may be due at least in part to contextual inputs that increase the probability of decisions with which they agree and decrease the probability of decisions with which they disagree.

A central aspect of the hypothesis of contextual guidance is that context can in principle influence processing but without any information that is specific to the context being transmitted through that influence. Thus any information that is used only for contextual guidance would not be explicitly available for processing in its own right. A dramatic demonstration of this possibility comes from a stroke patient HJA who has been studied for many years (Humphreys & Riddoch, 1987). As well as being agnosic this patient no longer sees the world in colour but only in black and white. It has now been discovered that, although he no longer sees the world in colour, colour does have implicit influences on his detection of luminance contrasts. In one task he had to say whether the top and bottom halves of a rectangular display differed in the second or the first of two intervals. Sometimes the two halves differed only in luminance, sometimes only in colour, and sometimes in both. When the two halves differed only in luminance performance improved as luminance contrast increased. When a colour difference was added, however, then the increase in performance with increases in luminance contrast was much greater than when these contrasts were presented without colour differences. Thus the presence of a colour difference has increased sensitivity to luminance differences. When the colour difference was presented without any luminance difference then performance was at chance. This illustrates his achromotopsia. Similar implicit effects of color upon the detection of luminance differences have also been shown with another achromotopsic patient, WM (Troscianko, Landis, & Phillips, 1993).

A simple interpretation of these results is that the colour streams modulate the luminance streams, but with their own feed-forward outputs no longer functioning properly. This assumes that connections between the color and luminance streams have learned that colour differences often predict luminance differences. Furthermore, the results support the view that the visual system can use predictions without confusing them with the evidence. These findings therefore illustrate a key difference that is hypothesized to distinguish RFs and CFs. Outputs are "seen" by later stages of processing as conveying information about their RFs, not as conveying information about their CFs. The patients described here report that in this case those later stages include conscious experience.

5 The Discovery of Distal Variables as a Foundation for Representation Proper

5.1 The Discovery of Distal Variables in Diverse Proximal Data Sets

The maximization of predictable variation can be seen as an extension of the well established practice of averaging to reduce noise. The basic idea is simple; any mutual information shared by diverse data sets must have some distal origin. The more diverse the data the more distal those origins are likely to be. If features of facial appearance and of emotive aspects of the tone of voice can be found that are predictably related to each other then they are likely to have their common origin in the emotional state of the person perceived. If information common to a heard speech signal and to visually perceived mouth movements can be found then that information is likely to reflect common causes very distant from the proximal sensory data. Evidence that this could be used to discover speech categories without the aid of any supervisor that already knows them is provided by de Sa (1994) whose approach is similar to ours in spirit, though differing in various important respects. The epistemological argument being presented here also applies within modalities. For example, aspects of shading and stereo depth that are mutually predictive will arise from their shared origins in surface shape. It also applies within sub-modalities, as shown by Becker and Hinton (1992) who describe an algorithm that discovers stereo depth using the mutual information shared by separate parts of a visual field that have nothing else in common.

5.2 Why Representation Proper Requires more than the Discovery of Distal Variables.

The word "representation" is generally used to describe what sensory and perceptual systems do, but it can carry inappropriate connotations. In that general use it is synonymous with "anything that transmits information". In that sense all neural signals are representations. "Representation" also has a more specific meaning, however, such that the distinction between representation and referent is crucial. Representation proper is using one thing, the representation, to refer to something else, the referent. It implies a user that knows about and distinguishes both representation and referent. This relation is usually asymmetrical, even where representation and referent are very similar. For example, a picture of a pipe is often used as a representation of a real pipe, but a real pipe is rarely if ever used as a representation of a picture of a pipe; furthermore, a photographic reproduction of Magritte's painting of a pipe is more likely to be seen as a representation of the painting than vice versa. Despite first appearances, this asymmetry does not apply to the notion of information transmission, which is defined simply as the mutual information that is shared between input and output, and this is symmetrical.

Representation proper plays an important role in human cognition, but most cortical function may proceed without it, nevertheless. We know of no observations at the level of local cortical circuits suggesting that the structures concerned treat their inputs as standing for something other than themselves. Thus it will not matter if neurophysiologists use the word "representation" when all they are dealing with is signal processing, because they have not yet found ways of studying representation proper. Psychologists do sometimes study representation proper, however, so for them indeterminate use of the word "representation" can lead to unnecessary confusion. Phylogenetic studies of representation proper show it to be rare or absent outside of the primate line and to progressively emerge within it (e.g. Chavalier-Skolinkoff,1983; Byrne & Whiten, 1992). In children different aspects of this skill develop during the years 1 to 6, gradually becoming more flexible, internalised, and differentiated (e.g. Piaget,1954; Wimmer and Perner, 1983; De Loach, 1987; Zaitchik, 1990; Campbell and Olson, 1990). De Loach (1987), for example, showed children a toy being hidden in a scale model of a room, then asked them to find a similar toy that had been hidden in the corresponding place in the room itself. De Loach found that the ability to do this emerges rapidly between the ages of 2 and 2.5 years, and she suggested that this is because the younger child cannot think of the model both as a thing in itself and as a representation of something else.

A quite different line of evidence on the possible role of representation proper comes from studies of the computational capabilities of simulated neural nets. So far, none of these treat their inputs as standing for something else, so the notion of a referent is not relevant to an analysis of their dynamics. They have considerable computational power, nevertheless.

Thus the ability to compute distal variables does not by itself constitute representation proper. It could contribute to that higher function, however, by making available information about distal variables that are quite distinct from the proximal data upon which they are based. Representation proper might then develop from the ackowledgement of that distinction at some higher level of organization.

Our conclusion is that representation proper is not a common feature of cortical computation, but arises late in the development of both child and species, and perhaps upon foundations such as the implicit form of realism that has been hypothesized here to result from the maximization of coherent variation by local cortical processors. If so, a better understanding of the capabilities and limitations of those foundations will help us understand how the higher constructions are possible, and why they are needed.

References

Artola, A., Brocher, S. & Singer, W. (1990) Different voltage-dependent thresholds for the induction of long-term depression and long-term potentiation in slices of the rat visual cortex. *Nature* 347, 69-72.

Atick, J. J. & Redlich, A. N. (1993) Convergent algorithm for sensory receptive field development. *Neural Computation* 5, 45-60

Baddeley, R. J. & Hancock. P. J. B. (1991) A statistical analysis of natural images matches psychophysically derived orientation tuning curves. *Proceedings of the Royal Society of London* B246, 219-223.

Baldi, B. & Hornik, K. (1989). Neural networks and principal component analysis: learning from examples without local minima. *Neural Networks* 2, 53-58.

Barlow H. B. (1961) Possible principles underlying the transformations of sensory messages. In Rosenblith, W. A. (ed.) *Sensory Communication* Boston: MIT Press.

Barlow, H. B. (1989) Unsupervised learning. *Neural Computation* 1, 295-311.

Barlow, H. B.& Foldiak, P. (1989) Adaptation and decorrelation in the cortex. In Durbin, R. & Miall, C. (eds.,) *The Computing Neuron* Wokingham: Addison-Wesley.

Becker S. & Hinton G. E. (1992). Self-organizing neural network that discovers surfaces in random-dot stereograms. *Nature* 355, 161-163.

Biederman, I. (1972) Perceiving real-world scenes. *Science* 177, 77-80.

Bienenstock E. L., Cooper L. N., & Munro P. W. (1982). Theory for the development of neuron selectivity: Orientation specificity and binocular interaction in visual cortex. *Journal of Neuroscience* 2, 32-48.

Brousse, O. & Smolensky, P. (1989) Virtual memories and massive generalization in connectionist combinatorial learning. In *Proceedings of the 11th Annual Conference of the Cognitive Science Society*. Hillside, NJ: Lawrence Erlbaum.

Byrne, R. W. & Whiten, A. (1992) Cognitive evolution in primates: evidence from tactical deception. *Man* 27, 609-627.

Campbell, R. N. & Olson, D. R. (1990) Children's thinking. In R. Grieve & M. Hughes (eds.) *Understanding Children: Essays in honour of Margaret Donaldson*. Oxford: Blackwell.

Chevalier-Skolinkoff, S. (1983) Sensori-motor development in orang-utans and other primates. *Journal of Human Evolution* 12, 545-546.

Cohen J. D. & Servan-Schreiber D. (1992) Context, cortex, and Dopamine: A connectionist approach to behaviour and biology in schizophrenia. *Psychological Review* 99, 45-77.

Craver-Lemley, C. & Reeves, A. (1987) Visual imagery selectively reduces vernier acuity. *Perception*, 16, 599-614.

De Sa, V. (1994) *Unsupervised Classification Learning from Cross-Modal Environmental Structure* PhD Thesis, University of Rochester, NY.

De Loach, J. (1987) Rapid change in the symbolic functioning of very young children. *Science* 238, 1556-1557.

Foldiak, P. (1990) Forming sparse representations by local anti-Hebbian learning. *Biological Cybernetics* 64, 165-170.

Fox K., Sato H. & Daw N. (1990) The effect of varying stimulus intensity on NMDA-receptor activity in cat visual cortex. *Journal of Neurophysiology* 64, 1413-1428.

Gibson, J. J. & Radner, M. (1937) Adaptation, after-effect and contrast in the perception of tilted lines. *Journal of Experimental Psychology* 20, 453-467.

Gilbert, C. D. (1992) Horizontal integration and cortical dynamics. *Neuron* 9, 1-13.

Gilbert, C. D., & Wiesel, T. N. (1990) The influence of contextual stimuli on the orientation selectivity of cells in primary visual cortex of the cat. *Vision Research* 11, 1689-1701.

Giffins, R. (1985) *Canonical Analysis: A Review with Applications in Ecology* Biomathematics 12. Berlin: Springer-Verlag.

Goodall, W. C. (1995) *Neuropsychological studies of Reading and Writing.* PhD Thesis, University of Stirling, Scotland, UK.

Goodall, W. C. & Phillips, W. A. (1995) Three routes from print to sound: Evidence from a case of acquired dyslexia. *Cognitive Neuropsychology*, in press.

Hancock P. J. B., L. S. Smith, & Phillips W. A. (1991). A biologically supported error-correcting learning rule. *Neural Computation* 3, 201-212.

Hirsch J. A. & Gilbert C. D. (1991) Synaptic physiology of horizontal connections in cat's visual cortex. *Journal of Neuroscience* 11, 1800-1809.

Hirsch J. A. & Gilbert C. D. (1993) Long-term changes in synaptic strength along specific intrinsic pathways in the cat visual cortex. *Journal of Physiology* 461, 247-262.

Hobson J. A. (1990) Activation, input source, and modulation: A neurocognitive model of the state of the brain-mind. In Bootzin R. R., Kihlstrom J. F. & Schacter D. L.*Sleep & Cognition.* 2: 25-40.

Hotelling, H. (1936) Relations between two sets of variables. *Biometrika* 28, 321-77.

Humphreys, G. W. & Riddoch, M. J. (1987) *To see but not to see: A case study of visual agnosia.* London: Lawrence Erlbaum.

Kay J. (1992) Feature discovery under contextual supervision using mutual information. *International Joint Conference on Neural Networks 4, 79-84.*

Kay, J. & Phillips, W. A. (1994) Activation functions, computational goals and learning rules for local processors with contextual guidance. *Technical Report CCCN-15,* University of Stirling, Centre for Cognitive and Computational Neuroscience.

Kay, J. & Phillips, W. A. (1995) Activation functions, computational goals and learning rules for local processors with contextual guidance. Manuscript submitted, & available from authors.

Li, Z. & Atick, J. J. (1994) Efficient stereocoding in the multiscale representation. *Network* 5, 157-174.

Linsker, R. (1988). Self-organization in a perceptual network. *Computer* 21, 105-117.

Lowel, S., & Singer, W. (1992) Selection of intrinsic horizontal connections in the visual cortex by correlated neuronal activity. *Science* 255, 209-212.

Marr, D. (1982) *Vision .* San Francisco: Freeman.

McClelland, J. L. (1978) Perception and masking of wholes and parts. *Journal of Experimental psychology: Human Perception and Performance* 4, 210-223.

Moran, J. & Desimone, R. (1985) Selective attention gates visual processing in the extrastriate cortex. *Science,* 229, 782-784.

Phillips, W. A. (1971) Does familiarity affect transfer from an iconic to a short-term memory? *Perception and Psychophysics* 10, 153-157.

Phillips, W. A. & Goodall, W. C. (1995) Lexical writing can be non-semantic and fluent without practice. *Cognitive Neuropsychology* (in press).

Phillips, W. A., Hay, I. M., & Smith, L. S. (1993) Lexicality and pronunciation in a simulated neural net. *British Journal of Mathematical and Statistical Psychology* 46, 193-205.

Phillips, W. A., Kay, J., & Smyth, D. (1995) The discovery of structure by multi-stream networks of local processors with contextual guidance. Manuscript submitted, & available from authors.

Piaget, J (1954) *The Construction of Reality by the Child* New York: Basic Books.

Plaut, D. C. & McClelland, J. L. (1993) Generalization with componential attractors: Word and nonword reading in an attractor network. In *Proceedings of the 15th Annual Conference of the Cognitive Science Society*. Hillside, NJ: Lawrence Erlbaum.

Redlich, A. N. (1993) Redundancy reduction as a strategy for unsupervised learning. *Neural Computation* 5, 289-304.

Sagi, D & Julesz, B. (1986) Enhanced detection in the aperture of focal attention during simple discrimination tasks. *Nature* 321, 693-695.

Singer, W. (1990) Search for coherence: A basic principle of cortical self-organization. *Concepts in Neuroscience* 1, 1-26.

Singer, W. (1993) Synchronization of cortical activity and its putative role in information processing and learning. *Annual Review of Physiology*, 55, 349-374.

Smyth, D. (1994) Simulations of networks of local processors with contextual guidance. Master's Thesis, CCCN, University of Stirling.

Troscianko T, Landis, T. & Phillips W. A., (1993). Chromatic discrimination in cerebral achromotopsia: Additional evidence favouring magno-based perception, and a neural-net model. *Perception* 22 supplement, 8-9.

von der Malsburg, C & Schneider, W. (1986) A neural cocktail-party processor. *Biological Cybernetics* 54, 29-40.

Wang, D., Buhmann, J, & von der Malsburg, C. (1990) Pattern segmentation in associative memory. *Neural Computation* 2, 94-106.

Weisstein, N. & Harris, C. S. (1974) Visual detection of line segments: An object-superiority effect. *Science* 186, 752-755.

Wimmer, H. & Perner, J. (1983) Beliefs about beliefs: representing and constraining function of wrong beliefs in children's understanding of deception. *Cognition* 13, 103-128.

Zaitchik, D. (1990) When representations conflict with reality. *Cognition* 35 41-68.

Audition and Vision

Using Complementary Streams in a computer model of the abstraction of Diatonic pitch

Niall Griffith

Department of Computer Science, University of Exeter

Exeter, UK.

Abstract

Two computational models using ANN's are described that extract statistical representations of pitch use in melodies across various keys. These representations are equivalent to abstract pitch (degree) identities. The research is focussed on how the differences between pitch use in different keys can be represented and outlines two simple mechanisms through which these descriptions can be constructed. The research supports the view that inductive processes concerned with extracting statistical representations of pitch use are able to create stable and consistent representations equivalent to categories that delineate tonal structure.

1   Introduction

Much research directed at the modelling and simulation of musical cognition has concentrated on how formal corollaries of musical processes and representation are encoded, e.g. the identification of the key of a piece. Various models have been proposed to simulate this process [27, 31, 21, 16, 30, 19, 17]. These models have assumed a fully developed sense of key, and little attention has been paid to how our sense of tonality develops. Recently, inductive models based on artificial neural network (ANN) paradigms have been used to model aspects of the processes involved in *learning* about musical structure via simulated exposure to pieces of music [1, 20]. This paper concerns itself principally with how an abstract scale, such as the tonic-solfa or diatonic scale may be learned[1]. Musical Tonality seems to involve a complex of processes operating over various timescales. The models described here concentrate on one relatively neglected aspect of tonality - the way in which pitches are used in music. Much work has focussed on the processes involved in identifying pitch from harmonic components [28, 22]. However, it is difficult to argue that the abstraction of diatonic pitch proceeds from the intrinsic nature of tones. Mechanisms other than the purely psychoacoustic, operating over timescales longer than those involved in perceptual integration are required [13]. The models described here explore two ways of extracting descriptions of pitch use that allow the identification of abstract pitches. The motivation and assessment of the simulations are described in more detail than is possible here in [13].

Being able to identify the key of a piece is a skill associated with trained musicians. However, people with no musical training are still able to perform music. Research into melodic memory and tonality [9, 10], suggests that tonality involves representing the relationships between pitches, the memorisation of tunes in terms of abstract scales,

---

[1]This paper describes some of the research towards a PhD thesis at the University of Exeter, supervised by Noel Sharkey and Henry Shaffer, and supported by an award from the British Science and Engineering Research Council.

138

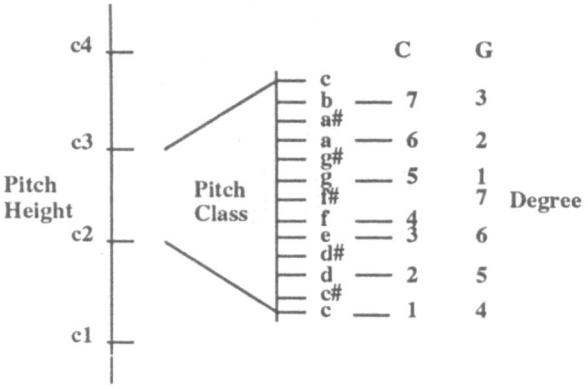

Figure 1: The various kinds of pitch abstraction.

and a close relationship between tonal skill and the ability to identify a key [6, 24]. The work of Krumhansl [19] stresses the emergence of hierarchies of pitch relations correlated with pitch frequency and duration. The work of Butler and Brown [6, 5, 3] has emphasised the role of pitch transitions and patterns of intervals implicit in these transitions, and shares with Krumhansl the view that tonality uses descriptions of pitch use, rather than deriving it entirely from the intrinsic relationships between pitches.

2 Abstract Pitch

Pitch abstraction progresses initially via the identification of discrete pitches and pitch-classes [28, 22]. These are prerequisites for the abstraction of a pitch-class's scale position or function. Abstract pitch is described mnemonically in the tonic-solfa, e.g. **Do Re Mi Fa So La Ti**, and numerically as degrees[2] of the scale, e.g. $\hat{1}\,\hat{2}\,\hat{3}\,\hat{4}$ $\hat{5}\,\hat{6}\,\hat{7}$. These abstract schemas share three characteristics. (i) They describe a scale that spans a single octave. (ii) They do not specify the pitch height of the octave. (iii) They do not specify the starting pitch of the scale within the octave. The relationship between pitch height, pitch-class, and degree is illustrated in Figure 1.

One proposal is that degrees emerge from the action of a gating mechanism [2, 25], through which combinations of pitch and key are mapped to particular degrees. The question remains as to how we *learn* that the pitch **g** in the scale of **C** is equivalent to **c** in the scale of **F**, namely degree $\hat{5}$? Also, a gating mechanism tells us nothing about the relations between degrees. These relationships cannot be derived directly from the harmonic constituents of the pitches involved as these do not vary according to their position in a scale. Also, as musical systems use different scales, this suggests that there is a general mechanism able to induce pitch functions from a particular musical system. This is the sort of approach advocated by Bharucha [1] - that musical schemas arise from the exposure of general categorical mechanisms to musically structured sounds. The use made of pitches and intervals are two basic descriptors we might

---

[2]The term degree is used throughout this paper.

expect to define significant aspects of tonal structure.

A very general description of pitch use is the frequency of occurrence of pitch-classes [27, 8]. By tracking the frequency of pitch occurrence, patterns of pitch use can be identified with scales or keys [13]. However, underlying such general patterns there are phrases, from which the overall pitch profile arises. The repeated use of phrases forms patterns that vary with the key, and reflect the position of a pitch as a degree of the scale [6, 5], and its identity in abstract scales. The models to be described classify the patterns of pitch and interval use that arise within the context of keys to identify this kind of functionality.

Interval is the first order difference between pitches, and the representation of pitch use in terms of intervals facilitates direct comparisons between pitch use in different keys. The purpose of this paper is to highlight the complementary nature of the information associated with streams encoding pitch and interval. The arguments for the primacy of pitch representations [9, 10, 2, 29] in melodic memory, and the difficulties [13] associated with accepting in full the *rare interval* argument of Browne [4, 6], does not exclude interval from a role in tonality in the encoding of abstract pitch itself.

3 Outline of the Model

The model outlined is a two-stage developmental model, in which the identity of abstract pitch is *bootstrapped* via the identification of tonal centres. The identification of tonal centres (keys) has been described in [13, 14]. In brief, the classification of melodies into keys uses a tracking memory that develops values that reflect the frequency of occurrence of pitch-classes over time. When this memorised pattern is classified in an ART2 network, twelve key nodes are created, each largely (93% - 98%) populated by melodies in a single key. The classes are stable across a range of η rates that determine the responses of the tracking memory.

Subsequently, the degrees of the scale are identified from patterns of pitch-class use *within* the identified keys. This has been modelled in two ways. Firstly, by comparing the representation of pitch-class transitions in the context of different keys with these transitions across all keys. Secondly, by comparing the patterns of intervals associated with pitch-classes in different keys. These two approaches share the view that pitch function arises via the identification of a general pitch context (key) and the description of pitch-class use within it. The identification of the degrees of the scale is facilitated by the use of the identities (keys) derived within one process of categorisation to guide another related process. The models described use two different network paradigms - Simple Recurrent Nets (SRN's) and ART networks.

4 Representing pitch use through Pitch Transitions

The first approach to pitch abstraction assumes that pitches are used in ways that consistently reflect their place or function in a scale, and the resulting patterns can be used to identify this scale position. These relationships are described by looking at the transitional probabilities between successive pitches [23]. In the case of the tunes in the current experimental set of diatonically limited nursery rhymes[3], the pitch set in

---

[3]60 nursery rhymes were used to train the networks and a further 25 were used to test them. All the rhymes were presented in all possible transpositions.

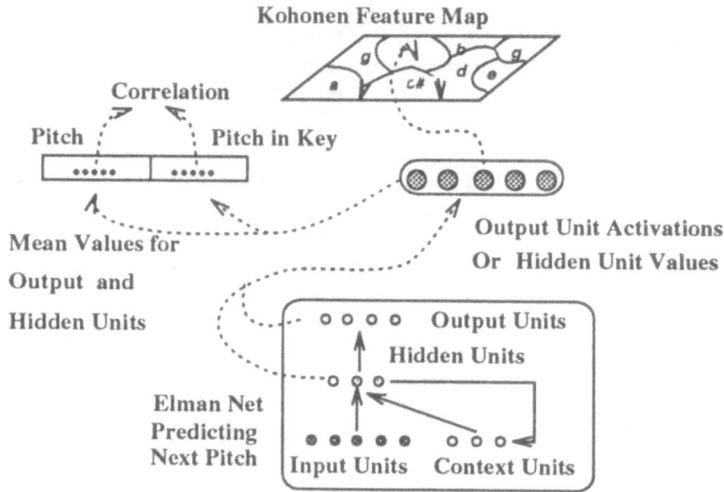

Figure 2: An outline of the model using an SRN to learn pitch transitions.

any key is seven pitch-classes.

SRN's [11] have been quite widely used in learning tasks which model sequential expectation. Typically, a network is expected to *predict* from the current item the next item in a sequence [26]. In this case, a complication arises because songs were presented in every transposition. Any *'grammar'* implicit in the pitch use within a song in a particular key, needs to be disentangled from global representations developed in the SRN from pieces performed in all twelve keys.

The simulations were as follows. A SRN, shown in the bottom of Figure 2, was trained on the task of *predicting* the next pitch in a song[4]. Because each song is presented in all keys and because pitches are shared between keys, this learning task involves many-to-many mappings. Consequently, the SRN only learns to predict repetitions of pitches - the most frequently ordered pair of pitches. The network is also able to learn[5] to predict a *legitimate pitch*, i.e. a pitch that is a member of the pitch set for the current key. Once the network had learned to predict to this extent the simulation was stopped, and the network was tested using the training and test set. The resulting hidden unit representation for each of the predictions was kept and used to train a Kohonen Feature Map (KFM) [18]. The relations between hidden unit representations that emerge in the organisation of the KFM shown in Figure 3 reflect surface temporal structure. The inputs associated with particular positions on the map are tagged by the name of the *predicting* pitch. The hidden units for a particular pitch are, in eleven out of twelve cases, localised on the map, indicating that the hidden units for a pitch are generally more similar to each other than they are to other pitches. Eleven of the 27 borders between pitch areas are between pitches separated by an M2.

---

[4]The simulations performed constituted a perm of 21 experiments, 3 seeds (1,13,19) by 7 hidden unit counts (6,16,26,36,46,56,66). Typically the networks used a learning rate of 0.01 and a momentum of 0.1. The results described here are confined to the simulation using 66 hidden units and a seed of 19.

[5]After ten cycles (each cycle consists of 29736 predictions spread over 720 sequences)

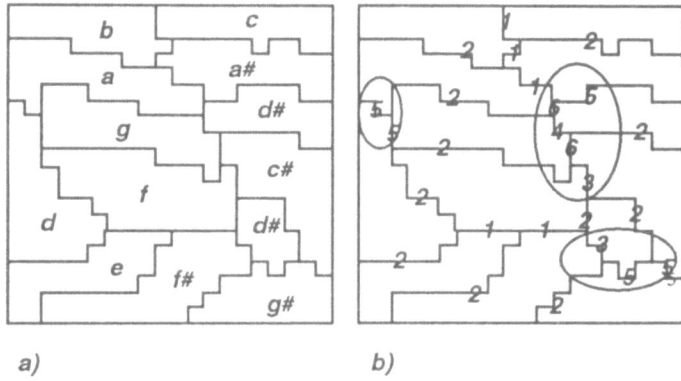

a)   b)

Figure 3: KFM of the hidden unit representations extracted from a SRN trained to predict next pitch. a) Shows areas identified with predicting pitches. b) Shows the interval in semitones between the pitch areas. The map is a 2D, 20 by 20 surface, trained for 10000 cycles using a rate of 0.3, an update area of 15, and a seed of 13.

After repetition, M2 is the most frequently occurring interval in this set of songs, being five of the seven intervals in the major scale.

The musical interest of the network representations is more apparent when we consider what has been achieved by the SRN. The original vector descriptions are just lists of 0's and 1's; each being equidistant from, and orthogonal to the others. These represent pitch classes in terms of membership of the chromatic set, dissociated from any harmonic content. The predictive SRN has constructed internal representations that are most similar when the pitches share their context, i.e. the pitches that precede them, which in melodies tend to be the same pitch or one adjacent in the scale.

It is encouraging that the SRN is capturing this statistical regularity. However, the hidden unit representations do not reflect either key or functional pitch use directly. However, as the SRN is extracting statistical regularities reflecting the transitions between pitches, the representations within the area for each pitch-class should also be differentiated. To investigate this, the mean hidden unit representations for a pitch-class, calculated from all the songs across all the keys, were correlated with the mean hidden unit representations for a pitch-class within the songs in a single key. For example, the overall mean vector for pitch c was correlated to the mean vector for c in C Major, G Major, etc. Table 1 shows the correlations[6] ranked by descending level of correlation from left to right. The pattern that emerges is a ranking of pitches in scale positions $\hat{2}$ ($\hat{1}$ $\hat{6}$) $\hat{3}$ $\hat{4}$ $\hat{7}$, although there are deviations from this, particularly in the case of $\hat{1}$ and $\hat{6}$. However, over the whole set of simulations this pattern indicates the relationships amongst the representations developed by the SRN are consistent, and reflect the way that pitches are used in different keys.

These ordered correlations have two drawbacks. Firstly, the range of variation in the correlations is quite small - between 0.98 and 0.77[7]. The mixing of $\hat{1}$'s and $\hat{6}$'s reflects this. More importantly, the actual significance of a pitch within a key is not

---

[6]Pearson Product Moment Correlation
[7]The correlations are all significant at the 0.001 level.

Key	1		2		3		4		5		6		7	
A	2	b	5	e	1	a	6	f#	3	c#	4	d	7	g#
A#	2	c	5	f	1	a#	6	g	3	d	4	d#	7	a
B	2	c#	5	f#	1	b	6	g#	3	d#	4	e	7	a#
C	2	d	5	g	1	c	6	a	3	e	4	f	7	b
C#	2	d#	5	g#	1	c#	6	a#	3	f	4	f#	7	c
D	2	e	5	a	1	d	6	b	3	f#	4	g	7	c#
D#	2	f	5	a#	6	c	1	d#	3	g	4	g#	7	d
E	2	f#	5	b	1	e	6	c#	3	g#	4	a	7	d#
F	2	g	5	c	6	d	1	f	3	a	4	a#	7	e
F#	2	g#	5	c#	1	f#	6	d#	3	a#	4	b	7	f
G	2	a	5	d	1	g	6	e	3	b	4	c	7	f#
G#	2	a#	5	d#	6	f	1	g#	3	c	4	c#	7	g

Table 1: Correlations between the mean hidden unit vectors for pitches over all keys and in particular keys. The ranking shows the order of the pitches and degrees.

congruent with musical or psychological understanding, which asserts that the most important pitch in a scale is Degree $\hat{1}$ not $\hat{2}$. Degree $\hat{2}$ is ranked first in this case because its representation is closest to the mean representation of all degrees.

5 Representing pitch use through patterns of Interval Use

A second approach to modelling pitch abstraction as a process that differentiates the way that pitches are used in different keys is shown in Figure 4. A process of memorisation using echoic and tracking memory models develops pitch-in-key representations of intervals guided by the key identified for a song. The memorisation of interval patterns was implemented using four similar memory models that produced very similar results. The general form of the memory is shown in the bottom of Figure 4. It comprises two stages. The first stage traces the occurrence of intervals over all the pitch-classes. This *echoic* (ECH) memory, is of the shunting (Multiplicative), adding type [15, 12]. Here, one shunting, adding, memory is described. Where values in the input vector $\mathbf{X}$ are either 0 or 1, $\mathbf{x}_j$ is the input value and $\mathbf{w}_j$ is the echoic memory value, initialised to zero, and η is the memory rate:

$$\text{if} \quad \mathbf{x}_j(t) > 0 : \mathbf{w}_j(t) = (\mathbf{w}_j(t-1) + (\eta \mathbf{x}_j(t)))$$
$$\text{else} \qquad\qquad : \mathbf{w}_j(t) = \eta \mathbf{w}_j(t-1)$$

The ECH memory models are described in more detail in [13]. They produce a trace of events in which the recency of each interval is reflected by a value between 0 and 1. The second stage is a set of TRK memories, like that used to track the frequency of occurrence of pitch and identify key (see section 3). One memory is dedicated to each pitch-class and receives input from the initial ECH memory. Learning takes place in the TRK memory associated with a pitch-class *only* when that pitch-class occurs.

The two-stage memory computes two things. Firstly, the ECH memory contains a vector that continually reflects the recency of intervals at each point in a melody. The actual values reflect the η rate and the configuration of the adding and shunting elements. Intervals that are more recent have larger values in the ECH memory. Secondly, the TRK memories are specific to pitch, and track the pattern of intervals in the ECH memory, emphasising the intervals that are consistently prominent in a pitch's context by scaling up the tracking of the more recent intervals relative to older, lower valued intervals. As the TRK memory for a pitch is only activated when that pitch occurs, the intervals associated with less frequent pitches are tracked less often, and the pattern that is tracked in the TRK memory is sensitive to the idiosyncrasies of pitch use in particular songs over the short term. However, the model is not limited to learning the pitch representations during a song in isolation. The key of each song, identified in the process described in Section 3, is used to guide the attention of a further process in which the representations developed in the TRK memories are learned[8] in a layer of memories in which the recipient node is determined by the current key and pitch-class. The representations developed within these nodes can be classified by an ART2 network.

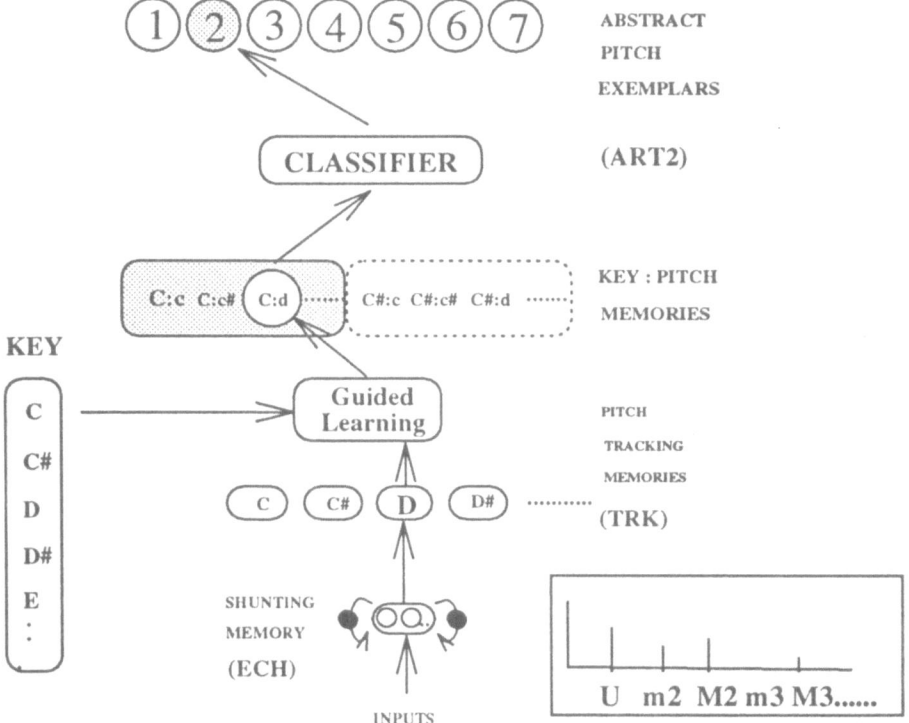

Figure 4: Outline of the classification of patterns of interval, using key identity to guide the memorisation of interval.

The integration of intervallic patterns over keys was simulated for a range of η rates for the echoic (0.25, 0.5, 0.75) and tracking memories (0.005, 0.01, 0.05, 0.1, 0.5). When the developed pitch-in-key representations were classified, seven clear categories of interval use emerged. These categories are identified with the degrees of the diatonic major scale. The hierarchical similarity relations between the degree exemplars developed in this way are shown in Figure 5. Degrees $\hat{1}$, $\hat{5}$ and $\hat{4}$, are the most similar. Degrees $\hat{2}$, $\hat{6}$ occur as a pair quite close to the core trio, while $\hat{3}$ and $\hat{7}$ are more distant. This pattern conforms well to the functional similarities between degrees

---

[8]Using the same slow learning as an ART2 network [7].

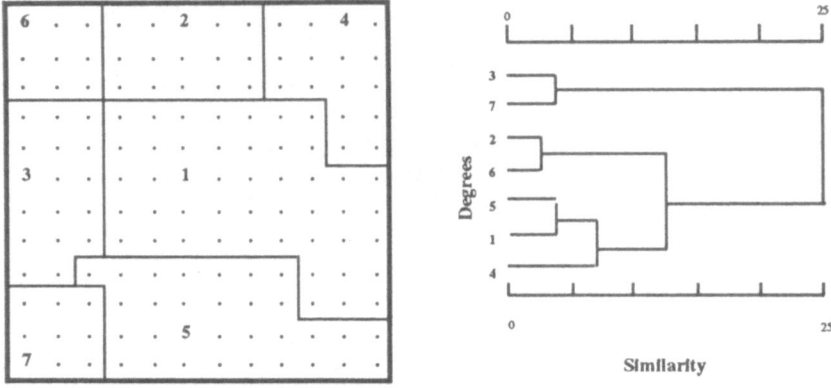

Figure 5: a) Cluster analysis of the abstract pitch exemplars developed from patterns of interval associated with pitches in an ART2 network. b) A Kohonen feature map showing areas associated with different degrees of the scale.

of the scale, but does not measure the importance of each degree in the scale. This is implicit in the relative size of the areas associated with each degree representation when these are mapped on a KFM (see Figure 5a), and it is explicit in the frequency of occurrence of the degrees in the melodies.

6   Conclusion

The models described here illustrate how connectionist models can induce from melodies, representations of the order of pitch-classes that reflect some of the relations between degrees of the diatonic major scale. Using an SRN model to predict pitch orders allows the derivation of representations which reflect patterns of pitch use in melodies. The comparison of local key and global representation of pitch-classes indicate that these patterns can be equated with pitch functions in keys, and in this way models the abstraction of pitches into an abstract tonic-solfa like form. However, the global statistical reference of the SRN has its drawbacks. It is both fragile and orders the degrees in the wrong way. Using the patterns of intervals between pitches allows a more direct comparison between the ways that pitches are used in different keys. The memorisation of patterns of interval in memories that are dedicated to particular pitches in particular keys allows the development of patterns that reflect very clearly the degree identity of a pitch class within a scale. The categories learned from these patterns reflect the relationship between degrees fairly well. For all their limitations the two models outlined above are of interest because they show how two co-operating processes, categorising different streams of information over different timescales, can be used to derive functional representations in an unsupervised way.

References

[1] J.J. Bharucha. Music cognition and perceptual facilitation: A connectionist

framework. *Music Perception*, 5(1):1–30, Fall 1987.

[2] J.J. Bharucha. Pitch, harmony and neural nets: A psychological perspective. In P.M.Todd and D.G.Loy, editors, *Music and Connectionism*. MIT Press/Bradford Books, Cambridge, MA, 1991.

[3] H. Brown and D. Butler. Diatonic trichords as minimal tonal cue-cells. *In Theory Only*, 5(6-7):39–55, 1981.

[4] R. Browne. Tonal implications of the diatonic set. *In Theory Only*, 5(6):3–21, July 1981.

[5] D. Butler. Describing the perception of tonality in music: A critique of the tonal hierarchy theory and a proposal for a theory of intervallic rivalry. *Music Perception*, 6(3):219–242, Spring 1989.

[6] D. Butler and H. Brown. Tonal structure versus function: Studies of the recognition of harmonic motion. *Music Perception*, 2(1):5–24, 1984.

[7] G.A. Carpenter and S. Grossberg. Art2: Self-organization of stable category recognition codes for analog input patterns. *Applied Optics*, 26(23):4919–4930, December 1987.

[8] D. Deutsch. Music recognition. *Psychological Review*, 76(3):300–307, 1969.

[9] W.J. Dowling. Assimilation and tonal structure: Comment on castellano, bharucha, and krumhansl. *Journal of Experimental Psychology*, 113(3):417–420, 1984.

[10] W.J. Dowling. Tonal structure and children's early learning of music. In J. Sloboda, editor, *Generative Processes in Music*. Oxford University Press, 1988.

[11] J.L. Elman. Finding structure in time. CRL Report 8801, Centre for Research in Language, University of California, San Diego, La Jolla, California 92093, April 1988.

[12] R.O. Gjerdingen. Categorisation of musical patterns by self-organizing neuron-like networks. *Music Perception*, 7(4):339–370, Summer 1990.

[13] N.J.L. Griffith. *Modelling the Acquisition and Representation of Musical Tonality as a Function Of Pitch-Use through Self-Organising Artificial Neural Networks*. PhD thesis, University of Exeter, Department of Computer Science, October 1993. Unpublished.

[14] N.J.L. Griffith. The development of tonal centres and abstract pitch as categorisations of pitch-use. *Connection Science*, 6(3&4):155–176, 1994.

[15] S. Grossberg. Behavioral contrast in short term memory: Serial binary memory models or parallel continuous memory models. *Journal of Mathematical Psychology*, 17:199–219, 1978.

[16] S. R. Holtzmann. A program for key determination. *Interface*, 6, 29-56 1977.

[17] D. Huron and R. Parncutt. An improved key-tracking method encorporating pitch salience and echoing memory. *Psychomusicology*, In Press, 1994.

[18] T. Kohonen. *Self-organization and Associative Memory*. Springer Verlag, Berlin, 1989.

[19] C.L. Krumhansl. *Cognitive Foundations of Musical Pitch*. Oxford University Press, Oxford, 1990.

[20] M. Leman. The theory of tone semantics: Concept, foundation, and application. *Minds and Machines*, 2(4):345–363, 1992.

[21] H.C. Longuet-Higgins and M.J. Steedman. On interpreting bach. *Machine Intelligence*, 6:221–239, 1970.

[22] R. Meddis and J. Hewitt, M. Virtual pitch and phase sensitivity of a computer model of the auditory periphery. i: Pitch identificationb. *The Journal of the Acoustical Society of America*, 89(6):2866–2882, June 1991.

[23] M.C. Mozer. Connectionist music composition based on melodic, stylistic, and psychophysical constraints. In P.M.Todd and D.G.Loy, editors, *Music and Connectionism*. MIT Press/Bradford Books, Cambridge, MA, 1991.

[24] H. Panion. An experimental study of relationships among selected musical abilities. Master's thesis, The Ohio State University, 1983.

[25] D.L. Scarborough, O.M. Miller, and J.A. Jones. Connectionist models for tonal analysis. *Computer Music Journal*, 13(3):49–55, Fall 1989.

[26] D. Servan-Schreiber, A. Cleeremans, and J.L. McClelland. Encoding sequential structure in simple recurrent networks. Technical Report CMU-CS-88-183, Carnegie Mellon, November 1988.

[27] H. A. Simon. Perception du pattern musical par auditeur. *Science de l'art*, V(2):28–34, 1968.

[28] E. Terhardt, G. Stoll, and M. Seewann. Pitch of complex signals according to virtual-pitch theory: Test,examples, and predictions. *The Journal of the Acoustical Society of America*, 71(3):671–678, March 1982.

[29] P.M. Todd. A connectionist approach to algorithmic composition. *Computer Music Journal*, 13(4):27–43, Winter 1989.

[30] W. Ulrich. The analysis and synthesis of jazz by computer. In *Proceedings of the 5th. IJCAI*, pages 865–872, 1977.

[31] T. Winograd. Linguistics and the computer analysis of tonal harmony. *Journal of Music Theory*, 12(3):2–49, 1968.

Data-driven Sound Interpretation: its Application to Voiced Sounds.

Leslie S. Smith

CCCN/Department of Computing Science, University of Stirling

Stirling FK9 4LA, Scotland

Abstract

As part of an investigation of how sound processing may be driven by the characteristics of the sound, we consider the processing of voiced sounds. We consider the (physical) parameters characterising such sounds, how these map into the perceptual space, and how early auditory processing may perform this mapping. The way in which the auditory system is sensitive to phase relationships between nearby harmonics is investigated using using computer generated stimuli in which phase differences between the partials alter only the amplitude modulation envelope. The results fit with a model in which cochlear nucleus neurons detect this amplitude modulation.

1 Introduction

Data driven sound interpretation is concerned with extracting information useful in sound interpretation directly from the sound itself. Much work on speech interpretation starts by transforming the sound from the time to the frequency domain by Fourier transforming short (25-50ms) sections of the sound into a large number of bands. Although this in itself does not lose information (since the sound can be resynthesised from this complex data), the way in which it is used particularly emphasises the power/frequency structure of the signal. Although this is clearly important, we submit that this initial processing tends to ignore other features which can also be useful. For example, precise timing information is lost, as is phase information. To some extent, these losses can be made up for by using top-down processing (where the interpretation is guided by what is likely to be correct); however, adding top-down processing is always possible, and is most likely to be effective when the best possible use is made of the original data.

What are the alternatives to the Fourier transform approach? There are two possible directions for research into appropriate features for suitably characterising sound for interpretation: one may either consider the sound itself, looking carefully at the characteristics of sound produced in different ways, as in the ecological approach [1], or one may look at what it is that biology appears to have chosen to emphasise in animal auditory processing, as attempted by auditory modelling techniques [2, 3, 4, 5]. Earlier work by the author considered onset and offset times in biologically plausible frequency bands, inspired by auditory modelling techniques, but also influenced by the sharp onset associated with many types of sound [6].

In this work, we concentrate on processing of sounds which are the result of low frequency excitation, but which have a rich harmonic structure. These are described in section 2. Such sounds occur frequently: voiced elements of speech (as well as the noises made by many animals), and sounds from many musical instruments have this characteristic. Since voiced elements in speech are critical for speech understanding, it seems reasonable that our auditory systems should be specialised towards their interpretation, particularly since they have been exposed to such sounds since early infancy.

This paper illustrates how features of sounds with this type of structure can be found using techniques based on cochlear models. We discuss possible neural models which are helpful in the discovery of particular characteristics of such sounds, and we develop a neurobiologically inspired model which explains some psychophysical results on phase sensitivity. We conclude by considering why this may be important in producing more effective synthetic sound interpretation systems, and discussing what further research might be done.

2 Sound characteristics

Signals produced by low frequency excitation with a rich harmonic structure have the form:

$$S(t) = \sum_{i=1}^{\text{Top}} A_i \sin(2\pi i F_0 + \phi_i) \tag{1}$$

where F_0 is the excitation frequency, the A_i are the strengths of the different harmonics, and ϕ_i the phases of the different harmonics. Such sounds come from a wide variety of sources. Voiced speech, sung notes, many animal noises, and the sounds from some blown musical instruments such as a saxophone all have this form. However, percussive sounds tend to have a noisier spectrum, and sounds which are unpitched (such as running water, wind noise, or hissing) have a spectrum in which the energy is distributed evenly (rather than discretely) over a range of frequencies. A complete physical description of the sound signal $S(t)$ consists of the F_0, and the two vectors $\mathbf{A} = (A_i : i = 1..\text{Top})$ and $\phi = (\phi_i : i = 1..\text{Top})$.

Perceptual systems are rarely interested in these precise values, but the need to distinguish many different voiced sounds (to distinguish different vowels, different speakers, different musical instruments, etc.) means that we need sounds produced using different parameters to sound different. As F_0 changes, we perceive the pitch of the sound to alter; for a voiced speech sound, this might help us distinguish a male from a female or a child speaker. As $|A|$ alters, we perceive the volume of the sound to alter. As the A_i alter, we perceive changes in the timbre of the sound, changes which can help us to distinguish different musical instruments, or different vowels. The ear is sensitive to changes in the ϕ_i, under certain conditions [7], and these are perceived as changes in timbre.

3 The auditory model

The auditory model used is shown in figure 1. This consists of the Patterson and Holdsworth AIM model [2], which is used to find the basilar membrane motion, followed by a very simple inner–hair–cell model, performing pure rectification.

This is followed by low-pass filtering, and then either the re-use of the AIM filterbank, to provide a display of the spectral content of the envelope, or by a bank of bandpass filters, modelling the output of some chopper cells of the cochlear nucleus.

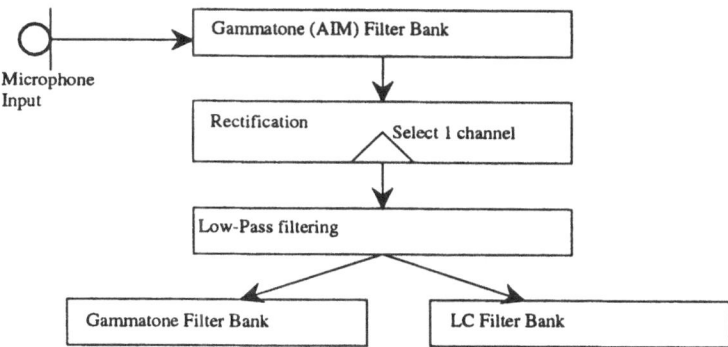

Figure 1: The early auditory processing model.

The AIM model was chosen because of its availability, and because it is easy to use. Recent work in auditory neurophysiology [8] suggests the model lacks sophistication, in that it ignores the effect of the outer hair cells: we return to this in the discussion. The use of simple rectification for modelling the neural transduction by the inner hair cells is unrealistically simplistic: however, we wanted to focus on what happens at cochlear nucleus cells innervated by that part of the auditory nerve coding signals above about 1KHz, so the interest is not in the pulses in a single nerve, but in those in a population of tonotopically close nerves. For this, we believe simple rectification is a reasonable simple approximation.

The model's output at this stage simulates the signal in the auditory nerve. Real auditory nerve output is processed by the cochlear nucleus (CN), which contains a number of neurons whose output appears to sum up certain factors about the sound. In this work, we are interested in aspects which are particularly relevant to the processing of voiced sounds. The output of onset and offset cells is relevant to the start of finish of such sounds, and also to alterations in the A_i over time. We are particularly interested in the processing of steady-state voiced sounds, and we believe that some of the chopper cells in the CN may allow perceptually useful information about the sound to be found. These cells appear to be particularly sensitive to amplitude modulations [9].

We have modelled this possible function of these cells by firstly low-pass filtering the rectified signal from one bandpassed channel, then using bandpass filters, tuned to a range of frequencies. The LPF used has a sharp cutoff at 700Hz, and the bandpass filters used were tuned to between 50 and 500Hz. The product of filter Q (the filters used are inductance/capacitance (LC) tuned resonators) and filter period was kept constant, so that all the filters would resonate for the same length of time. The low-pass filtering is not strictly necessary, since the bandpass filters used act as an LPF; however, it allows the spectrum of the AM signal to be either listened to (by replaying this signal) or displayed using the AIM software. The LC resonators provide a simulation of a set of chopper cells with a range of chopping frequencies, approximately modelling the chop-S chopper cells of [10]. Since they resonate when presented with an amplitude modulated signal, they amplify the amplitude modulation element of their input, as in [9].

4 Processing sounds with the model

When a voiced sound is input to the model, a glance at the display produced by the filterbank software shows that most channels above 1KHz display amplitude modulated signals. The filters used have a bandwidth based on [11], namely $24.7(4.37F_c + 1)$Hz, where F_c is the centre frequency of the filter in KHz. If we consider the filter to have a rectangular frequency response, the result of applying a signal produced from equation 1 will be

$$S(t) = \sum_{i=L}^{H} A_i \sin(2\pi i F_0 + \phi_i) \tag{2}$$

If different signals differ in the A_i in equation 2, then, since the inner hair cell frequency responses overlap, different hair cells will be differently stimulated, leading to the signals sounding different. However, as Patterson [7] noted, signals which differ in only the ϕ_i can also sound different, and as this alters only the phase, and not the amplitude of the harmonics, the degree of stimulation of the hair cells will be unaltered. Patterson noted that one mode whereby the alteration of the ϕ_i could affect the perception was at the nonlinearity at the hair cell: the cell output would be modulated by the envelope of the sound.

We have investigated this possibility by generating sounds with $L = 20$ and $H - L$ either 1 or 2, using $F_0 = 100$, so that the harmonics will be within the frequency response of a single hair cell.

In the case when $H - L = 1$, we can set $\phi_L = 0$ and replace ϕ_H by $\phi_H - \phi_L$ without loss of generality. We also set $A_L = A_H = 1$ so that equation 2 becomes

$$
\begin{aligned}
S(t) &= \sin(2\pi L F_0 t) + \sin(2\pi H F_0 t + \phi_H) \\
&= \sin(2\pi L F_0 t)(1 + \cos(2\pi F_0 t + \phi_H)) \\
&\quad + \cos(2\pi L F_0 t)\sin(2\pi F_0 t + \phi_H)
\end{aligned} \tag{3}
$$

The first part of equation 3 is a signal at LF_0 modulated by a signal at F_0, and the second part is the product of a signal at LF_0 and a signal at F_0. The effect of the second part is to produce a signal at LF_0 modulated by a signal at approximately $2F_0$. The relative strengths of these two signals is unaltered by altering ϕ_H, although the exact phase relationship of the signals does change.

In the case where $H - L = 2$, we can set the phase of the centre harmonic (ϕ_{L+1}) to 0, without loss of generality. We also set $A_L = A_{L+1} = A_H = 1$, and write $M = L + 1 = H - 1$ so that equation 2 becomes

$$
\begin{aligned}
S(t) &= \sin(2\pi L F_0 t + \phi_L) + \sin(2\pi M F_0 t) + \sin(2\pi H F_0 t + \phi_H) \\
&= \sin(2\pi M F_0 t)(1 + \cos(2\pi F_0 t - \phi_L) + \cos(2\pi F_0 t + \phi_H)) \\
&\quad + \cos(2\pi M F_0 t)(\sin(2\pi F_0 t + \phi_H) - \sin(2\pi F_0 t - \phi_L))
\end{aligned} \tag{4}
$$

The first part of equation 4 is primarily a signal at MF_0 modulated by a signal at F_0 (with some additional modulation at $2F_0$ if $\phi_H + \phi_L$ is small), and the second part is a signal at MF_0 modulated by a signal at $2F_0$. However, in this case, the relative strengths of these two modulations depends on ϕ_H and ϕ_L; for example, if we set $\phi_H = \phi_L = n\pi$, the F_0 component of the modulation is dominant, and if $\phi_H = \phi_L = (n+0.5)\pi$, the $2F_0$ component is dominant.

The theoretical prediction is thus that given A_i constant, altering the ϕ_i in the case where $H - L = 1$ should have no effect, but should have an effect when $H - L = 2$.

So far, only some provisional psychophysical experiments have been carried out. Using the parameters as above, the author was unable to differentiate between sounds produced using $H - L = 1$ with different values of ϕ_H, but could easily and unambiguously differentiate between sounds produced using $H - L = 2$ with $\phi_L = \phi_H = n\pi$ and $\phi_L = \phi_H = (n+0.5)\pi$. This suggests that it is the spectrum of the amplitude modulation which the auditory system uses to accomplish this form of phase sensitivity.

As discussed briefly in section 3, the effect of the rectification followed by the low-pass filtering is to demodulate the amplitude modulation in the channel selected. Displaying the result of this using the AIM filterbank, the way in which the relative amounts of power in the different frequency bands changes with variation in ϕ_H and ϕ_L when $H - L = 2$ is clearly visible. However, the filter bank is a model of the basilar membrane movement, and we do not suggest that the demodulated signal is fed back in to the cochlea. Instead, we propose that some of the chopper cells of the CN provide the relevant frequency selectivity by acting as resonant filters at low frequencies. Modelling a population of these cells using a bank of bandpass filters, different filters resonate as ϕ_H and ϕ_L are changed when the signal has 3 components, but there is no change when the signal has two components.

One can apply real sounds to the model as well: applying a sequence of spoken /CVC/ syllables, and choosing a filter band between about 1500Hz and 2500Hz, the result of the lowpass filtering and the filter bank is to produce very much the same resonance for each vowel. What does change is the amount of energy in the cochlear filter band, as the spread of energy in the original sound varies from vowel to vowel. The final output reflects primarily the fundamental frequency of the voiced sound. This could be useful as part of a system to separate concurrent speakers monaurally using their different excitation frequencies. When there are concurrent voiced sounds, not only will more than one resonator resonate, but in addition it is likely that some frequency bands will contain more of one vowel than the other, allowing the fundamental of each to be found from different bands. This is really an alternative way of implementing what Meddis and Hewitt [12] do with autocorrelations; it has the advantage of being more firmly based in the neurobiology.

When sung speech, or sound from (e.g.) a saxophone is applied to the system, the result is to isolate the fundamental of the sound. The resultant signal has also some of the first harmonic as well, and has, on occasion, also contained a subharmonic of the perceived fundamental (from the saxophone). Input from other instruments such as a glockenspiel or a guitar results in unpitched output: the system reacts to the initial attack of the sound, but not to the sustained signal. Such instruments have a higher fundamental frequency, and so do not produce amplitude modulated outputs from the cochlear filters.

5 Discussion

We have shown that the auditory system has some sensitivity to the ϕ_i as well as the F_0 and the A_i in sounds produced from equation 1. Purely place-coding theories of sound would lead to these signals sounding identical. Considering speech as input, it is clear that sensitivity to F_0 helps identify speakers, and sensitivity to the A_i helps identify the particular vowel. It is not clear what advantage sensitivity to the ϕ_i confers. Articulator movement certainly affects the harmonic content (i.e. the A_i), but whether it also alters the phase relationships (ϕ_i) between nearby harmonics is not clear. It is clear that the sensitivity to the phase relationship can only be useful in interpreting sounds from a single stream: the ear is not sensitive to phase relationships between non-harmonically related sounds. The sensitivity is, we suspect, relevant in the identification of the timbre of particular musical instruments: however, further investigation would require experiments on the actual phase relationships between nearby harmonics generated by musical instruments.

In Dallos's work [8] it appears that the basilar membrane selectivity characteristic alters with sound intensity, becoming much more sharp at low sound intensity. Yet both [7] and our own work (along with everyday experience) find that sounds do not alter in timbre with volume (until they become extremely loud). In particular, the phase sensitivity mechanism suggested in section 4 will not work if the bands become much narrower. One possible mechanism is that the inner hair cells do not all have the same size of receptive field: the amplitude modulation effects only require that some of the hair cells have wideband receptive fields. Another mechanism is that the innervation pattern of the chopper cells allows them to receive input from a range of tonotopically nearby auditory nerve fibres.

The model discussed is a very simple model of a selected part of early auditory processing. The CN chopper cells have been modelled with LC resonators. Much more sophisticated neuron modelling by Hewitt and Meddis [13] and Lorenzi and Berthommier [14] suggests that these vestibulocochlear nucleus (VCN) stellate cells actually amplify amplitude modulations in the range of 50 to 500Hz. The LC resonator used is not intended to be more than illustrative. It is clear that the ear is receptive to the fine temporal structure of sound.

The model also explains some of the monaural 'missing fundamental' effects [15]. The pitch sensation comes from the nonlinear rectification of the wideband filtered signal, and this is emphasised by the amplification of amplitude modulation at the chopper cells. In our own experiments, it appears easier to find the fundamental from the amplitude modulations present in medium to high frequency bands than from the low frequency bands: this is particularly true when there is interfering noise.

6 Conclusions and Further Work

The amplitude modulation detecting output of the chopper cells has been proposed as part of a mechanism for separating concurrent voiced sounds. A mechanism whereby phase-based features of voiced sound can be found using an auditory modelling technique has been presented. Its usefulness from an ecological viewpoint is uncertain: however, it is probably used in discriminating between speakers, and between different vowels spoken by speakers. It is likely to be used in detecting the timbre of some musical instruments as well.

Further work on the psychophysics of the phase sensitivity would be useful for attempts to characterise the precise nature of the mechanisms underlying it: for example, the different harmonics could be applied to different ears. In this case, the model proposed here would suggest that the phase sensitivity should disappear, and experiments have shown this to be the case. Houtsma and Smirzynski [16] have found sensitivity to low pitch to be stronger when more low harmonics are present. These are not resolved at the cochlea, but may be resolved at the CN, depending on the innervation pattern at the chop-S cells. Alternatively, they may be resolved at the inferior colliculus, itself innervated by choper calls from the CN [17]. This would give an alternative to a system using interspike interval histograms.

Maintaining precise timing in the filtered output is important for decoding the amplitude modulation and phase relationships in the harmonics of a voiced signal, as well as being critical for onsets and offsets [6]. Auditory modelling front-ends for sound interpretation systems must thus maintain precise timing, expensive though this is in CPU time. In the author's view, the advantages in (e.g.) the ability to find the fundamental excitation frequency in the presence of noise, or the capacity to interpret phase information in a similar way to people, or in having precise timing for acoustic events outweigh the problems. Any attempt to make such front-ends run in real time will clearly require parallelism. Direct silicon implementation is one way of achieving this. Not only can the cochlea be implemented this way (as Lazzaro et al [18], Mead and Lyon [19] and others have done) but the different cell types of the cochlear nucleus can be implemented directly. We believe that understanding and replicating the functionality of the early auditory processing structures and neurons is the best way of synthesising work in auditory modelling and synthetic sound interpretation.

References

[1] W.W. Gaver, What in the world do we hear?: an ecological approach to auditory event perception, Ecological Psychology, 5(1), 1-29, 1993.

[2] R. Patterson, J. Holdsworth, An Introduction to Auditory Sensation Processing, in Air Applications Model of Human Auditory Processing, Progress report 1, Annex 1, 1990

[3] P. Cosi, On the use of auditory models in speech technology, in Intelligent Perceptual Models, LNCS 745, Springer Verlag, 1993.

[4] M. Slaney, Lyon's cochlear model, Apple Technical report 13, Apple corporate computer library, Cupertino, CA, USA, 1988.

[5] O. Ghitza Auditory models and human performance in tasks related to speech coding and speech recognition, IEEE Trans Speech and Audio Processing, 2, 1 part 2, 115-132, 1994.

[6] L.S. Smith, Sound segmentation using onsets and offsets, Journal of New Music Research, 23, 1, 11-24, 1994.

[7] R.D.Patterson, A pulse ribbon model of monaural phase perception, J. Acoust Soc Am, 82, 5, 1987.

[8] P. Dallos, The active cochlea, J Neurophysiology, 12, 4575-85, 1992.

[9] D.O. Kim, J.G. Sirianni, S.O.Chang, Responses of DCN-PVCN neurons and auditory nerve fibres in unanesthetized decerebrate cats to AM and pure tones: analysis with autocorrelation/power-spectrum, Hearing Research, 45, 95-113, 1990.

[10] C.C. Blackburn, M.B. Sachs, Classification of unit types in the anteroventral cochlear nucleus: PST histograms and regularity analysis, J. Neurophysiology, 62, 6, 1989.

[11] B.R. Glasberg, B.C.J. Moore, Derivation of auditory filter shapes from notched-noise data, Hearing Research, 47, 1-2, 103-138, 1990.

[12] R. Meddis, M.J. Hewitt, Modeling the identification of concurrent vowels with different fundamental frequencies, J. Acoust Soc Amer, 91, 1, 233-245, 1992.

[13] M.J. Hewitt, R. Meddis, A computer model of the cochlear nucleus stellate cell:responses to amplitude modulated and pure tone stimuli, J Acoust Soc Amer, 91, 2096-2109, 1992.

[14] C. Lorenzi, F. Berthommier, A computational model for amplitude modulation extraction and analysis of simultaneous amplitude modulated signals, Journal de Physique IV, Colloque C5, 4, 379-382, May 1994.

[15] B.C.J. Moore, An Introduction to the Psychology of Hearing, 3rd edition, Academic Press, 1989.

[16] A.J.M. Houtsma, J.Smurzynski, Pitch identification and discrimination for complex tones with many harmonics, J Acoust Soc Amer, 87, 1, 304-310, 1990.

[17] M.J. Hewitt, R. Meddis, A computer model of amplitude modulation sensitivity of singel units in the inferior colliculus, J Acoust Soc Amer, 95, 4, 2145-2159, 1994.

[18] J. Lazzaro, J. Wawrzynek, M. Mahowald, M. Silviotti, D. Gillespie, Silicon auditory processors as auditory peripherals, IEEE Trans Neural networks, 4, 3, 1993.

[19] C. Mead, Analog VLSI and Neural Systems, Chapter 16, Addison Wesley 1989.

Computer Simulation of Gestalt Auditory Grouping by Frequency Proximity

Michael W. Beauvois
Laboratoire de Psychologie Expérimentale (CNRS URA 316),
Université René Descartes, 28, rue Serpente, F-75006 Paris, France and
IRCAM, 31, rue St-Merri, F-75004 Paris, France

Ray Meddis
Dept. of Human Sciences, University of Technology,
Loughborough LE11 3TU U.K.

Abstract

A computer model is described that is able to reproduce two examples of auditory-streaming phenomena normally accounted for by the Gestalt auditory grouping principle of *proximity*. These are: 1) the fission boundary of human listeners, and 2) the stream-organisation process exhibited by human listeners when presented with ABC tone sequences. Whereas auditory-streaming phenomena are generally accounted for in terms of an auditory scene-analysis process that works using Gestalt perceptual principles (e.g. *proximity*, *good continuation*), the operation of the model suggests that some Gestalt auditory grouping may be the product of low-level processes, and that physiological and peripheral-channelling factors are responsible for Gestalt auditory grouping by frequency *proximity*.

1 Introduction

If listeners are presented with isochronous alternating-tone sequences composed of two pure tones of different frequencies (ABAB...), two percepts are possible. At long TRTs (tone-repetition times, or the time interval between the onset of consecutive tones), or if there is a small frequency separation (Δf) between the tones, an observer will perceive the sequence as a connected series of tones, or a musical trill (see Figure 1A). This property of continuity is known as *temporal coherence* [1]. However, at short TRTs, or when there is a large Δf, the trill seems to split into two parallel sequences or 'streams', one high and one low in pitch, as if there were two different, but interwoven, sound sources. Here, the observer's attention is focussed on only one tone stream (A or B), and the stimulus appears to have a longer periodicity equal to twice the TRT (see Figure 1B). The attended stream is subjectively louder than the unattended stream, producing an auditory figure-ground percept in terms of amplitude. This phenomenon is known as *auditory stream segregation* [2].

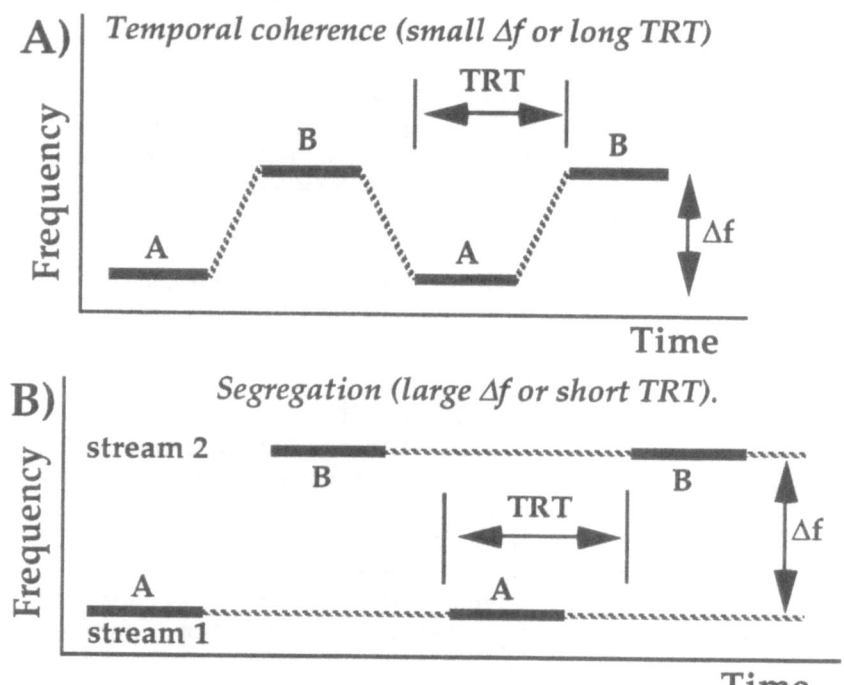

Figure 1. A) The percept of a temporally coherent ABAB tone sequence, and B) the percept of a segregated ABAB tone sequence.

Van Noorden [1] plotted the occurrence of segregated and coherent percepts as a function of Δf and TRT, and found three separate perceptual areas defined by two perceptual boundaries (Figure 2). Above the *temporal coherence boundary* it is impossible to integrate A and B into a single perceptual stream. Below the *fission boundary* it is impossible to hear more than one stream, and the tone sequence forms a coherent whole. The region between the two boundaries is an ambiguous region perceptually, since either a segregated or a coherent percept may be heard depending upon the observer's attentional set.

1.1 Auditory Scene Analysis and Stream Formation

Bregman's [4] theory of auditory scene analysis postulates that the auditory system decomposes a sound mixture by using Gestalt perceptual principles to group the mixture's resolvable frequency components into separate perceptual structures that are used to represent individual sound sources.

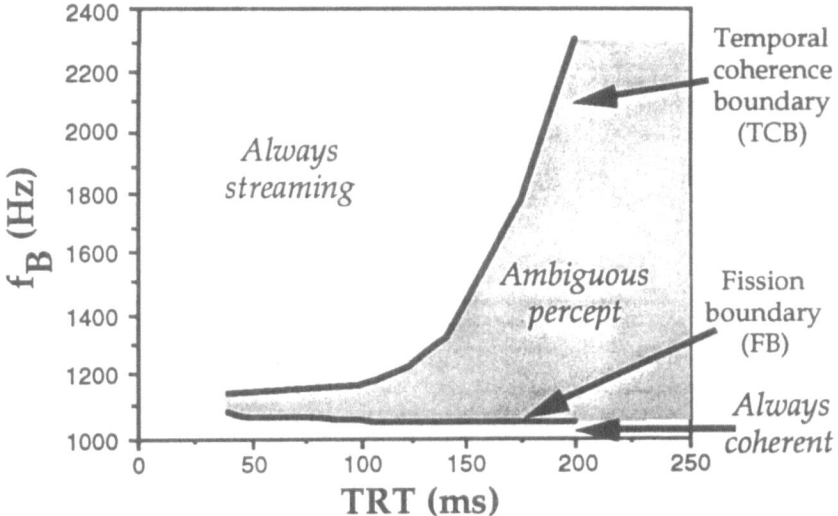

Figure 2. Temporal coherence and fission boundaries for ABAB sequences composed of alternating 40-ms pure tones, redrawn from McAdams & Bregman [3]. Three perceptual regions are present. Here, f_A=1000Hz.

For example, the Gestalt principle of *good continuation* states that elements that follow each other in a given direction are perceived together. This can be demonstrated by connecting the tones of an ABAB sequence by glides. This connection by glides reduces the tendency to hear A and B as separate streams [5]. Likewise, the Gestalt principle of *proximity* states that nearer elements are grouped together in preference to those that are spaced further apart. This is demonstrated by the tendency of tones to form streams when they are in the same frequency region and there is a small Δf (e.g. below the fission boundary).

1.2 A Physiological Approach to Auditory Stream Formation
An alternative approach to using Gestalt perceptual principles to explain auditory grouping is to consider the processes operating at low levels of the auditory nervous system, and the possibility that the physiology of the lower auditory system is responsible for some segregation phenomena. This approach would suggest that some Gestalt auditory grouping could prove to be the emergent properties of a simple low-level processing system.

To implement this approach, a computer model of the auditory system is demonstrated below, which simulates Gestalt auditory grouping by frequency *proximity* in alternating pure-tone sequences. The computer model is based upon simple circuits analogous to physiological systems present in the lower auditory system and auditory periphery, exhibits similar behaviour to that of human listeners for certain simple stimuli, and contrasts with other models of auditory grouping - e.g. [6] - by virtue of its simplicity. This approach can be seen as being complementary to the Gestalt approach, but at a different level of explanation.

2 Summary of Model Features

The model is similar to the model described by Beauvois & Meddis [7] and Beauvois [8], except that further components have been added to make the model more physiologically plausible. Figure 3 shows the construction of one channel of the model. A summary of the model features follows.

1. The acoustic signal is first subjected to a peripheral frequency analysis which establishes 'channels' characterised by a bandpass frequency response to stimuli.

2. The output of each bandpass filter is fed into a simulation of a group of inner hair-cell/auditory-nerve (AN) synapses.

3. Each model channel subdivides into three pathways:

   3.1. A temporal fine-structure path preserves all aspects of the hair-cell/AN output to enable the signal to be processed by higher levels, and to preserve all AN information for pitch extraction purposes.

   3.2. A temporal-integration path temporally integrates the hair-cell output (3-ms time constant).

   3.3. An excitation-level path adds a cumulative random element to the output of the temporal-integration path, and then subjects it to a temporal integration process with a longer, arbitrary time constant (70-ms).

4. The output of the excitation-level paths are examined to see which one has the highest excitation level compared to the other channels. The channel with the highest excitation level is then defined as the 'dominant channel'.

5. The activity in all amplitude-information pathways is then attenuated by a factor of 0.5, except for the dominant channel.

6. The model amplitude output is the sum of the outputs of the attenuated and non-attenuated amplitude-information paths.

7. The model assesses stream segregation on the basis of the relative amplitude levels of the two tones. If the levels are comparable over a 1-s period, the percept is judged to have been coherent over the course of that second. Otherwise, a 'segregated' percept is reported.

In the model itself, stream segregation is assumed to occur when the amplitude ratio of A and B in the system output exceeds a critical value (Z). The amplitude imbalance between the two tones is created by a suppression mechanism where the action of a preceding tone suppresses the output of a following tone. The attentional mechanism that attenuates all frequency-selective channels except the dominant channel gives rise to an auditory figure-ground effect, where the information coming through the attenuated channels is heard 'in the background'. The attenuation principle is that very active channels suppress less active channels. The simple amplitude-attenuation mechanism used by the model is suitable for pure-tone stimuli, and contrasts with the more complex lateral-inhibition mechanism used by Shamma [9] to process speech stimuli. In addition, the model's assessment of channel 'activity' is over a long time period, and is only loosely coupled to instantaneous signal levels. Furthermore, the channel activity is not wholly deterministic, but is conditioned by the cumulative random element incorporated into the model.

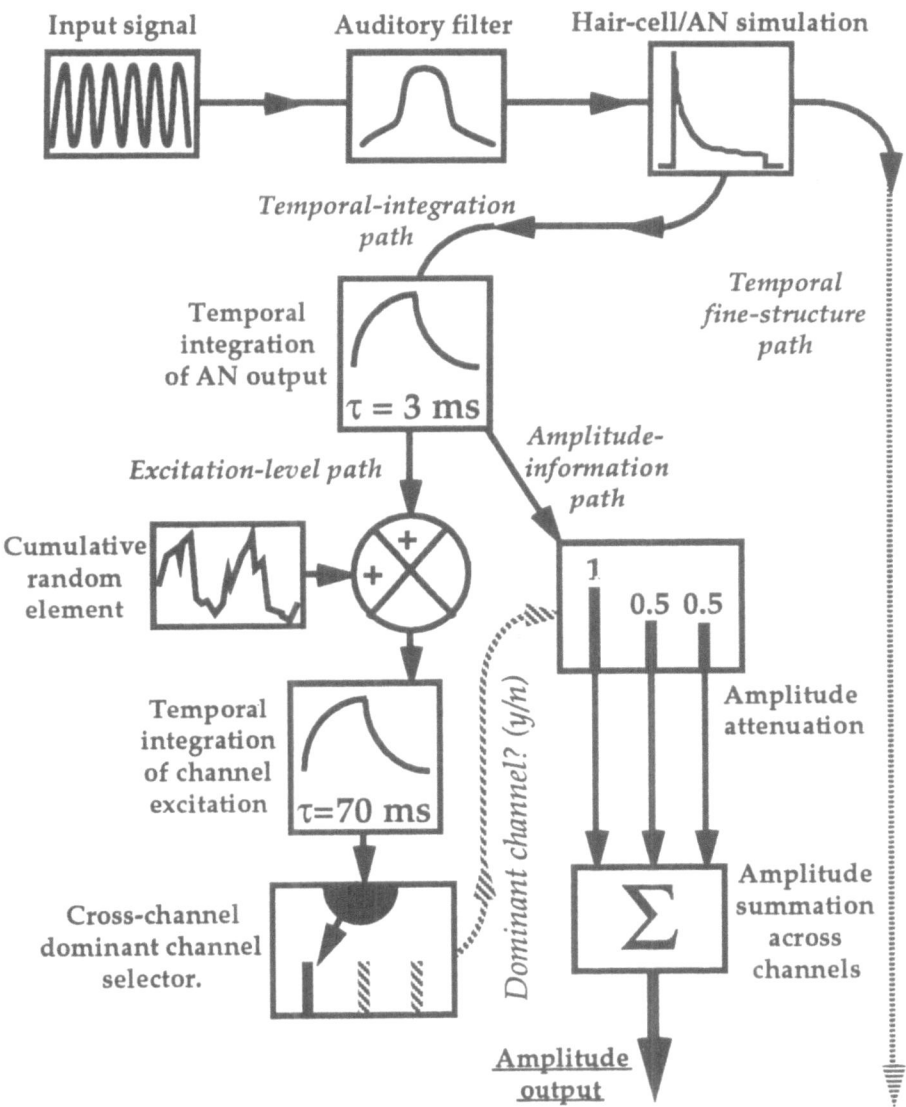

Figure 3. *Diagram showing the arrangement of one model channel.*

3 Model Simulations

The results of two experimental studies carried out on human listeners were simulated using the model, where both experiments demonstrated Gestalt auditory grouping by frequency *proximity*.

3.1 Fission Boundary

The model was presented with 15-s ABAB tone sequences composed of 40-ms tones, where f_A = 1000 Hz, and TRT = 50, 100, 150, or 200 ms. The value of f_B was increased systematically for each TRT value, and there were 100 trials for each combination of TRT and f_B. The number of coherent responses given by the model for the last second of each sequence was totalled for each TRT/f_B combination, and the totals converted to percentages. The model fission boundary (MFB) was taken to be the f_B value where the model output dropped below 100% coherent responses. This criterion was suggested by the nature of the fission boundary, which defines a region where the percept is always one of permanent temporal coherence - i.e. the model output will always be 100% coherent responses. When the model output drops below 100% coherent responses, a segregated/coherent mix is indicated which corresponds to the percept heard in the ambiguous region.

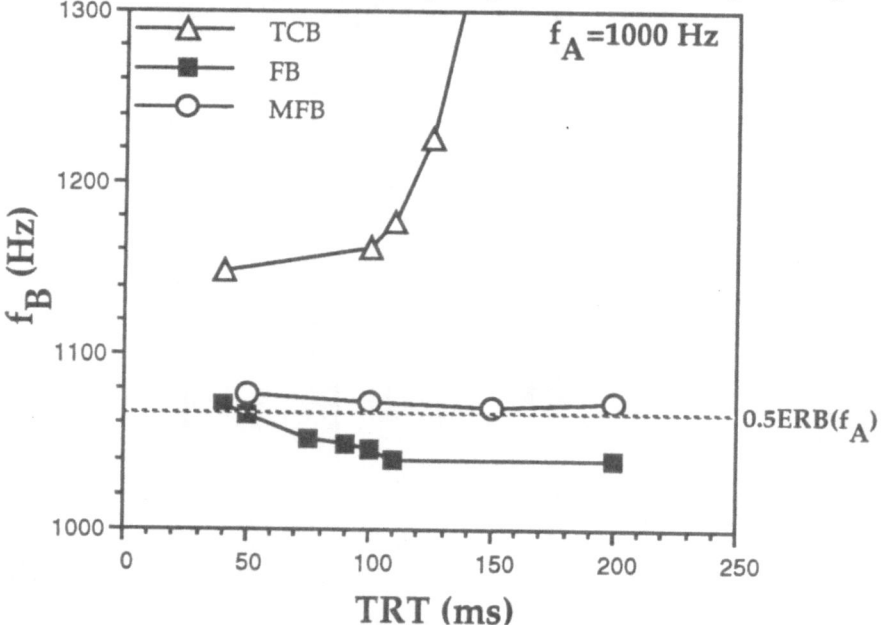

Figure 4. The model fission boundary (MFB) compared with the TCB and FB from Figure 2.

Figure 4 compares the fission boundary (FB) with the MFB for each TRT value. Also shown is 0.5ERB(f_A), half of the equivalent rectangular bandwidth of the auditory filter whose centre frequency equals f_A. We can see that both fission boundaries are relatively constant when TRT>100 ms, and both show a gradual increase when TRT<100 ms. Figure 4 also indicates a close correspondence between 0.5ERB(f_A) (1066 Hz), the MFB (≈1073 Hz), and the fission boundary. This suggests that 1) the MFB corresponds to the fission boundary, and 2) the fission boundary is connected with auditory-filter (i.e. physiological and peripheral-channeling) factors.

3.1 Stream Organisation in ABC Tone Sequences

Baker *et al.* [10] investigated stream formation, as a function of frequency *proximity*, to determine the metric the auditory system uses to group together consecutive frequency components into the same stream. They presented subjects with 11-s ABC tone sequences where A and C were fixed at 929 Hz and 1973 Hz, TRT=120 ms, and the tone durations were 110 ms. In each sequence, f_B was fixed at a value between 929 Hz and 1973 Hz (Figure 5).

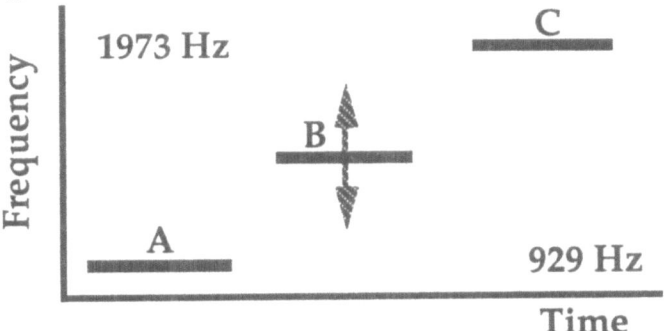

Figure 5. The stimulus arrangement used by Baker et al. [8].

With this stimulus, an AB stream will be heard accompanied by a separate C stream when A and B are close in frequency. However, when B and C are close in frequency, a BC stream will be heard accompanied by a separate A stream. Baker *et al.* [10] found that the midpoint for the changeover of AB and BC stream organisations occurs when $f_B \approx 1283$ Hz. This midpoint value was surprising, as Baker *et al.* [10] expected the midpoint to be directly related to the frequency-mapping characteristics of the basilar membrane, which suggest a value of ≈ 1377 Hz.

Baker *et al.* 's [10] stimuli were presented to the model 90 times. The last second of the model output was examined to find the amplitude values of A, B, and C, in order to determine the amplitude ratios for each dyad (AB, BC, or AC). If a dyad's amplitude ratio exceeded Z, then that dyad was considered to have segregated into separate streams. The amplitude values were used to give the 'segregated or coherent' decision for the AB, BC, and AC dyads, and the model results were totalled to plot the percentage of coherent responses for each dyad against f_B (Figure 6). The model equivalent to the midpoint of Baker *et al.* [10] will be the value of f_B where the model output shows an equal probability of AB, BC and AC streams forming, due to the overall temporal coherence of the sequence given by the absence of a dominant AB or BC stream. This approach suggests that the dominant 'percept' which is 'heard' by the model will be the dyad that shows the highest probability of coherence (in terms of the percentage of coherent responses).

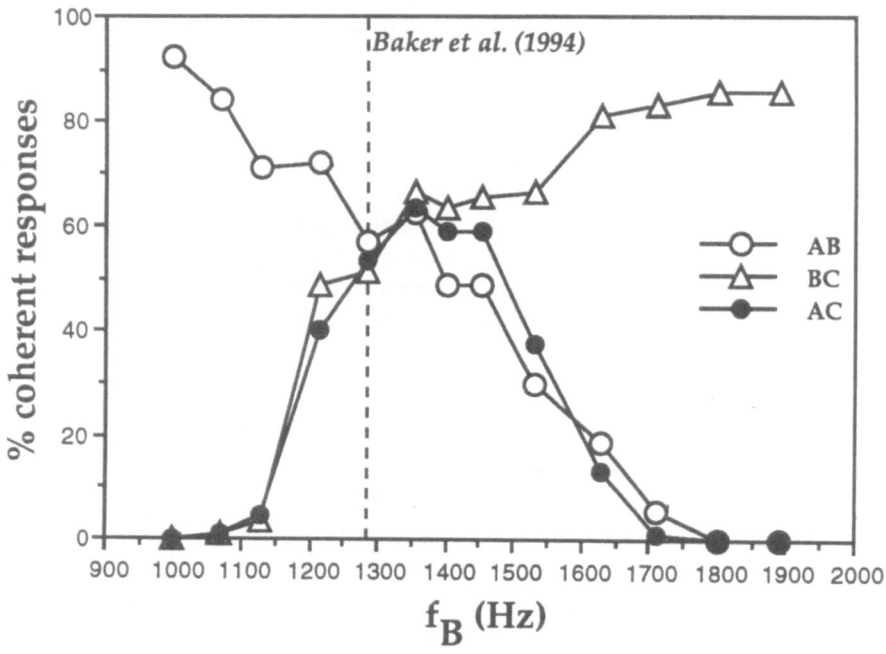

Figure 6. % coherent responses for AB, BC, and AC dyads against f_B (Hz) for the stimuli shown in Figure 5. Baker et al.'s midpoint [10] is also shown.

Figure 6 shows that the model successfully reproduces the transition between AB and BC stream organisations. That is, when A and B are close in frequency, the dominant model 'percept' (in terms of the percentage of coherent responses) is an AB stream, and when B and C are close in frequency, the dominant 'percept' is an BC stream. When $f_B \approx 1320$ Hz, the coherence probabilities for all dyads are equal. This f_B value is the model equivalent to the midpoint of Baker *et al.* [10]. Figure 6 indicates that the model midpoint is roughly equivalent to that of their listeners, with only a ≈ 37 Hz difference between the two.

Baker *et al.* [10] found that B had to be closer in frequency to A than either the linear or logarithmic halfway points (1451 and 1354 Hz respectively) in order to 'release' itself from BC-stream formation. That is, B is more easily captured into a stream by C than by A. This phenomenon, and the slight discrepancy between the model and listeners' midpoints, may be due to the shape of human auditory filters. Whereas the bandpass filters used by the model are symmetrical around a centre frequency, human auditory filters have an asymmetrical bandpass function that is characterised by a short high-frequency skirt and a long low-frequency skirt, where the size of the low-frequency skirt increases with signal level [11]. This would suggest that the difference between the two midpoints is due to auditory-filter (i.e. physiological and peripheral-channeling) factors, and that the addition of asymmetrical filters to the model will be necessary to achieve an exact numerical fit to their data.

4 Gestalt Auditory Grouping and the Model

We have seen that the model is able to simulate the fission boundary and the stream-organisation process found in ABC tone sequences, both of which are normally accounted for in terms of Gestalt auditory grouping by frequency *proximity*. It is important to note that the *same* model parameter values were used for each replication, and that these parameter values also enable the model to reproduce other auditory-streaming phenomena not described here [12]. This would indicate that, for the stimuli described above, the model is imitating listeners' responses fairly accurately, and may be processing the stimuli in a similar manner to the human auditory system.

Bregman [4] views stream formation as the result of the grouping performed by a primitive segregation mechanism (PSM) that works using Gestalt perceptual principles. Bregman [4] also states that the PSM is automatic and unlearned, and involved in *involuntary* attention. The model is able to simulate auditory-streaming phenomena normally thought to occur due to Gestalt auditory grouping by frequency *proximity* by using an *involuntary* attentional mechanism determined solely by the channel excitation level. The similarity between the model and Bregman's PSM suggests that the model may correspond, in part, to the PSM, and that some Gestalt auditory grouping is the product of processes that are located at a relatively low level of the auditory system, and which work in a similar manner to the model.

Although Bregman's [4] PSM uses Gestalt perceptual principles to explain stream formation, the model simulations described here indicate that grouping by frequency *proximity* is closely related to auditory-filter factors. This implies that Gestalt auditory grouping by frequency *proximity* could equally be understood in terms of physiological and peripheral-channelling factors, and *involuntary* channel-suppression at a relatively low level. These findings agree with those of Hartmann & Johnson [13], who found that peripheral-channelling factors were of "paramount importance" in determining stream segregation. The convergence of their findings with the low-level processing of the model would suggest that, with respect to Gestalt auditory grouping by frequency *proximity*, peripheral-channelling factors largely determine the percept heard by listeners.

The success of the model in simulating the responses of human listeners justifies the potential value of a low-level analysis for explaining psychological phenomena otherwise accounted for in Gestalt terms. However, the power of the model should not be exaggerated. It represents only a preliminary effort to complement Gestalt explanations of perceptual phenomena, and only a limited range of data has been considered here.

Acknowledgements
This research was supported by grants to the first author from the CNRS (France) and the Fyssen Foundation, Paris, France.

References

1. Van Noorden LPAS. Temporal coherence in the perception of tone sequences. Ph.D thesis, Institute for Perception Research, Eindhoven, The Netherlands 1975.

2. Bregman AS, Campbell J. Primary auditory stream segregation and perception of order in rapid sequences of tones. Journal of Experimental Psychology 1971; 89:244-249.

3. McAdams S, Bregman AS. Hearing musical streams. Computer Music Journal 1979; 3:26-43,60.

4. Bregman AS. Auditory Scene Analysis. MIT Press, Cambridge, MA, 1990.

5. Bregman AS, Dannenbring GL. The effect of continuity on auditory stream segregation. Perception and Psychophysics; 1973; 13:308-312.

6. Brown GJ, Cooke M. Perceptual grouping of musical sounds: A computational model. Journal of New Music Research 1994; 23:107-132.

7. Beauvois MW, Meddis R. A computer model of auditory stream segregation. Quarterly Journal of Experimental Psychology 1991; 43A(3):517-541.

8. Beauvois MW. A Computer Model of Auditory Stream Segregation. Ph.D thesis, Loughborough University of Technology, Loughborough, U.K., 1992.

9. Shamma SA. Speech processing in the auditory system II: Lateral inhibition and the central processing of speech evoked activity in the auditory nerve. Journal of the Acoustical Society of America 1985; 78:1622-1632.

10. Baker KL, Williams SM, Nicolson RI. Evidence for the frequency metric used in stream segregation. Dept. of Psychology Report, Sheffield University, Sheffield, U.K., 1994.

11. Glasberg BR, Moore BCJ. Derivation of auditory filter shapes from notched-noise data. Hearing Research 1990; 47:103-138.

12. Beauvois MW, Meddis R. Computer simulation of auditory stream segregation in alternating-tone sequences. Journal of the Acoustical Society of America (in preparation).

13. Hartmann WM, Johnson D. Stream segregation and peripheral channeling. Music Perception 1991; 9(2):155-184.

Mechanisms of Visual Search : An Implementation of Guided Search

K.J. Smith and G.W. Humphreys
School of Psychology, University of Birmingham,
Birmingham, U.K.

Abstract

An implementation of the Guided Search theory [1] was developed using a Boltzmann Machine architecture. The model assessed the ability of Guided Search to predict various visual search phenomena. The model successfully simulated the data from basic feature and conjunction searches found in human subjects. Further simulations evaluated search for a subset of items and for the case where two targets were present. The data with two targets failed to fit human data. We suggest that the failure to simulate human data on this task emerges from the architecture of Guided Search itself.

1 Introduction

Visual search experiments typically focus on two forms of search tasks - feature and conjunction tasks. Feature search involves the detection of a target in a visual display which differs from the surrounding distractors by a single feature such as colour, orientation or size. This type of search is very efficient and is usually independent of the number of items in the visual display [2].

Conjunction search involves the detection of a target which differs from each of the distractors along one of two dimensions. For example, a conjunction search might involve the detection of a green, vertically oriented target amongst red, vertical and green, horizontal distractors.

Conjunction search often shows reaction times (RTs) increasing linearly with increasing number of items in the display. In addition, it is often found that the time to respond to target absence is twice as long as that for target presence [2]. However, conjunctions of some features may show relatively efficient search functions and an absent:present ratio less than 2:1. For example relatively efficient conjunction search has been found for conjunctions of colour with curved or straight lines [3] and colour and form conjunctions [4]. Serial, self-terminating types of visual search theories, such as Feature Integration theory (FIT) [2], have difficulty explaining the latter findings.

1.1 Guided Search

An alternative to FIT, the Guided Search model [1], proposes a parallel stage of processing which provides a continuous activation map for the guidance of a serial stage. The activation map is created by summing bottom-up and top-down information from feature modules to give a measure of the probability that the target is present at each location. The location with the highest level of activation in the activation map, has the highest probability of being the target, so the serial stage of processing is directed to this location first.

The serial stage identifies the item at the highlighted location by comparing its feature attributes with that of the target. If the item is found to be the target, processing stops and a response is made. If the item is found *not* to be the target, the location is removed from the search and the serial stage continues to process the locations on the activation map in descending order of activation. Only the subset of the items most likely to be the target are processed, which reduces the number of items that need to be identified before a response is made and means that the search may be carried out faster, and more efficiently, than would be predicted by FIT.

Cave and Wolfe suggest that the parallel stage of processing is noisy and may result in locations other than the target receiving high activation levels. If no noise is present, the target will always stand out amongst the distractors and search would not differ for feature and conjunction tasks.

2 Implementing Guided Search

2.1 Architecture

Guided Search was implemented using a Boltzmann Machine activation function where each unit can be placed in one of two states (1 or 0). The state of each unit is determined stochastically, depending on the states of connecting units and weights on the connections between them.

A Boltzmann Machine usually uses a simple learning procedure to assign the best set of connection weights to a fully connected set of units [5, 6]. In this implementation, however, the connections and weights are hand-wired in accordance with the Guided Search theory to give a set of hierarchically connected maps each with nine locations (Figure 1). The connections and weight settings are described below.

The model was implemented in the C programming language on a Hewlett Packard Workstation.

2.1.1 Maps, Connections and Weights

Retina. The identity of items in the search display are directly entered into the retina. The codes mark the items in the display as red or green, horizontal or vertical or empty. The retinal codes are not of the Boltzmann Machine type (i.e. 1 or 0) instead they contain a separate value for each feature type within one modality. The item identities are only known at the retinal level; the other maps mark interesting locations for the driving of attention but do not contain specific knowledge of the identities of the items at these locations.

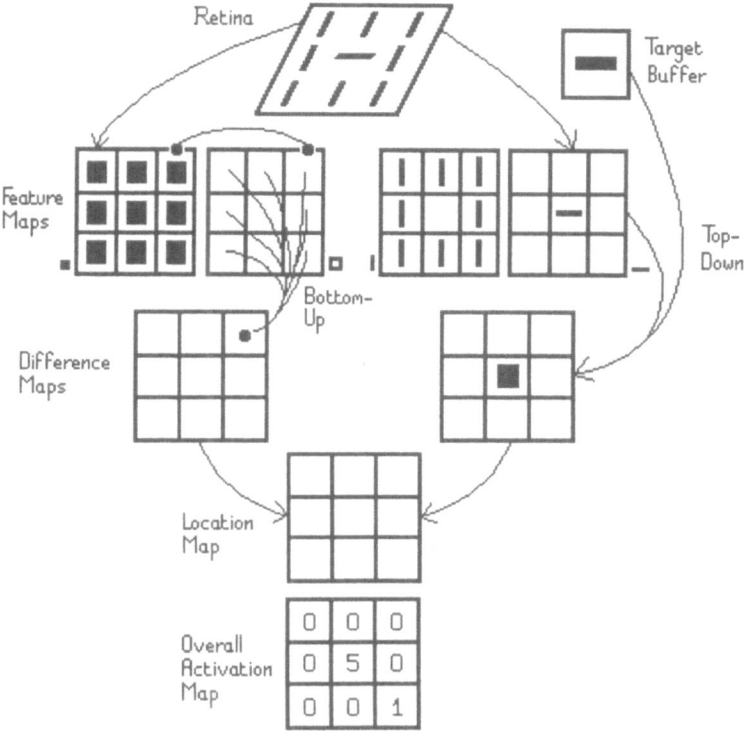

Figure 1: The architecture of the Guided Search implementation. Inhibitory connections are shown by stopped lines (—•). Excitatory connections are shown by lines ending with arrows (→).

Target Buffer. The target buffer encodes the target information made available to the model. The colour and/or orientation of the target may be marked as unknown.

Feature Maps. Feature maps encode the presence of colour or orientation features. There are two feature maps for each modality in this model, however, more maps could be incorporated. The presence of colour is encoded onto a red or a green map and the presence of orientation is encoded onto a vertical or a horizontal map.

Each location in a feature map is connected to the corresponding location in the retinal array. The feature maps encode the presence of the particular feature they represent in the retina. An inhibitory connection is present between the same location in both feature maps within the same modality reducing the probability that an item becomes encoded, for example, as both red and green.

Difference Maps. The difference maps are so-called because they compute activation levels by comparing an item to the target (top-down information) and to the other items in the array (bottom-up information). The activation of a location in the difference map is dependent, therefore, on the *difference* between one item and other array items or the target.

There are two difference maps: one for colour information and one for orientation information. Each difference map is connected to the feature maps within the same modality. For example, the colour difference map is connected to the red and green feature maps. A unit in the difference map is activated if the evidence from either feature map suggests that it represents an interesting location; the actual feature make-up of the item is not important.

Top-down excitation is added if the unit in the feature map under consideration matches a feature attribute of the target. For example, if the target item is red, all locations in the difference map which are connected to on-units in the red feature map will receive top-down excitation.

Bottom-up inhibition is calculated via inhibitory connections with every unit in the feature map being processed. If many locations in the feature map are in an on-state, the inhibition is high and reduces the chance of the location in the difference map being activated. If the number of on-locations in the feature map is low, some inhibition is still present, but it is not of a high enough level to reliably prevent the difference map unit from being activated in the presence of top-down excitation, or the basic level of activation.

Location Map and Overall Activation Map. The formation of an overall activation map was broken into two stages, the first concerning the production of a location map to point to locations of interest by summing evidence from the difference maps. The second stage takes one activated unit in the location map at random and increments an activation measure in an overall activation map. The overall activation map is not part of the Boltzmann Machine-type architecture; the units are not activated using a probabilistic function and can take whole number values from 0 to 5. This should provide a measure of overall activation as the units in the location map which are reliably in an on-state should have a higher probability of being incremented over a number of cycles.

The units in the overall activation map have a threshold value of 5. Once this value is reached, the serial stage of processing is initiated, and 'attention' is directed to the item at the activated location. The identity of the item is discovered by referring to the retinal display and the item is then compared to the target. If the item is found to match the target, processing is stopped and the target item is said to have been found. If the item being processed does not match the target, the location is removed from further processing and search continues.

2.2 The Activation Function

The state of the units in the maps (except the retina and the overall activation map) is determined by a stochastic activation function:

$$probability = \frac{1}{1 + \exp(-Input/Systemp)}$$

This calculates the probability that a particular unit should be placed in an on-state. 'Input' represents the activation level given by the weighted input. 'Systemp' is the system temperature and affects the influence of random activation. High system temperatures increase the effect of random activation and thus the probability that a unit is placed in an on-state when its input is lower than a threshold value. Low system temperatures tend to reduce the effect of random activation so that the thresholds approximate to a binary function [7].

2.3 Testing the Implementation

2.3.1 Method

The weights to the feature maps were set so that each unit would be placed in the correct state for the retinal information approximately 95% of the time. The top-down and bottom-up weights were then systematically manipulated over a range of values. A set of weights were chosen which resulted in a relatively efficient feature search function and a slower, display size dependent conjunction search function. The two forms of search task function should be significantly different.

Each type of search was tested using 4 blocks of 25 runs for each display size. Display size was manipulated between 1 and 9 items in the search set. Search was terminated when the target was found, or after 500 cycles without the target location being chosen. Only target present trials were investigated since the termination procedure for target absent trials for the model is unclear.

2.3.2 Results and Discussion

Feature search was relatively flat and unaffected by the number of items in the display (slope = 0.32 cycles per item, R^2 = 40.0%) (Figure 2); the effect of display size was not significant (t = 2.00). In contrast, conjunction search was slower than feature search and it was effected by display size (slope = 1.34 cycles per item, R^2 = 81.0%, display size t = 4.12, $p < 0.05$). An 8x2x4 ANOVA shows that the two types of search differed significantly ($F(1, 21)$ =340.09, $p < 0.01$).

The results were similar to the descriptions of search functions for human subjects in which feature search is fast and efficient, and conjunction search is affected by the number of items in the display size. However, when nine items were present in a conjunction search display, no location was activated above threshold in the overall activation map within the 500 cycles. In this event, search was said to fail even when the target was present in the display. This occurred because the bottom-up inhibition for each feature type overrode the top-down excitation given by the target. At this point, locations in the difference map were unlikely to be activated within a resonable time and search was effectively stopped. This might suggest that only up to 8 items may be processed at once by Guided Search (at least in this implementation with these weights). Above this display size, another process may be needed to continue search.

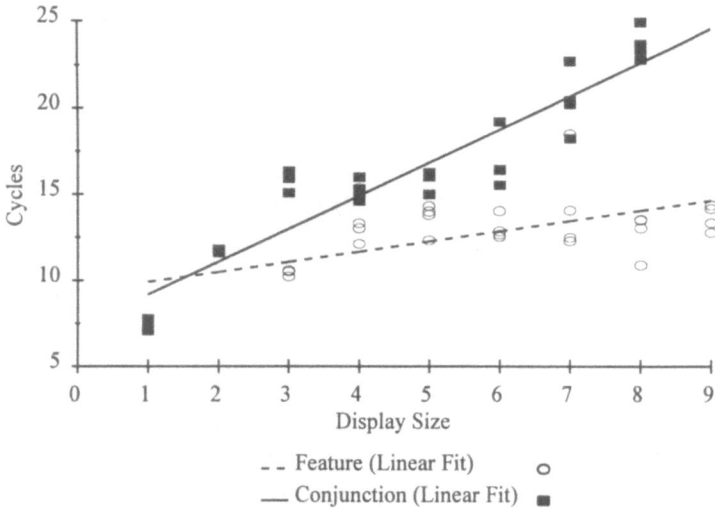

Figure 2: Feature and Conjunction Search Functions

3 Simulation 1 - Vertical Feature and Subset Searches

3.1 Introduction

The model as established was applied to tasks for which the weights were not specifically set. The first simulation involved subset and vertical feature search.

Friedman-Hill and Wolfe [8] investigated the performance of human subjects on subset and vertical feature searches. Subset tasks require the subject to search a subset of items in the display for a target. For example, the subject may be asked to find the odd red item in a display. Vertical feature tasks involve the detection of a vertical item amongst red and green, horizontal distractors. The target colour is not known. In both forms of search, only some of the target information is known to the subject so top-down information is restricted.

Human subjects show fast, efficient search functions for vertical feature search, but slow, display-size dependent search for subset search tasks [8]. Friedman-Hill and Wolfe suggest that subset searches are carried out by two, separate, parallel processes; the first parallel stage forming a subset of the features for which the target information is known, the second parallel process examining the chosen subset for the target which now only differs from the subset distractors along one feature dimension. It is suggested that subset search is effected by display size as the production of the initial subset is process limited in some way.

3.2 Method

The model was tested using vertical feature search and subset search tasks [8]. The number of items in the retinal display were manipulated between 4 and 8 items. Each type of search was carried out using 4 blocks of 25 runs for each display size. The weights and connections in the model are described above and remain unchanged. The results for the vertical feature search and the subset search tasks are compared to the standard conjunction search.

3.3 Results and Discussion

Vertical feature search was efficient (slope = 0.163 cycles per item, $R^2 = 8.3\%$), and there was no effect of display size (t=0.46) (Figure 3).

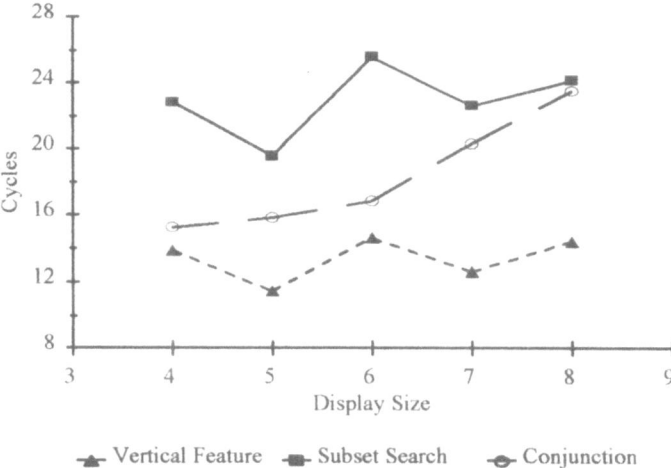

Figure 3: Vertical Feature, Subset and Conjunction Search Functions

Subset search was much slower and was affected by display size (slope = 0.584 cycles per item, $R^2 = 19.9\%$; display size t=6.45, p<0.05). Conjunction search was slower than vertical feature search but faster than subset search. A 3x5x4 ANOVA shows that the search types differed significantly ($F(2, 24)=158.76$, p<0.01).

These results are similar to those found be Friedman-Hill and Wolfe [8]. Human subjects show the same pattern of vertical feature, subset and conjunction searches, in that vertical feature search is fast and efficient whereas subset search shows the slowest response times.

The effect of display size on the subset search is not, perhaps as great as is found in human subjects. However, the orientations of the targets and distractors in the subset search carried out by Friedman-Hill and Wolfe were set at random with a constraint that the difference in orientations would be at least 30°. This suggests that more noise will be present, on average, than if the orientations were restricted to horizontal and vertical. The increased noise would be expected to increase the effect of display size which may account for the difference in performance of the simulation and human subjects.

It appears from the simulation results that a second-order parallel search as suggested by Friedman-Hill and Wolfe is not necessary to account for the human subject search functions. Although the overall activation map suggests that the most likely locations to be passed on for identification are part of the required subset, a second parallel search is not needed. Instead, one parallel process is sufficient to locate the target.

4 Simulation 2 - Redundant Target Search

4.1 Introduction

In a redundant target search task, the search display contains more than one target item. It has been found that the presence of two or more target items produces faster search RTs than a search set with only one target for human subjects [7, 9]. In addition, if Cumulative Density Functions (CDFs) of RTs are plotted, the actual function for two target displays is to the left and above both the function of one target displays and that predicted for two target displays if the target locations were processed independently of each other [7, 9]. We assessed whether Guided Search was capable of simulating these results.

4.2 Method

The model was tested using one or two targets present in the retinal display. Both feature and conjunction searches were investigated. The number of items in the retinal display were manipulated between 2 and 8 items. Each type of search was carried out using 4 blocks of 25 runs for each display size and number of targets.

4.3 Results and Discussion

Figure 4 show faster search for two targets than for one target, for both feature and conjunction tasks. The effect of the number of targets was significant to the 0.01 level ($F(1, 15) = 62.22$). Figure 5 shows CDFs for the number of cycles to find the target for one and two target displays (display size 2). Also included in the figure is the predicted CDF for two target displays that would be found if the two target locations were independent of each other. The obtained two target CDF is below and to the right of the predicted CDF, contrary to the human data for the same display size (see [9]).

In addition. redundant target, conjunction search failed for display sizes of 8 items or over as the target was not found within 500 cycles. This is due to the increased bottom-up inhibition produced by the two targets. Processing up to 7 display items was not affected as the additional inhibition does not reliably override any top-down excitation. A second process might, again, be needed to account for redundancy gain results for displays over 7 items.

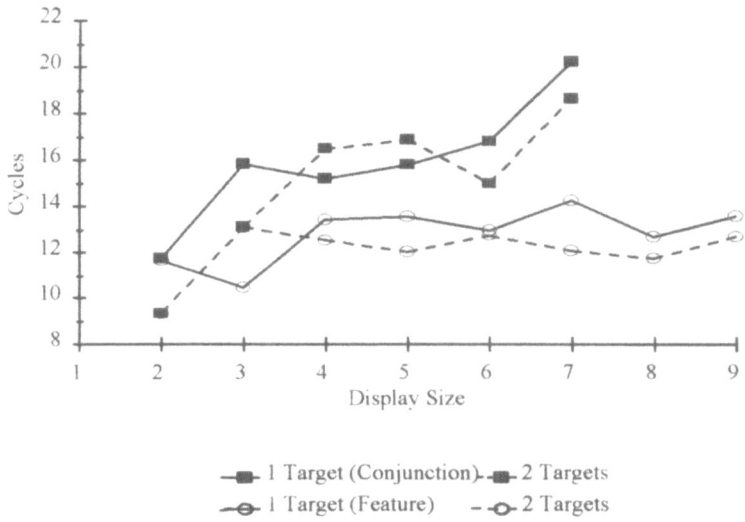

Fig 4: Feature and Conjunction Search with One and Two Target Items

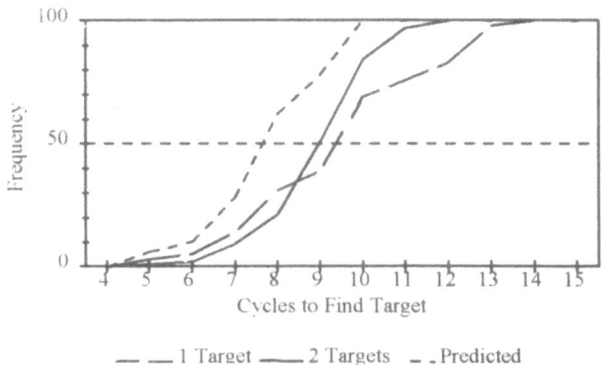

Fig 5: Cumulative Density Functions for one target and obtained and predicted two target displays

5 Conclusions

In conclusion, whilst the results of the vertical feature, subset and the basic feature and conjunction search tasks, provided support for the Guided Search [1], the model (at least in this implementation) cannot explain conjunction search with display sizes over or 8 items, and with redundant targets.

We suggest that the problem with simulating redundant target effects reflects a specific weaknesses in the model, since the model lacks mechanisms of grouping whereby multiple targets may link together. Alternative models, which incorporate grouping procedures, are successful in this respect [7, 11]

Acknowledgements

This work was supported by a SERC studentship to the first author and by a grant from the Joint Research Council Initiative in Cognitive Science to the second author

References

1. Cave KR and Wolfe JM. Modelling the Role of Parallel Processing in Visual Search. Cognitive Psychology 1990; 22:225-271.

2. Treisman A. Search, Similarity, and Integration of Features Between and Within Dimensions. Journal of Experimental Psychology: Human Perception and Performance 1990; 17, 652-676.

3. Wolfe JM Yee A. and Friedman-Hill SR. Curvature is a Basic Feature for Visual Search Tasks. Perception 1992; 21:465-480.

4. Wolfe JM Cave KR and Franzel SL. Guided Search: An alternative to the Feature Integration Model for Visual Search. Journal of Experimental Psychology: Human Perception and Performance 1989; 15:419-433.

5. Hinton GE and Sejnowski TJ. Learning and Relearning in Boltzmann Machines. In: Rumelhart DE. and McClelland JL. (Eds). Parallel Distributed Processing: Explorations in the Microstructure of Cognition. Vol 1: Foundations. The MIT Press; London 1986.

6. Iazzetta A Vaccaro R and Villano U. A Transputer Implementation of Boltzmann Machines. In: Caianiello (Ed) Parallel Architectures and Neural Networks: First Italian Workshop. World Scientific, London 1989.

7. Müller HJ Humphreys GW and Donnelly N. SEarch via Recursive Rejection (SERR): Visual Search for Single and Dual Form Conjunction Targets. Journal of Experimental Psychology: Human Perception and Performance 1994; 20:235-258 .

8. Freidman-Hill SR and Wolfe JM. Second-order parallel processing: Visual search for the odd item in a subset. Journal of Experimental Psychology: Human Perception and Performance, in press.

9. Mordkoff JT Yantis S and Egeth HE. Detecting Conjunctions of Color and Form in Parallel. Perception and Psychophysics 1990; 48:157-168.

10. Wolfe JM. Guided Search 2.0: A Revised Model of Visual Search. Psychometric Bulletin and Review 1994; 1:202-238.

11. Humphreys GW and Müller HJ. SEarch via Recursive Rejection (SERR): A Connectionist Model of Visual Search. Cognitive Psychology 1993; 25:43-110.

Categorical Perception as an Acquired Phenomenon: What are the Implications?

James M. Beale and Frank C. Keil
Department of Psychology, Cornell University
Ithaca, New York 14853 USA

Abstract

Previous research on categorical perception (CP) has focussed primarily on low-level sensory continua. In a series of recent studies, we have found CP effects for 'higher level' representations: individual face categories. These findings suggest that CP effects can be acquired through experience, since such effects appear to vary as a direct function of the level of familiarity with individual faces. Thus, CP boundaries need not be innately specified. As such, the phenomenon of CP is much broader than has previously been believed. In this paper, we discuss the implications of these findings and explore various possible mechanisms to account for the phenomena. We then describe a number of further studies designed to distinguish between competing accounts.

1 Introduction

Categorical perception (CP) effects have been found for a wide range of stimuli varying along natural sensory continua, including the perception of color boundaries, phonemes, and more recently facial expressions. Previous work on CP has stressed the importance of innate mechanisms for the processing of naturally occurring, 'low-level' continua such as these. All species are born with innate mechanisms for survival. Yet, the extent to which humans are endowed with innate abilities (or innate constraints on their learning mechanisms) has long been a point of debate since it is also clear that humans possess powerful and highly general learning mechanisms that apply to many novel situations.

This work was supported by NIH grant #5-R01-HD23922. Portions of this work were presented at the Psychonomic Society 34th annual meeting in Washington, D.C. on November 7, 1993. For a more complete report of the empirical aspects of this work see: Beale, J.M. & Keil, F.C. (Under review for publication). "Categorical effects in the perception of faces" E-mail correspondence with the authors may be addressed to: james_beale@cornell.edu or keil@theory.tc.cornell.edu

Perceiving and responding to objects in the environment is critical to the survival of any organism. The ability to ignore redundant sensory variation reduces processing demands and enables the organism to more easily cope with other relevant environmental information. Stimulus variation is generally much less important within a category than between categories since objects within a category can often be responded to in the same manner. By grouping objects into categories, the problems of acting on one's perceptions may be greatly simplified.

However, to the extent that we ignore within-category variation, our mental representations do not accurately represent our sensory information. Rather, what we perceive is a systematically distorted (nonlinear transformation) of our sensory input such that some information has become more salient while other information has been suppressed. The psychophysical phenomena of CP provide examples of such perceptual non-linearities.

The colors of a rainbow provide a good illustration of categorization along a natural, low-level sensory continuum. Even though a smooth range of light frequencies are present in the rainbow, we perceive bands of color rather than the gradual continuum we know it to be. It is actually easier to discriminate two colors of different shades when they cross color boundaries (such as between green and yellow) than when they are within the same color category (such as two shades of green), even though the differences in frequency are identical for the two pairs [1]. Rather than perceiving light frequencies accurately, the continuum is partitioned into hue categories that serve to simplify the sensory input. Neurophysiological evidence supports the notion that this color categorization stems from color-sensitive cells in the early stages of visual processing [2].

In one of the earliest examples of CP effects, Liberman, et al. [3] studied subjects' perception of the continua between phonemes. Stimuli consisted of stop-consonants which differed in their place of articulation (i.e., /be/, /de/, and /ge/); when produced, these sounds vary along a continuum of starting frequencies of the transition of the second formant. When subjects were presented with equally-spaced stimulus pairs along this continuum, pairs that crossed phoneme boundaries were easiest to discriminate. Other research on infants has demonstrated that the CP of speech sounds can be found within a few days after birth, suggesting that adult categories stem from innate mechanisms [4]. Interestingly, infants posses phoneme boundaries at six months which are lost by 12 months of age [5]. Infants appear to be born with categories that are then fine tuned by experience, although it is presently unknown precisely how such changes occur.

Etcoff and Magee [6] have found that facial expressions also appear to be perceived categorically. When viewing line drawings of faces that varied along continua between facial expressions (for example, angry to disgusted, or happy to sad), subjects perceived these stimuli as belonging to discrete categories and discriminated pairs of faces that straddled the category boundaries better than the within-category pairs. Faces naturally demonstrate great diversity in their expressive states; as such, the categorization of facial expressions serves to disambiguate along natural continua. Once again, evidence suggests that these CP phenomena stem from innate mechanisms. Newborn infants show a preference for more complex stimuli, and prefer faces most of all [7]. Researchers have identified cells in the temporal visual cortex that respond selectively to faces and facial expressions [8, 9] providing further support for biological innateness.

Children do show clear developmental changes in face processing. For example, they shift from representing isolated facial features at age 6 to configurational representations by age 10 [10]. If there is an innate mechanism for face processing, it must be capable of later fine tuning through experience, much as are speech categories. These changes in face processing have been explained as the result of gradually increasing expertise [11, 12]. An expertise-based theory of perception would explain changes in the nature of early processing as being due to quantitative shifts resulting from increased experience with particular categories of stimuli.

By carving up sensory input into manageable blocks of information, later processes might then pick out meaningful organizations among these blocks [13]. To the extent that categorization is a general means by which information can be made more easily manageable, we might expect to find CP effects at higher perceptual levels, with more artificial continua, and where no single dimension of variation is obvious. To determine whether or not all CP phenomena result from innate mechanisms for the perception of low-level natural continua, we chose to look at the acquisition of individual face recognition ability for several specific reasons: (1) discrete categories clearly exist, (2) categories for individual faces must be acquired through experience, (3) levels of familiarity can be enormous, and (4) all people normally become experts within this domain.

2 Are individual faces perceived categorically?

The task of recognizing any particular object is far from trivial since objects vary in appearance over time due to changes in lighting and orientation. In addition, faces commonly deform in shape due to changes in expression. In general, all faces share the same set of features (eyes, nose, mouth, etc.), yet vary in many subtle ways along numerous dimensions -- all of which may be important for distinguishing one face from another. Yet, despite these variations we easily recognize familiar faces with high levels of expertise from a very early age.

Given that facial expressions are categorically perceived, one might then ask whether individual faces are also perceived categorically. Since people in all cultures appear to exhibit the same types of facial expressions and since these expressions are interpreted to have roughly the same meanings [14], it is reasonable to suppose that we possess an innate mechanism for the recognition of facial expression. The ability to recognize each individual face, on the other hand, must be acquired through experience. It thus seems less reasonable to expect that individual faces would be perceived categorically. The question then becomes: Can psychophysical techniques for studying CP effects be applied to a non-natural continuum, such as the continuum from Clinton to Kennedy? If so, we can use these techniques to ask: Are Kennedy and Clinton perceived categorically?

Figure 1. A morph continuum from Clinton to Kennedy.

2.1 Using standard psychophysical techniques

In a series of studies, Beale and Keil [15] tested the nature of individual face representations using linear continua between individual faces; these stimuli were generated between exemplars of familiar faces using a 'morph' program (see Figure 1). In their first study, stimuli were taken from two morphed continua: William Clinton to John F. Kennedy (C/K) and Sylvester Stallone to Pete Townsend (S/T). A series of nine images were produced at 10% increments as a continuum between each face-pair, for a total of 11 base images per continuum. Each subject viewed stimuli from a single continuum (either C/K or S/T) in both a categorization and discrimination task (adapted from those used by Etcoff and Magee [6]).

In the categorization task, stimuli were presented one at a time in random order; for each stimulus subjects indicated to which category it belonged. During each trial of the discrimination task, three stimuli (A, B, and X) were presented in succession. Images A and B always differed by two steps (or 20%) along a single continua; image X was always the same as either A or B. The subject's task was to indicate whether the third image was the same as A or B.

Data from the categorization and discrimination tasks displayed classic characteristics of CP in both conditions. The C/K and S/T categorization data displayed clear shifts in categorization judgements; stimuli were judged to belong to distinct categories with sharp category boundaries between them. Thirty three and 66% accuracy cut-offs were imposed on the categorization data to define the category boundary. A peak in accuracy was predicted in the discrimination task for the 2-step pairs that had straddled the boundary in each categorization condition. Planned comparisons were performed on these pairs to determine if they were different from all within-category pairs; comparisons were significant in both the C/K and S/T conditions ($p < 0.05$).

These results suggest that face stimuli are perceived categorically. However, the level at which this CP effect occurs cannot be determined from this initial study. In the discrimination task, stimuli were presented sequentially in the same location on the computer screen; this would have allowed subjects to make use of changes in low-level features in the image (e.g., pixel intensities, contrast levels). Thus, the data may indicate the categorical perception of a low-level feature, rather than at the level of the individual face. What was needed was a task which reduced the availability of low-level cues and encouraged subjects to focus on higher-order information to make judgements of individual identity.

2.2 Developing a better methodology

When images were presented sequentially in the discrimination task, shifts in the locations of pixels or other low-level features were made salient to subjects. To bias subjects toward more holistic processing, a new method was developed in which stimuli were presented simultaneously. In this 'better-likeness' (or 'B-L') task, the two images of each face-pair were presented simultaneously side-by-side. Subjects were asked to indicate which was the better example of a particular person (i.e., which image was closer to a particular end of the continuum). As in the initial study, this B-L task was paired with a categorization task. Stimuli consisted of the original C/K and S/T continua, as well as an additional face-pair continuum from Clint Eastwood to Arnold Schwarzenegger.

Subjects were presented with three categorization tasks and a single B-L task containing face-pairs from all three continua. The methods of the three categorization tasks were identical to those of the initial study. On each trial of the B-L task, subjects indicated whether the left or right image more closely resembled the person who had been named at the start of the trial. Results of the categorization tasks again displayed distinct shifts in categorization judgements. Increased discriminability, as indicated by peaks in accuracy, was found for face-pairs which crossed the predicted category boundaries in all B-L task conditions ($p < 0.05$). Peak accuracies in the B-L task for cross-category pairs demonstrate that face stimuli are perceived categorically at the level of individual face processing.

These CP effects occur at a higher level of sensory processing than has previously been observed, suggesting that CP is not limited to simple, low-level perceptual continua. More generally, this shows that psychophysical techniques can be applied to the study of complex, higher-level continua which simultaneously vary along multiple dimensions. Given that all three continua were perceived categorically, one might then wonder if all faces are perceived categorically. It could be that all faces are represented in such a way that even after brief exposures they can be perceived in a categorical manner. Another likely possibility is that a certain amount of expertise is necessary before CP effects appear. Having established the appropriate methodology, we can now determine whether or not all CP phenomena result from innate perceptual mechanisms.

2.3 Are all faces perceived categorically or can CP be acquired?

A third study addressed the effects of familiarity on the categorical perception of faces. In an independent rating task, familiarity levels were determined for a database of 38 faces consisting of both famous and unknown people. From these faces, high-, moderate-, low-, and non-familiar faces were selected and paired: Michael Douglas / Dustin Hoffman (D/H), high; Carey Grant / Jack Lemmon (G/L), moderate; Christopher Atkins / Barry Tubb (A/T), low; Kevin Burns / Jason Harris (B/H), non-familiar. For each face-pair, morphed continua were then constructed for use as stimuli. Subjects' were presented with these four continua and judgements were recorded using the categorization and B-L tasks from the preceding study.

Results support the hypothesis of categorical boundaries for moderately and highly familiar faces. The categorization task data in all four conditions displayed sharp categorical shifts. Predicted peaks in the B-L task were significant in the high- (D/H) and moderate- (G/L) familiarity conditions conditions ($p < 0.05$). Peaks in the low- (A/T) and non- (B/H) familiar conditions were not significant. Thus, individual faces are perceived categorically only if they are familiar.

With the results of all seven B-L task conditions, in this and the preceding study, the correlation can be computed between the average familiarity of each face-pair and the magnitude of the CP effect (as indicated by the significance level, or p value, of the predicted peak). From the resulting measure, familiarity can be seen to play a major role in the categorization of individual faces ($r = -0.848$); the CP effect increases proportionately to subjects' level of familiarity with each individual face. Level of familiarity was highly predictive of the degree of the categorization effect; familiar faces were perceived categorically, while unfamiliars were not. CP effects can be acquired through experience and appear to vary systematically with the level of previous experience.

3 How do we account for acquired CP?

Standard interpretations of CP phenomena have argued for the existence of innate mechanisms for the processing of low-level, naturally occurring continua. Such theories have taken the form of either prototype theories or a part-based (feature-based) theories in which categories are defined by a set of necessary and sufficient features [4]. In presenting our findings on the acquisition of CP for faces, we do not argue that these earlier theories are incorrect, but rather extend the phenomena of CP to higher levels of processing. We also provide new methods for examining the nature of categorical representations. It should also be noted that, although these accounts stress the importance of innate categories, they also acknowledge the importance of later fine timing through experience. Rather than debating the applicability of these earlier approaches, we would like to provide an overview of a number of approaches which are derived from quite different perspectives.

3.1 Structural Invariants Hypothesis

All objects vary in appearance over time. Some changes are incidental to objects (e.g., changes in lighting), while others are defining (e.g., relative motions of parts). The nervous system might take advantage of these variations to determine which properties of objects are defining. Objects could then be represented in terms of component structures. Any object can be described in terms of properties that remain constant due to underlying structure and those that vary. For faces, invariant structures result from the structures of the skull, while variations result from deformations of the muscles and skin (as well as motions of the jawbone) [15]. As structural invariants of an object are learned, the range of acceptable deformations would become easier to compute. Consequently, the category boundaries would be set. Unfamiliar objects would not have category boundaries since the range of acceptable deformations would be unknown. In the present studies, the Structural Invariants Hypothesis would predict no CP effects for novel face-pairs since the bone structure invariants are unknown for these individuals.

If the Structural Invariants Hypothesis is correct, we would expect to find CP effects for other face-like stimuli which are capable of deforming (i.e., which vary along a number of dimensions which allow underlying structures to become apparent). Conversely, we would predict no CP effects for stimuli which normally exhibit little variation, thus providing no information concerning underlying invariant properties, or when variations in appearance are not defining of category membership.

Figure 2. Muppets: Animal to Big Bird continuum.

Many people are familiar with the muppets of Jim Henson and are able to recognize them as individuals. Muppets' 'faces' have many of the same basic features as human faces, yet are greatly simplified; their primary deformations are limited to a few dimensions and consist of a rigid motions (e.g., the opening and closing of their mouths). Preliminary data from studies using continua between muppet faces (see Figure 2) do not appear to show CP effects, thus providing support for the Structural Invariants Hypothesis. While this approach is useful for generating testable hypotheses (see Section 4 below), it has little or nothing to say concerning the nature of the underlying mechanisms.

3.2 An expertise-based account

Even where strong evidence of innate mechanisms for CP has been found, it must also be conceded that experience plays a role in shaping category bounds. The effects of expertise have been examined for a wide variety of domains. In general, experts have been found to be better than novices at recognizing meaningful sub-units, or chunks, of information within their domain of expertise [16]. Experts categorize problems according underlying principles, while novices pay more attention to surface feature similarities suggesting that experts possess much more well organized, domain-specific schemas than do novices [17]. Experts use of abstract information allows them to process larger chunks of information more quickly and easily. Experts are also more adept at perceiving structures in their environment which trigger the application of specific schemas [18]. Sweller, Mawer, and Ward [19] have proposed that experts possess a hierarchy of schemas from general to solution-specific principles. As such, schemas should not be expected only for specific types of information. Rather, it is thought that categorization and schema formation are probably characteristic of knowledge organization at all levels.

Recent research has shown that the 'basic level' at which objects are represented appears to shift downward (to previously subordinate levels) as a function of expertise within a given domain [20]. Other research suggests that as experts learn to focus on task-specific information, they also learn to disregard information which is not relevant. For example, while expert radiologists' ability to remember abnormal x-rays increases with experience, their memory for normal x-ray images actually decreases proportionally [21]. Not only does information become more organized as a result of experience, but is organized such that some information becomes more salient while other information is suppressed. This chunking appears to occur at the time of encoding and might take the form of automatic processes which distort experts' perception of information. In other words, within their domain of expertise experts actually perceive sensory information differently than do novices. As such, it may be that the same underlying mechanisms give rise to both CP phenomena and expertise.

The literature on expertise provides a valuable resource to those interested in the stages through which novices gain experience. However, although many studies have examined changes in knowledge structures and access to them as expertise is acquired, few have focussed on the processes and mechanisms by which such changes occur.

3.3 Neural Code Theory

Populations of cells which respond selectively to specific categories of stimulus features have been discovered at numerous locations in the visual system, including: center-surround receptive fields of retinal ganglion cells, color receptors in the LGN, oriented line receptors in the LGN and primary visual cortex, and cells responsive to faces in areas of the temporal visual cortex. It is likely that such feature tuning is common to other domains as well (e.g., phonemes), and may be a mechanism common to many levels of neural processing. It may in fact be that all CP phenomena are produced by simple processes of individual neurons.

In all cases when a cell is said to be 'tuned' for a particular stimulus, its activity is greatest for that stimulus. The cell also responds vigorously for all items which are very similar to its preferred stimulus, not at all for stimuli that are sufficiently different, and in a graded fashion for those that are in between. Within a narrow range, on the 'edges' of the cells preferred response range, the cell's output gradually decreases as the similarity to the preferred stimulus decreases. Even though single cells are specifically tuned, their output levels do not discriminate well between stimuli at or near their peak activity (i.e., for the best exemplars of the category); rather discrimination is best where the slope of the activity is the steepest (i.e., at the category boundary). Although these phenomena have primarily been studied in single cells representing single stimulus dimensions, they are likely to apply for populations of cells and for representing multiple features as well.

An explanation of CP effects in terms of the neural activity is appealing. Not only does such an approach provide an explanation of the basic underlying mechanisms, it also lends itself to computational modelling. Computer models have been used successfully to categorize faces on the basis of sex, to discriminate familiar from unfamiliar faces [22], and to recognize individual faces even when partially occluded [23]. The recent development of neural networks and parallel processors have greatly contributed to our understandings of brain representations and will undoubtedly continue to do so.

The explanatory power of this approach comes with a cost. At present, the details of neural processes are not understood in sufficient detail to generate any but the most general predictions. We would predict the existence of cells tuned to specific categories at all levels of processing with increasing complexity at higher levels, but cannot yet predict the precise nature of these categories. Despite its current limitations, this perspective may prove useful in pointing out avenues for future research and guiding our formulation of research questions. None of the three approaches are mutually exclusive. Since they offer descriptions at different levels, any or all of them may turn out to be correct.

4 Directions for further research

Numerous questions remain to be answered concerning the nature of CP phenomena and perceptual representations in general. We have found that CP effects can be acquired for higher level continua. As such, these studies provide a means by which modified psychophysical methods (such as those of the B-L task) may be used to tests the boundaries of high-level representations.

CP effects were not found for the unfamiliar faces we chose. However, these stimuli were carefully matched such that variations were limited. Are there conditions under which unfamiliar face might be expected to exhibit category boundaries? Had we used stimuli which cross other familiar category boundaries (e.g., cross-gender, or cross-race), CP effects might have been found even for the unfamiliar faces. Further research along these lines is certainly in order.

Is the phenomenon of higher-level CP face-specific, or can it be found for other objects in other domains? If it is a more general phenomenon, which seems likely, for what other domains might we expect to find these effects? According to an expertise-based account, we might expect to find CP effects anywhere there are clear categories within a single domain, such as for different types of animals or artifacts (see Figures 3 and 4). As such, we might expect all other highly familiar classes of objects to display CP effects -- so long as continua can be generated between them.

Figure 3. Animals: Tarantula to Crab continuum.

Figure 4. Artifacts: Axe to Hammer continuum.

Once a category boundary has been established, discrimination is better across category than within category. Does this result solely from an improvement in discrimination ability across the boundary? Or is there a corresponding decrease in discrimination ability within-category equal to the increase across-category? This second possibility would be consistent with the idea of an acquired non-linear transformation of the sensory information. If this is the case, it should be directly observable in the data from the trained familiarity studies mentioned above. In some sense, these findings might not seem particularly surprising. However, if there is always a direct trade-off in discrimination between items at CP boundaries and those within a category, it might logically follow that children should be better at discriminating within-category items -- or rather, items which are within-category items for the average adult.

All recognizable faces have become familiar through previous exposure. It would be quite informative to determine exactly what types of exposure are necessary for categorical representations to appear As suggested by the Structural Invariants Hypothesis, variation in the input may be critical to category formation. This could be tested by experimentally training subjects on previously unfamiliar face-pairs which vary on a number of dimensions. For example, training stimuli might consist of faces which exhibit a variety of facial expressions and orientations. Control subjects could be exposed to stimuli of the same individual's faces with variations in orientation but not in expression. The Structural Invariants Hypothesis would predict that subjects should be able to acquire representations which exhibit CP in the experimental but not the control condition.

Further refinements of category training procedures using a wide range of stimuli and stimulus variations could be used to specify precisely which dimensions are relevant for individual objects. By pursuing answers to these many questions we hope to not only deepen our understanding of CP, but of the process of knowledge acquisition in general.

The authors would like to thank Ulric Neisser, Stevan Harnad, Grant Gutheil, and Bruno A. Olshausen, whose insightful comments and discussions were particularly helpful in the development of the ideas presented here. We would also like to thank Daniel J. Simons for help in acquiring images and Peter M. Vishton for comments on drafts.

References

1. Bornstein, M.H. & Korda, N.O. (1984). Discrimination and matching within and between hues measured by reaction times: Some implications for categorical perception and levels of information processing. *Psychological Research, 46,* 207-222.
2. DeValois, R.L. & DeValois, K.K. (1975). Neural coding of color. In E.C. Carterette and M.P. Friedman (Eds.). *Handbook of Perception, 5.* New York: Academic Press.
3. Liberman, A.M., Harris, K.S., Hoffman, H.S, & Griffith, B.C. (1957). The discrimination of speech sounds within and across phoneme boundaries. *Journal of Experimental Psychology, 54,* 358-368.
4. Eimas, P.D., Miller, J.L., & Jusczyk, P.W. (1987). On infant speech perception and the acquisition of language. In S. Harnad (Ed.). *Categorical Perception: The Groundwork of Cognition.* New York: Cambridge University Press.
5. Werker, J.F. & Tees, R.C. (1984). Cross-language speech perception: Evidence for perceptual reorganization during the first year of life. *Infant Behavior and Development, 7,*49-63.

6. Etcoff, N.L. & Magee, J.J. (1992). Categorical perception of facial expressions, *Cognition, 44,* 227-240.

7. Morton, J. & Johnson, M.H. (1991). Conspec and conlern: A two-process theory of infant face recognition. *Psychological Review, 98(2),* 164-181.

8. Hasselmo, M.E., Rolls, E.E., & Baylis, G.C. (1989). The role of expression and identity in the face-selective responses of neurons in the temporal visual cortex of the monkey, *Behavioral Brain Research, 32,* 203-218.

9. Perrett, D.I., Smith, P.A.J., Potter, D.D., Mistlin, A.J., Head, A.S., Milner, A.D., & Jeeves, M.A. (1984). Neurons responsive to faces in the temporal cortex: Studies of functional organization, sensitivity to identity and relation to perception. *Human Neurobiology, 3,* 197-208.

10. Diamond, R. & Carey, S. (1977). Developmental changes in the representation of faces. *Journal of Experimental Child Psychology, 23,* 1-22.

11. Carey, S. (1992). Becoming a face expert. *Philosophical Transcripts of the Royal Society of London, B, 335,* 95-103.

12. Diamond, R. & Carey, S. (1986). Why faces are and are not special: An effect of expertise. *Journal of Experimental Psychology: General, 155(2),* 107-117.

13. Harnad, S. (1987). *Categorical Perception: The Groundwork of Cognition.* New York: Cambridge University Press.

14. Ekman, P., Freisen, W.V., & Ellsworth, P. (1982). What are the similarities and differences in facial behavior across cultures? In P. Ekman (Ed.). *Emotions in the Human Face.* New York: Cambridge University Press.

15. Beale, J.M. & Keil, F.C. (Under review for publication). Categorical effects in the perception of faces.

16. Barfield, W. (1986). Expert-novice differences for software: Implications for problem solving and knowledge acquisition. *Behaviour and Information Technology, 5,* 15-29.

17. Chi, M.T.H., Feltovich, P.J., & Glaser, R. (1981). Categorization and representation of physics problems by experts and novices. *Cognitive Science, 5,* 121-152.

18. Lesgold, A., Rubinson, H., Feltovich, P., Glaser, R., Klopfer, D., & Wang, Y. (1988) Expertise in a complex skill: Diagnosing x-ray pictures. In M.T.H. Chi, R. Glaser, & M.J. Farr (Eds.). *The Nature of Expertise.* Hillsdale, NJ: Erlbaum.

19. Sweller, J. Mawer, R.F. & Ward, M.R. (1983). Development of expertise in mathematical problem solving. *Journal of Experimental Psychology: General, 112(4),* 639-661.

20. Tanaka, J.W. & Taylor, M. (1991). Object categories and expertise: Is the basic level in the eye of the beholder? *Cognitive Psychology, 23,* 457-482.

21. Myles-Worsley, M., Johnston, W.J., & Simons, M.A., (1988). The influence of expertise on X-ray image processing. *Journal of Experimental Psychology, Learning, Memory, and Cognition, 14(3),* 553-557.

22. O'Toole, A.J., Abdi, H., Deffenbacher, K.A., & Valentin, D. (1993). Low-dimensional representation of faces in higher dimensions of the face space. *Journal of the Optical Society of America A, 10,* 1-7.

23. Turk, M. & Pentland, A. (1991) Eigenfaces for recognition. *Journal of Cognitive Neuroscience, 3,* 71-86.

Sequence Learning

A Computational Account of Phonologically Mediated Free Recall

Peter J. Lovatt

Centre for Cognitive and Computational Neuroscience,
University of Stirling
Stirling FK9 4LA, Scotland, U.K.

Dimitrios Bairaktaris

Department of Computing Science,
University of Stirling
Stirling FK9 4LA, Scotland, U.K.

1 Introduction

This paper investigates, by means of experimentation and simulation, *Phonological Mediation* in Immediate Free List Recall. It consists of two parts. The first part presents novel experimental evidence on Phonological Similarity and Word Length effects in free recall. The second part describes the architecture and simulation results of a novel connectionist model of free recall.

In previous modelling work on serial list recall, [4] presented a connectionist model of serial list recall which reproduced all the major effects of serial recall. Such effects as the phonological similarity effect, originally proposed by Baddeley [1], whereby subject's serial list recall of phonologically similar items (e.g. **cat, mat, rat**) is considerably worse than that of their recall for non–phonologically similar items, and the word length effect, whereby immediate serial list recall is significantly impaired when the list items are polysyllabic rather than monosyllabic, (e.g. **establishment** versus **bed**) [2]. The model also demonstrates those characteristics of the List Length, Primacy and Recency effects (originally highlighted by Postman and Phillips [13]) and proposes that such characteristics are due to the dynamics of the model's recall mechanism. This contrasts with the Word Length and Phonological Similarity effects which, they argue, are primarily due to the model's input representation and encoding scheme. Based on this differentiation the model makes a strong prediction regarding phonological mediation in short term memory, such that:

- *If word length and phonological similarity effects in serial recall are due to the encoding mechanism, they should also be found in other experimental situations relevant to short term memory performance.*

The closest experimental design to serial list recall is that of free recall. In serial recall subjects are asked to recall the list items in the order of presentation while in free recall subjects are asked to recall the list items in any order. This fundamental difference in the two tasks certainly requires storage and recall mechanisms with different dynamics, but does not exclude the possibility of a common (*phonological*) encoding mechanism. If the model's prediction is correct one should expect to discover that phonological similarity and word length also reduce free recall performance.

Craik & Levy [7] have investigated how acoustic similarity affects primary memory. In their experiments they presented subjects with lists of 20 items which contained *clusters* of acoustically similar words. These clusters were included either in the middle or the end part of the list. They reported improved recall probabilities in performance for the acoustically similar part of the list. When the acoustically similar cluster was included in the middle of the list the standard *U*-shape serial position recall curve [13] was distorted with the cluster items reaching levels of recall probabilities similar to those of items at the beginning of the list. Craik & Levy draw an analogy with the results from Baddeley [1], but they conclude that acoustic similarity does not affect primary memory. Their conclusion would seem to run counter to our predictions. However, their experiments test phonological similarity in only one part of the list at any one time. We believe that because subjects are free to adopt their own recall strategies in free recall, they choose to recall the distinctive aspects of the lists, i.e. the acoustically similar cluster, first. Validation of this belief comes from the finding that the levels of recall for such clusters are equal to the levels of recall of the terminal items (items which are generally recalled first) in free recall experiments which do not contain distinctive clusters.

Dalezman [8] has shown that when subjects are instructed to free recall list items from a particular part of the list, those items are recalled at a higher probability when compared with the control condition where subjects are free to start recall from any list item they wish. In view of this evidence, the Craik & Levy results can be explained as an recall strategy effect which does not test acoustic similarity but instead tests subjects implicit adoption of different recall strategies. Even though Craik & Levy did not take into account the results reported by Dalezman, in their final discussion they postulate the possibility of a strategy selection effect.

The *aim* of the following experiment is to test whether phonological similarity and word length effects exist in free recall; and if they do, to determine the levels at which the disruption is significant so that an existing connectionist model can be appropriately adapted to incorporate such characteristics.

2 Method

2.1 Materials

Three lists of 20 words were used for the recall stimuli. The first list contained 20 unrelated monosyllabic words, the second list contained 20 phonologically similar monosyllabic words, and the third list contained 20 unrelated polysyllabic words. Each list was generated by random selection (without replacement) from a large pool of appropriate words. For the pool of unrelated monosyllabic words, five words were slected starting with each letter of the alphabet, with the exception of the letter "x", (which contained an insufficient number of monosyllabic words). The words were matched for frequency and they were phonologically, and, where possible, semantically unrelated. For the pool of phonologically similar monosyllabic words, words were selected according to their ending. Words in this pool ended in either –uck, –ock, or –ack. For the pool of unrelated polysyllabic words, words were chosen in much the same way as for the first group. However, the constraint of a three syllable minimum length was enforced. No words were longer than five syllables and they were both phonologically and, where possible, semantically unrelated.

2.2 Design

A repeated measures design was used with three experimental conditions. No practice was allowed for each subject and each subject was tested on each condition only once. Both these measures were considered to be essential in order to avoid the possibility of subjects developing recall strategies specific to the task material. For each subject, three lists of 20 words were generated. Each of the three lists was generated by randomly selecting (without replacement) words from a different pool of words. After the presentation of each list the subjects were tested on their free recall of that list. Each subject was tested individually and the sequence of the three conditions was randomised.

2.3 Procedure

The words in each list were presented individually at a 2 second interval on a computer screen. Subjects had been instructed that at the end of each list they were to recall as many words as possible by writing them down on a sheet of A4 paper. There was no time limit on the recall task but no subject took more than a few minutes to exhaust their recall. Once the subjects had completed all of the experimental conditions they were thanked for their time and paid. Subjects responses were entered into the computer and then electronically compared with the experimental stimuli.

2.4 Subjects

58 subjects were recruited from The University of Stirling. The majority of the subjects were either undergraduate or postgraduate students, and their ages ranged from approximately 17 to 25. However, no personal details were recorded.

3 Results

The results of the free recall tasks can be seen in Figure 1. It shows clear primacy and recency effects for each of the experimental conditions. It also shows the detrimental effects of word length and phonemic similarity on recall and the characteristic trough in the middle section of the list.

A computer program scored each list recall sheet from every subject and tabulated the results. ANOVA tests were carried out on the tabulated results. ANOVA summary tables are shown in Figures 2 - 5.

Figure 2 shows the within subjects ANOVA summary table. It can be seen that both the experimental **condition** (normal, long and similar list

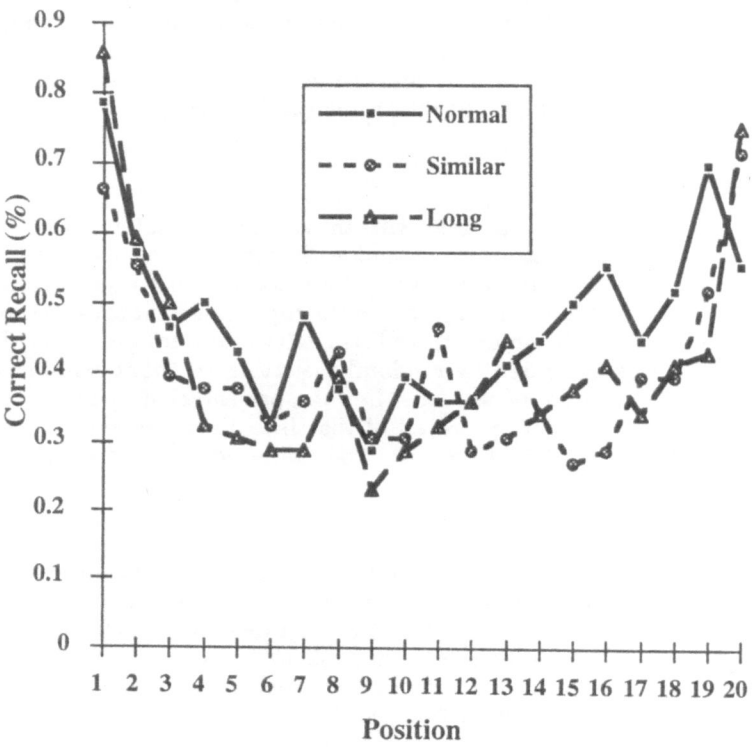

Figure 1: Serial position curves in free recall of 20 words as a function of word length and phonological similarity.

Source of Variation		SS	df	MS	F	P-value	F crit
	Condition	3.269643	2	1.634821	7.092567	0.000844	2.998448
	Position	48.07143	19	2.530075	10.97657	9.67E-33	1.589662
	Interaction	10.87321	38	0.286137	1.241388	0.148003	1.408527
	Within	760.6429	3300	0.230498			
	Total	822.8571	3359				

Figure 2: ANOVA summary table comparing all three experimental conditions for all list positions.

Source of Variation	SS	df	MS	F	P-value	F crit
Condition	2.78616	1	2.78616	11.8769	0.00058	3.84568
Position	26.4192	19	1.39048	5.92739	7.2E-15	1.59124
Interaction	5.82991	19	0.30684	1.308	0.16696	1.59124
Within	516.089	2200	0.23459			
Total	551.125	2239				

Figure 3: ANOVA summary table comparing normal and similar word lists for all list positions.

Source of Variation	SS	df	MS	F	P-value	F crit
Condition	2.06429	1	2.06429	8.94171	0.00282	3.84568
Position	36.3839	19	1.91494	8.29481	6.3E-23	1.59124
Interaction	6.11429	19	0.3218	1.39394	0.11869	1.59124
Within	507.893	2200	0.23086			
Total	552.455	2239				

Figure 4: ANOVA summary table comparing normal and long word lists for every list position.

items) and the **position** of each word in the input list have a significant effect on subject's recall ($F = 7.0925, P < .01[F_{crit}(2, 19) = 2.99845]$) and ($F = 10.9766, P < .01[F_{crit}(2, 19) = 1.58966]$). However, there is no interaction ($F = 1.24139, P > .01[F_{crit}(2, 19) = 1.40853]$).

Figures 3-5 show pair-wise ANOVA summary tables for each combination of condition pairs. Figure 3 shows the effect that the experimental condition and the position have on recall when only normal and similar words are considered together. It shows that both the condition and the position have a significant effect on item recall ($F = 11.877, P < .01[F_{crit}(1, 19) = 3.8457]$) and ($F = 5.9274, P < .01[F_{crit}(1, 19) = 1.5912]$) and that there is no significant interaction ($F = 1.308, P > .01[F_{crit}(1, 19) = 1.5912]$). Figure 4 shows the ANOVA summary table for the normal and long words. It again shows that both condition and position have a significant effect on recall ($F = 8.9417, P < .05[F_{crit}(1, 19) = 3.8457]$) and ($F = 8.2948, P < .05[F_{crit}(1, 19) = 1.5912]$) and again there is no interaction ($F = 1.3939, P > .05[F_{crit}(1, 19) = 1.5912]$). The ANOVA summary table of Figure 5 shows the effects of condition and position on the recall of similar and long words. It shows that the experimental condition has no effect on recall ($F = 0.239, P > .05[F_{crit}(1, 19) = 3.8457]$) but that the position of the word has a significant effect on recall ($F = 9.0285, P < .05[F_{crit}(1, 19) = 1.5912]$). Figure 5 also shows that there is no interaction

Source of Variation	SS	df	MS	F	P-value	F crit
Condition	0.05402	1	0.05402	0.23897	0.625	3.84568
Position	38.7763	19	2.04086	9.02847	1.9E-25	1.59124
Interaction	4.36562	19	0.22977	1.01647	0.43757	1.59124
Within	497.304	2200	0.22605			
Total	540.5	2239				

Figure 5: ANOVA summary table comparing long and similar word lists for every list position.

$(F = 1.0165, P > .05[F_{crit}(1, 19) = 1.5912])$.

4 Discussion

The aim of these experiments was to establish whether free list recall performance is affected by word length and phonological similarity. The statistical analysis of the experimental findings clearly shows that free recall is adversely affected by both word length and phonological similarity. These results confirm our original prediction concerning the existence of a phonologically mediated encoding process which is not exclusive to serial recall.

From an experimental point of view these findings give rise to a number of significant predictions regarding free recall experiments and short term memory recall performance. If as is suggested by these results, there is a common encoding process in both serial and free recall then free recall should also be affected by lexical status. Free recall of lists consisting of non–words should also result in decreased recall performance. Perhaps most significantly, if the encoding processes common to serial and free recall are also common to other short term memory tasks such as homophone and pseudohomophone judgement, serial recall experiments can be used as a general performance indicator for similar encoding process available in reading and word translation.

From a modelling point of view these findings pose a significant challenge regarding our existing model of serial recall. Can this model be modified to account for the effects observed in free recall? This challenge is not restricted in reproducing the word length and phonological similarity effect, but also includes the standard list length, primacy and recency effect also present in free recall. In the following sections of this paper we describe a connectionist model of free list recall. We begin our presentation by considering some general representation issues regarding connectionist models of list learning.

5 Representing Serially Ordered Information

List learning is a typical example of serially ordered information, where encoding the list items themselves is just as important as encoding the order in which these items occur during list presentation. Encoding and recall of serially ordered patterns requires that during encoding each member of the sequence is associated with appropriate contextual information, which can then be used to retrieve each pattern. There are two possible ways in which one may represent this contextual information:

- One possibility is to assign an externally provided *time-stamp* to each item of the sequence. In this case, a temporally varied pattern is assigned to every pattern of the sequence and during recall this pattern is used as a cue to retrieve the actual pattern from the sequence. By appropriately selecting the context patterns correct recall of the original sequence of patterns can be achieved [6].

- An alternative possibility is to use every pattern of the sequence itself as the context for the following patterns. This approach has been used successfully in a number of variations of the standard back- propagation algorithm, most notably in the work on recurrent networks by Elman [9] and in the Back-Propagation Through Time algorithm [15]. In these cases, the hidden layer representation developed by the network to represent the current input pattern is used as the contextual cue for the next pattern in the sequence. A similar approach has also been used successfully with a local representation self-organised Hebbian learning algorithm [3].

Serially ordered information processing is required in a variety of cognitive tasks. Tasks like sentence processing and immediate list recall have a specific context associated with the input sequence (e.g. discourse, experimental procedure). In other tasks however, such as the recall of a telephone number from long term memory, no specific context can be identified as recall may occur some days or even months later to the time of encoding of the original sequence. For this latter case, the *time-stamp* approach cannot explain how, in the absence of the original context, recall is still possible. One possibility is to claim that contextual information is stored together with the patterns themselves. In this case each separate sequence in memory must have a different contextual sequence stored with it.

The second approach, which uses the patterns themselves as context does not suffer from this problem, because all the information required for recall is included within the memory trace of the sequence itself. However, this approach has obvious similarities to a chaining algorithm and it fails to recall the sequence in cases where many copies of the same input pattern are present. Consider the following sequence of numbers:

$$1223$$

The context of the first number 2 is the number 1, the context for the second 2 in the sequence is the number 2 again. A simple forward chaining algorithm which assumes that each possible pattern in the sequence is only represented once cannot encode and recall this sequence. It will either ignore the second number 2, or it will chain 2 to itself and never produce number 3. The same problem is encountered if the same pattern occurs twice at non-consecutive positions in the sequence.

There is, however, a simple solution to this problem. If instead of representing repeated sequence items only once, we have a separate representation for each occurrence of the item. In this case a forward chaining algorithm works fine. This solution is implicitly implemented in both of the recurrent network variations of back- propagation mentioned above. The hidden layer pattern which is used as context for the next input pattern conveys information not only about the current pattern, but also about all the previous patterns. It is therefore the case that, a different hidden layer representation is generated for every pattern in the sequence, including repeated sequence items.

Having a separate representation for each occurrence of every input pattern can very quickly lead to a combinatorial explosion problem if all the possible positions in a sequence where a pattern may occur, are allocated statically. Dynamic Adaptation Scheme (DAS) is a self-organised constructive learning algorithm which detects novelty, adapts continuously and dynamically allocates resources to represent new information. The availability of this algorithm provides an effective solution to the combinatorial explosion problem mentioned above. The system optimises its performance by allocating nodes to represent each item of the sequence dynamically.

Next, we present the DAS network architecture and its dynamics.

6   The Dynamic Adaptation Scheme

6.1   Representation

The architecture of our model is shown in Figure 6. An input layer of units holds the representation of words as sets of phonemic features. The sequence of phonemes within a word are encoded by position specific coding [3]. Unlike the network of Burgess & Hitch [6] where words are represented by individual letter nodes and therefore the representation of the words **bat** and **tab** is the same, in our network each phoneme of the word is represented by a different input node depending upon its relative position in the word. In this way, **bat** and **tab** have completely different representations, although **bat** and **batsman** have similar representations.

Another layer of units, the Short Term Store (STS), holds the identities of the words through connections to their phonological specification in the input layer and their sequence in terms of relation within the STS layer. The STS layer nodes are fully interconnected with excitatory connections. Memory models with similar architectures, which emphasise different aspects of short-term memory, are described in [16];[14]. The input layer is supplied with a sufficient number of nodes in order to store all the significant phonological features of every list item. Each phonetic feature or phoneme of a list item is represented in the input layer by setting the activation of a specific input node to 1. It is assumed that a pre-processor is used for the conversion of the auditory or visual stimulus into the phonological code. Such a simple pre–processor network architecture is described in Burgess & Hitch [6]. It must be made clear however that the generation of the phonological code is a complex process which possibly requires the generation of intermediate phonetic codes [5] as well as the use of a lexicon [12]. It should also be mentioned that the quality of the phonological code used by the short term store layer is subject to modality

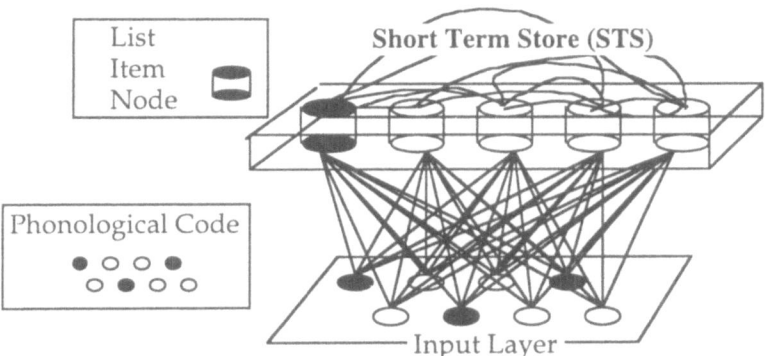

Figure 6: The architecture of Dynamic Adaptation Scheme. An input layer is fully connected to the STS layer via bi-directional modifiable connections. Each node in the STS layer is connected to every other STS node via uni-directional modifiable connections.

effects and various reception conditions such as articulatory suppression [10]. We are currently developing a model which deals explicitly with the generation of the phonological code. For the purposes of the current model the following design constraints apply to the generation of the phonological code:

- The code of each list item is generated sequentially over a period of time (t). In this way long duration words take longer to complete their representation at the input layer than short duration words. It must be emphasised that the model assumes a constant rate of word presentation and does not attempt to model effects which relate to variable rates of word presentation.

- Phonologically similar list items generate similar codes. This constraint is easily satisfied by the entactical input representation scheme described above.

6.2   Architecture

When the input pattern is completed the input nodes propagate their activation to the STS layer where a node is allocated to represent it.
Each STS node encodes two forms of information and for this it has two separate reception sites. Site (A) where feature information from the input nodes arrives and site (B) where serial order information from the other STS nodes arrives. The node activation ($Act_i^a(t)$) at site (A) is computed as follows:

$$Act_i^a(t)) = \Sigma_j W_{ij}^a(t)P_j(t) \tag{1}$$

where $P_j(t)$ is the activation of input node (j) at time (t) and $W_{ij}^a(t)$ is the weight value at time (t) of the connection between input (j) and STS node (i).

The STS node activation ($Act_i^b(t)$) and the corresponding *floating* threshold $T_i^b(t)$ at site (B) are computed as follows:

$$Act_i^b(t) = \Sigma_j W_{ij}^b(t) O_j(t) \tag{2}$$

and

$$T_i^b(t) = \epsilon(\mathring{A}ct_i^b(t-1)) \tag{3}$$

where $1 \geq \epsilon \geq 0$ and $T_i^b(t = 0) = 0$

and $O_j(t)$ is the output of STS node (j) at time (t) and $W_{ij}^b(t)$ is the weight value at time (t) of the connection between STS node (i) and STS node (j). During list presentation the STS node output signal is computed as follows:

$$if\, Act_i^b(t) \geq T_i^b(t)\ \&\ Act_i^a(t) > 0$$
then

$$O_j(t) = 1 \tag{4}$$

$$elseif\, Act_i^b(t) < T_i^b(t)\ \&\ Act_i^a(t) > 0$$
then

$$O_j(t) = Act_i^a(t) \tag{5}$$

else

$$O_j(t+1) = O_j(t)\frac{\delta}{e^{\delta - O_j(t)}} \tag{6}$$

where δ is a constant

Weight modifications and threshold updates occur only during the list presentation-encoding phase and only for the STS nodes which satisfy $Act_j(t) \geq 0$. The network encodes information about the current list of items by modifying the weight values on its connections. The weight values on the connections between the input nodes and the STS nodes ($W_{ij}^a(t)$) encode feature-based information about the list items themselves and are modified every time a STS node (i) emits an output signal $O_i(t) = 1$ as follows:

$$W_{ij}^a(t) = W_{ij}^a(t-1) O_i(t) P_j(t) \tag{7}$$

The weight values on the connections between the STS nodes themselves ($W_{ij}^b(t)$) encode serial order information about the order in which list items appear and are modified every time a STS node (i) emits an output signal $O_i(t) = 1$ as follows:

$$W_{ij}^b(t) = \mu W_{ij}^b(t-1) O_i(t) O_j(t), \tag{8}$$
where $1 \geq \mu \geq 0$

During recall the STS nodes compute their activation and output levels as follows:

$$Act_i^b(t) = \Sigma_j W_{ij}^b(t) O_j(t) \tag{9}$$

$$\text{if } Act_i^b(t) \geq T_i^b(t)$$
$$\text{then}$$

$$O_j(t) = Act_i^b(t) \tag{10}$$

$$\text{else}$$

$$O_j(t+1) = O_j(t)\frac{\delta}{e^{\delta - O_j(t)}} \tag{11}$$

where δ is a constant

When an STS node i emits an output signal the value of every input node (P_j) is computed as follows:

$$P_j(t) = O_i(t)W_{ji}^a(t) \tag{12}$$

6.3 Dynamics

6.3.1 Encoding

Figure 7 shows how a different STS node is dynamically allocated to represent each list item. During list presentation the network starts with all the nodes in the input layer and only one node in the STS layer as shown in Figure 7A. A time (t), the first complete word representation (**bat**) is made available at the input layer.

The first STS node computes its activation $Act_1^a(t)$ according to (1) and sets its output $O_1(t)$ according to (5). Weight modifications occur on both sets of weights connected to the STS node according to (7) & (8) (Figure 7B). The new $Act_1^b(t)$ and $O_1(t)$ are computed and the threshold level $T_1^b(t)$ is set according to (3). The first STS node has been allocated for the representation of the current input pattern and the STS layer is then supplied with another STS node. The network is now ready for the next input.

Until the next input pattern is completed, the output $O_1(t)$ decays through time according to (6) because $Act_1^a(t) = 0$ and $O_1(t) < T_1^b(t)$. When the second input pattern (**tab**) is complete at the input layer both STS nodes compute their respective activations $Act_j^a(t)$ and outputs $O_j(t)$ according to (1) & (5) (Figure 7C)). Only the second STS node satisfies the condition that $O_j(t) > T_1^b(t)$. This is because the first STS node is tuned to respond the strongest to the previous input (**bat**) and doesn't respond with sufficient strength to the current input (**tab**). By setting the parameter $\epsilon = 1$, a STS node will satisfy the condition in (4) if and only if the input pattern is identical to the one that was present in the input when the node was allocated for its representation. As above the second node is allocated to represent the current input pattern (Figure 7D) and the relevant weight modifications and threshold setting operations take place. Another node is added to the STS layer and the network waits for the presentation of the next input pattern. Consider the case where the next input pattern is the same as the previous pattern (**tab**). In this case all the STS nodes compute their respective activations $Act_j^a(t)$ and outputs $O_j(t)$ as before. Although the current input pattern propagates maximum activation Act_2^a to the second STS node the condition of 4 is not satisfied because $Act_2^b < T_2^b$. This is because the context for the second STS node is not present when the word (**tab**) appears for the second time. However, the third node satisfies the

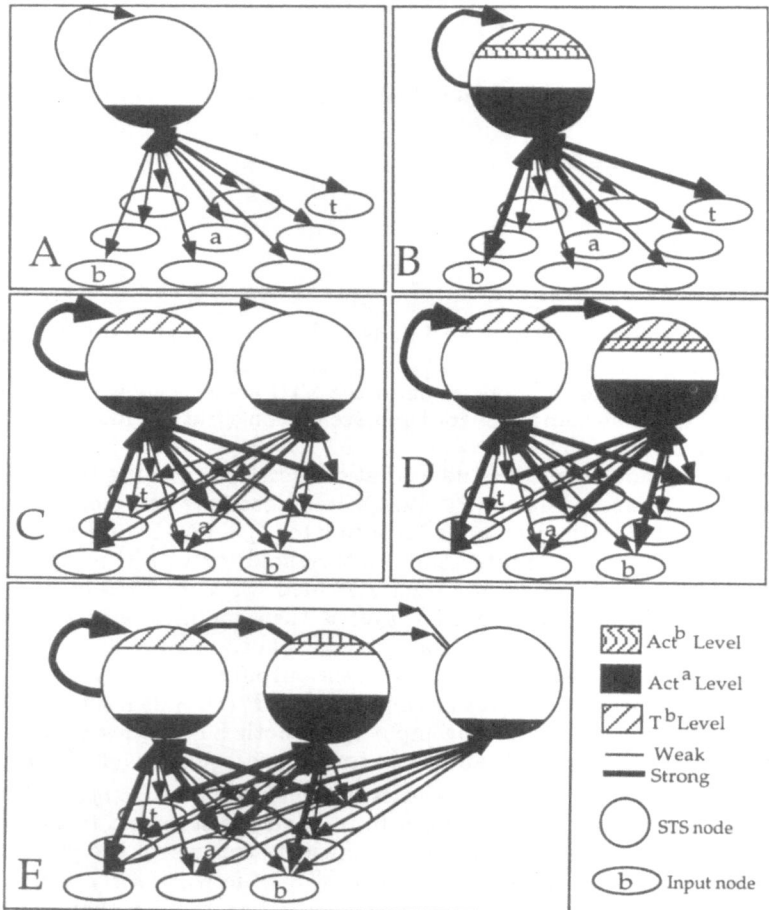

Figure 7: Dynamic allocation of STS nodes during list presentation.

condition of (4) and is allocated to represent the current input pattern. In this way, a separate STS node is allocated for the representation of the second occurrence of the word (**tab**) (Figure 7E).

6.3.2 Recall

Unlike recognition memory experiments where a cue pattern is made available to the subject in order to access previously stored memories, in immediate list recall experiments subjects are only given access to general contextual information about the experiment. This poses a boot–strapping problem with respect to connectionist models of memory. Unless feature information is available at the input layer we cannot access the information stored in the connections of the system. In order to overcome this problem we make the assumption that there exists a *Background Activation Level (BAL)* which is uniformly spread across all the STS (B) reception sites. By appropriately adjusting BAL we can ensure that only the STS node corresponding to the first list item will emit an output signal. The first node has a threshold value T_1^b smaller than any other STS node due the lack of previous context during list presentation. Once the first node has emitted an output signal the other nodes in the STS layer will receive activation at the (B) reception sites and they will in turn start emitting output signals according to (9, 10, & 11). When all the nodes have emitted an output signal random noise is induced and a winner-take-all mechanism finds a winner node which generates the corresponding input pattern according to (12).

7 Simulations

7.1 List Length

For all our simulations the network has the following parameter settings:

$$\epsilon = 0.04, \delta = 0.60, \mu = 0.5, BAL = 0.11$$

The setting of parameter ϵ is dictated by the requirement that every list item has to be represented by a separate STS node. Our previous research work [3] has established that the setting of the ϵ parameter influences the sensitivity (plasticity-stability) of the network to discover distinct categories in a given domain. Setting $\epsilon = 1$ forces the system to consider each input pattern as a separate domain category and allocate a separate node to its representation. For all the simulation results presented in this paper $\epsilon = 0.04$. The setting of parameter δ is fixed to give a range of recall roughly consistent with the range of the experimental data [11]. We have interpreted this finding in our model by limiting the influence of the decaying output of every STS node to the 7 ± 2 subsequent STS nodes. Parameter μ influences the strength of the synaptic enhancement during learning. The level of $BAL(= 0.11)$ was set to the minimum level which will force the first STS node to exceed its threshold and emit an output signal.

Activation is spread from the first STS node to all the other STS nodes. The STS node corresponding to the second list item receives the strongest activation signal because the first list item is the immediate context in which the second

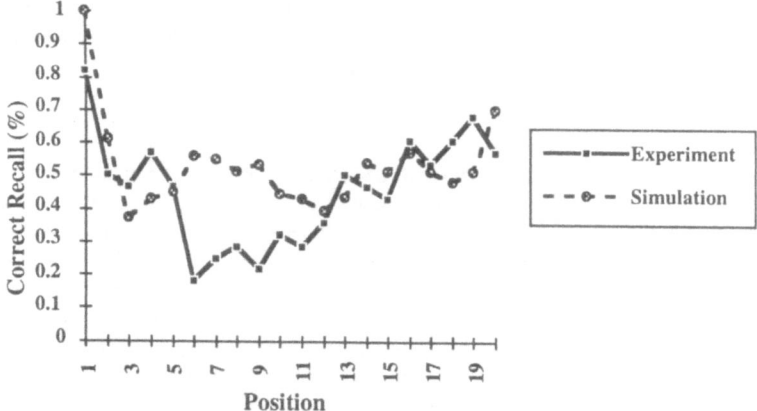

Figure 8: Experimental versus simulation recall probabilities for a list of 20 monosyllabic words.

list item occurred in the original list sequence. The STS node corresponding to the third list item receives the second strongest activation signal and the effect of the activation of the first STS node diffuses further as activation spreads to the other STS nodes representing list items further down in the original list sequence. This process of spreading activation we call *diffused chaining*. When all the STS nodes have emitted an output signal, noise is induced into the output value of each STS node and a winner-take all mechanism decides which list item is recalled.

We have simulated the network with a list of 20 short words, for ($M = 10000$) times. We have counted the times (N) each list item is recalled and calculated the relevant probability of correct recall as $\frac{N}{M}$. Figure 8 shows the recall probabilities for each of the 20 items in our list and compares them with the actual recall probabilities from the experimental data. There is no statistically significant $t(19df) = 1.95, P > t_{crit}(0.05, two - tail)$ difference between the experimental and simulation correct recall probabilities.

Figure 9 shows the recall probabilities for lists with 10, 20 and 30 items respectively. These results are in line with the experimental data; the recall curves have the standard primacy and recency shape for all three list lengths, while the middle part recall probabilities are getting smaller as list length increases.

7.2 Word Length and Phonological Similarity

We used the same parameter settings as above and simulated the network again for ($M = 10000$) times for lists of 10 short, 10 long, and 10 phonologically similar words. The recall probabilities from our simulations are shown in Figure 10.

During encoding, each phonologically similar word is allocated a separate STS

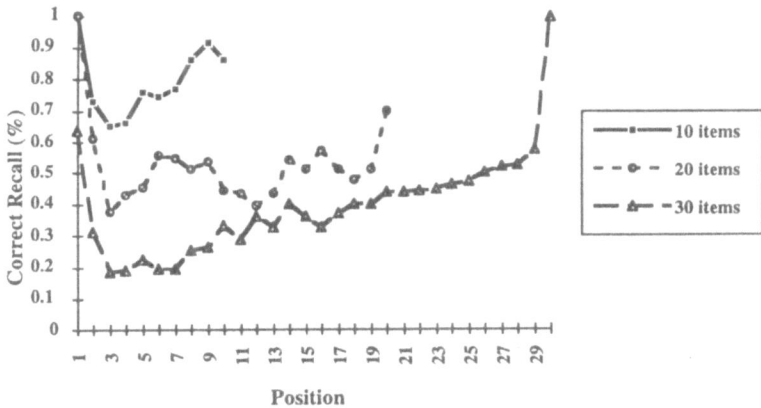

Figure 9: Recall probabilities for simulated lists of 10, 20 and 30 monosyllabic words.

node. At the same time activation is passed to all the other STS nodes which share some phonological features with current word. In this way, the level of output of each STS node escapes from its usual decaying through time routine according to (11) and is reset to the current activation level according to (10). There is a statistically significant $t(9df) = 4.38P < t_{crit}(0.01, two - tail)$ difference between the recall probabilities of list of 10 short and 10 similar words. Similar words cause the STS output nodes to be re–activated according to (5) and thus further enhance their intra– layer connections. This results in higher competition between the STS nodes and reduced overall recall probabilities.

When comparing short versus long duration words, there also is a statistically significant $t(4df) = 3.064, P < t_{crit}(0.04, two - tail)$ difference at the recency part of of the list (last 5 items). There is no statistically significant $t(4df) = 2.088P > t_{crit}(0.05, two - tail)$ difference however, at the primacy part of the list (5 first items) between short and long words. The lack of a condition effect in the primacy part of the list can be explained in two ways:

- The condition effect is stronger for the recency part of the curve than the primacy part of the curve in the experimental data themselves.

- The bi–syllabic words are not sufficiently long to produce a significant effect.

8   Conclusions

Previous work on a connectionist model of Word- Length and Phonological Similarity in Immediate Serial List Recall experiments proposed that these effects can be attributed to the encoding processes during list presentation. Based upon this proposition, a strong prediction about the existence of these

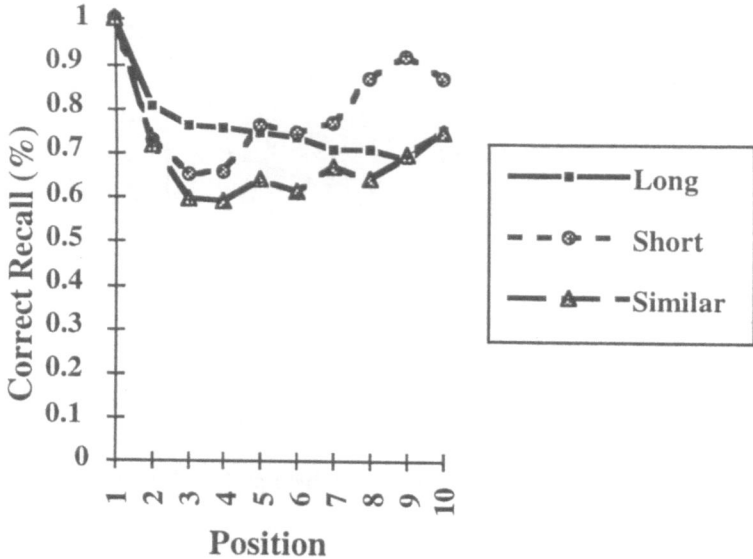

Figure 10: Recall probabilities for simulated lists of 10 monosyllabic, 10 long (bi-syllabic), and 10 phonologically similar words.

effects in other similar experimental designs was made. Immediate Free List Recall experiments were an obvious candidate for to test this hypothesis. In our experiments, subjects were shown lists of short, long and phonologically similar words. Analysis of the experimental results has shown that free recall performance is adversely affected when the list material comprises long or phonologically similar words. These findings confirm the prediction of our serial recall model. By modifying the parameter settings of the serial recall model, a new model of free recall was designed to simulate lists of varying length as well as lists comprising short, long and similar words. The new model replicated the experimental data accurately. Two major issues arise from the work presented in this paper:

- Phonological mediation is not exclusive to serial recall. Whatever encoding processes are activated during list presentation in serial recall are also activated in free-recall. This raises the interesting possibility that other serial recall effects (e.g. non– word effect) are also common to free recall. Furthermore, it seems to suggest that both serial and free recall experiments can be used as general purpose performance indicators for other STM related processes such as modality effects, encoding and recall strategies, etc.

- Psychological plausibility of explicit computational models with respect to established psychological effects is a worthy pursuit because it allows the development of theoretical predictions which can then be tested experimentally. In general, the more detail these models provide with respect to the experimental evidence the more complicated they become. Should model complexity be traded for model simplicity at the expense of modelling plausibility? In our view, a model's performance should not be solely judged upon its ability to replicate existing data, but also upon its ability to enable the formation of interesting predictions which can be tested with further experimentation.

References

[1] Baddeley, A.D., (1966), Short-term memory for word sequences as a function of acoustic, semantic and formal similarity, **Quarterly Journal of Experimental Psychology**, 18, 302-309.

[2] Baddeley, A.D., Thomson, & N. Buchanan, M., (1975), Word Length and the Structure of Short Term Memory, **Journal of Verbal Learning and Verbal Behaviour**, 14, 575–589.

[3] Bairaktaris, D., (1992), Discovering temporal structure using Hebbian learning. In Beale, R. and Finlay, J. (eds.), **Neural Networks and Pattern Recognition in Human Computer Interaction**, Ellis Horwood, 323–342.

[4] Bairaktaris D, Stenning K. (1992), A speech based connectionist model of human short term memory. **Proceedings of 14th Annual Conference of the Cognitive Science Society**, Lawrence Erlbaum Associates, 141–146.

[5] Besner, D., (1987), Phonology, Lexical Access and Reading and Articulatory Suppression: A critical review, **The Quarterly Journal of Experimental Psychology**, 39A, 467–478.

[6] Burgess, N., & Hitch, G., (1992), Towards a network model of the articulatory loop, **Journal of Memory and Language**, 31, 4, 429–460.

[7] Craik, F. I. M., Levy, B. A., (1970), Semantic and acoustic information in primary memory, **Journal of Experimental Psychology**, 86, 1, 77–82.

[8] Dalezman, J. J. (1967), Effects of output order on immediate, delayed, and final recall performance, **Journal of Experimental Psychology**, 2, 5, 597– 608.

[9] Elman, J, (1988), Finding Structure in Time, **CLR Technical Report 8801**, Centre for Research in Language, University of California, San Diego.

[10] Howard, D., Franklin, S., (1990), Memory Without Rehearsal". In **Neuropsychological Impairments of Short Term Memory**, G. Vallar & T. Shallice (Eds.), Cambridge University Press, 287– 320.

[11] Miller, G.A., (1956), The magical Number Seven, Plus or Minus Two: Some limits on Our Capacity for Processing Information, **Psychological Review**, 63, 81-97.

[12] Monsell, S., (1987), On the relation between lexical input and output pathways for speech, **Language Perception and Production**, 273–311.

[13] Postman, L., & Phillips, L.W., (1965), Short-term temporal changes in free recall, **Quarterly Journal of Experimental Psychology**, 17, 133-138.

[14] Wang, D., & Arbib, A.M., (1991), A neural model of temporal sequence generation with interval maintenance, **Thirteenth Annual Meeting of Cognitive Science Society**, 944-948.

[15] Williams, R. J., & Zipser, D. (1991), Gradient-based learning algorithms for recurrent networks and their computational complexity. In **Back- propagation: Theory, Architectures, and Applications**, Y. Chauvin & D. E. Rumelhart, (Eds). Hillsdale: Erlbaum.

[16] Zipser, D., (1991), Recurrent network model of the neural mechanism of short-term active memory". **Neural Computation**, 3, 179-193.

Interactions Between Knowledge Sources in a Dual-route Connectionist Model of Spelling

David W. Glasspool, George Houghton & Tim Shallice
University College London, England.

Abstract

It is now standard in the psychological literature to assume that the functional architecture for the system involved in spelling a word from memory uses two routes, a phonological route and a lexically based route. We describe a modular connectionist model based on this dual route architecture. Both routes in the model, tested in isolation, are able to simulate important aspects of the relevant psychological data. Some progress has been made towards combining the two routes into a single system. In attempting a coherent connectionist account, however, we are forced to address from first principles the difficult problem of the synchronisation and integration of information from each route into an output which combines the capabilities of both.

We believe that the interactions between cognitive modules may be more difficult to model than the modules themselves, and that connectionist approaches, by forcing these interactions to be addressed at a basic level, may help to focus attention on difficult problems of psychological modelling which might otherwise not be addressed.

1. Introduction - Solutions to the Spelling Problem.

Many intellectual problems may be solved by more than one method. In particular, one may distinguish "procedural" methods and memory based methods. Procedural methods provide a general mental resource for solving a problem or task, and are particularly important when faced with novel examples of a task. Memory based methods rely on having previously solved examples of a problem - if one can remember the problem and the solution, then the next time the same problem arises, the solution can be arrived at directly from memory. The two methods can be seen as different ways of trading off time/space costs against speed/flexibility benefits. The procedural method is typically slower and more computationally expensive, but can be applied to novel situations. A good procedure will also have a small memory load compared to the number of cases (possibly infinite) to which it can be applied. The memory method has the advantage of speed, but will not adapt well to novel situations and memory load increases with each solution learned. The two methods complement each other, and may be combined in various ways depending on circumstances. For instance, for familiar tasks the memory method may be preferred but can be supported by the procedural method when memory fails (as human memories are prone to do). If time is of the essence when faced with a novel problem, then memory for the most similar previously encountered example may provide a "quick-and-dirty" solution.

A good example of these methods occurs in learning to solve maths problems. For example, school children learn general procedures for multiplying numbers together, but these methods depend on the rote memorisation of multiplication tables for small numbers. In the same way, students of calculus learn a variety of procedures for differentiating and integrating functions, but with practice will come to memorise the solutions to commonly occurring examples. Similarly, in learning a language, people must memorise individual words and phrases, but the "generative aspect of language use" [1] requires the application of general procedures for combining these words into utterances. However, it is noticeable, generative linguistics notwithstanding, that simply learning the general rules of sentence structure of a foreign language does not make one an "idiomatic" speaker of that language. Native speakers of a language routinely employ a large collection of stereotypical phrases and expressions acquired during their lifetime.

It is now standard to assume that the cognitive skill of alphabetic spelling follows this general pattern: that is, fluent spellers of a language can employ two "routes" from word identity to spelling - a memory based, or "lexical" route, and a "constructed" route, using procedures for generating spellings. The lexical route employs a store of memorised spellings for familiar words. This provides "rapid access" spelling for well-known words, although it cannot be used to spell novel words. The constructed route, on the other hand, can produce spellings for novel words using generalised spelling procedures, but is unable to generate correct spellings for words which do not follow the usual spelling rules.

Apart from observational or "common-sense" evidence for multiple routes in spelling, there is also good evidence from neuropsychology. Patients have been described with "phonological agraphia" who spell words already known to them very well, but show poor spelling of dictated nonwords. For instance, patient PR studied by Shallice [2] achieved 91% correct spelling of known words, but only 18% correct spelling of nonwords. This suggests intact memory but disrupted procedural methods (sound-spelling conversion). Conversely, patients with "lexical agraphia" can spell nonwords perfectly well, but their spelling of a known word is worse the more irregular the word is. For instance, RG, studied by Beauvois & Derouesne [3], spelt nonwords perfectly, was 93% correct with regular words, but achieved only 36% correct when spelling exception words. Such "double dissociation" data provide strong support for that idea that normal spelling is subserved by multiple routes.

Putting these various solutions together, we can attempt to provide an overall "functional architecture" for alphabetic spelling as shown in Figure 1. This analysis of the

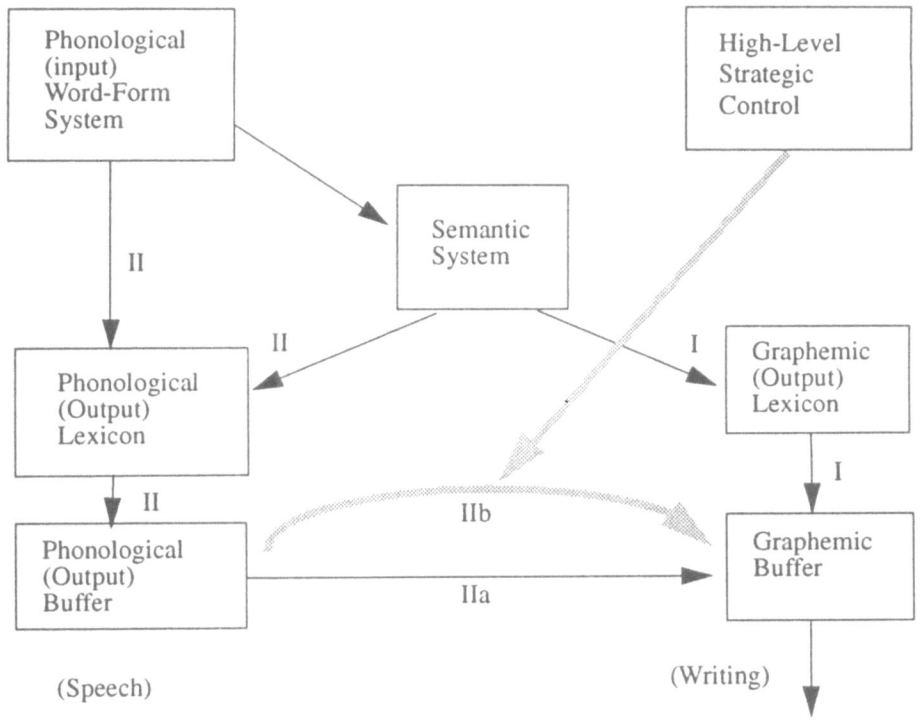

Figure 1: A functional diagram of the human spelling system.

spelling problem is closely related to several standard "dual route" formulations in the literature, such as those of [4] and [5].

Here, route I is a lexically based system, capable of spelling known words using learned spellings from a graphemic lexicon, and route II is an assembled route, using procedures to generate spellings. Two classes of spelling procedures are often discussed, sound-spelling conversion (IIa), and rule-based strategies (IIb).

Route IIa: Sound-spelling conversion. This is the most commonly discussed procedural spelling technique. Normal spellers are postulated to posses a mechanism for converting the sound of a word into a series of letters. This mechanism embodies the sound-spelling regularities of the language. It can be used to spell new words, and also seems to play a role in the spelling of familiar words. For instance, Kreiner & Gough [6] found that subjects made more spelling errors at points in words at which sound-spelling conversion rules would fail to unambiguously specify an appropriate letter (in particular, points at which the target word contained the vowel schwa, a vowel with no regular graphemic correspondence). However, this effect was found to interact with word frequency - high frequency words were much less affected than low frequency words, indicating an interaction with memory (on the assumption that more frequent words have better memorised representations). We return to this issue of the interaction between different systems later.

Route IIb: Conscious, rule-based, strategies. There are several possibilities here, for example:

1. Spelling rules. Spellers may use a variety of conscious rules to assist memory for words whose spelling does not accurately or consistently reflect their pronunciation, or which may depend on elements of grammar. For instance, the phoneme /i/ (as in *been*) is sometimes spelt "ie", as in *niece*. Occasionally it is spelt "ei" as in *receive*. Remembering which spelling is appropriate is aided by the conscious rule, "*i* before *e*, except after *c*". Grammar-based rules one may learn include that verbs ending in an *e* lose it when inflected with *ing* (*race-racing, believe-believing*, etc.), and do not repeat it when inflected with *ed* (*race-raced, believe-believed* etc.). Spelling rules are also essential in French for instance, where many written verb inflections are not pronounced, e.g., *Je donne, tu donnes, ils donnent* (I give, you give, they give). The verb form is pronounced the same in each case. The spelt form of the ending is dependent on the number and person of the subject (see [7] for discussion).

2. Spelling-based pronunciations: In discussing spelling strategies with friends and colleagues, it has been frequently reported to us that a favourite way of dealing with a troublesome word is to store a "special" pronunciation of that word which reflects its spelling more accurately than the standard pronunciation, and then to consciously use this pronunciation to guide spelling of it (by sound-spelling conversion). Examples reported to us include: remembering the word *friend* as (phonetically) fry-end, *business* as busy-ness, and *beautiful* as b-e-a-yootiful. This strategy is clearly a special case of the sound-spelling conversion procedure discussed above. However, it would appear to require additionally that the lexical entries for words spelled in this way be "tagged" in some manner, so that the strategy is evoked appropriately.

It is reasonable to conclude then that the spelling problem is solved by a number of methods (some probably idiosyncratic), and that the load placed on one method or another will depend on the particular problems presented by the orthographic system of the target language [8]. The remainder of this chapter briefly describes some ongoing work, which attempts to flesh out this picture by developing computational models of some of the component structures of the architecture shown in Figure 1; in particular we present results regarding the operation of the lexical route (including the nature of the "graphemic buffer"), the nature of the sound spelling conversion mechanism, and the issue of the mode of interaction between the various spelling routes, in particular the contrast between "controlled" and "automatic" interactions.

2. The Lexical Route

The lexical route represents spelling from memory, i.e., the orthographic lexicon stores a representation of the written form of known words from which their spelling may be generated. It is typically postulated that when a known word is accessed its constituent letter identities are loaded (in parallel) into the "graphemic output buffer" [9], [10]. Output processes convert abstract letter codes into an ordered series of actions. The actions will vary depending on the particular output medium (e.g., handwriting versus typing).

A number of questions arise about the nature of this route, concerning both representation and process. Representational questions involve the graphemic output lexicon - what is the precise form of the representation of a known word in memory? Two particular aspects are of central importance - serial order and constituent structure.

Serial Order: All the tens of thousands of words a writer of English knows are spelt using different combinations of the same 26 letters. A word is not considered to have been spelt correctly unless its constituent letters are produced in the correct order. In addition, the order of letters alone is enough to distinguish different words (anagrams), for instance, *rat, art, tar; trap, part, rapt; baker, brake, break*. Models of spelling must address the nature of these serial representations, and specify how they guide behaviour.

Constituent structure: It seems unlikely that words more than a few letters long are stored as unstructured strings. As is generally the case in human memory, they must be divided into "chunks". However, what the chunks are is unknown. Candidates include chunks corresponding to spoken syllables, purely orthographic "graphosyllables" [11], graphemes, etc.

In some recent modelling work we have attempted to address the first of these issues - the serial order problem [12]. The model addresses both the issue of how the serial order of letters might be coded in memory, and how this representation is used in the control of behaviour (in particular, the dynamics of the "graphemic buffer"). In this work, the "competitive queuing" (CQ) approach to serial order is taken [13]. CQ models are neural networks which store item and order information in the connections between nodes standing for some constituent, and nodes representing the items forming the constituent. These models do not use any serially-ordered structural primitives (such as serial buffers), or associative links between nodes representing successive items. At recall, the nodes representing a chunk are activated and activation spreads along learned weights to its constituent items, which become activated in parallel. However, a gradient of activation is established and maintained over these items, such that the sooner an item is to be output, the more active it is. Activated items compete for control of output by virtue of their activation level, more highly activated nodes being more likely to win. Once an item wins the competition and is output, its internal representation is inhibited. CQ models thus distinguish a stage of

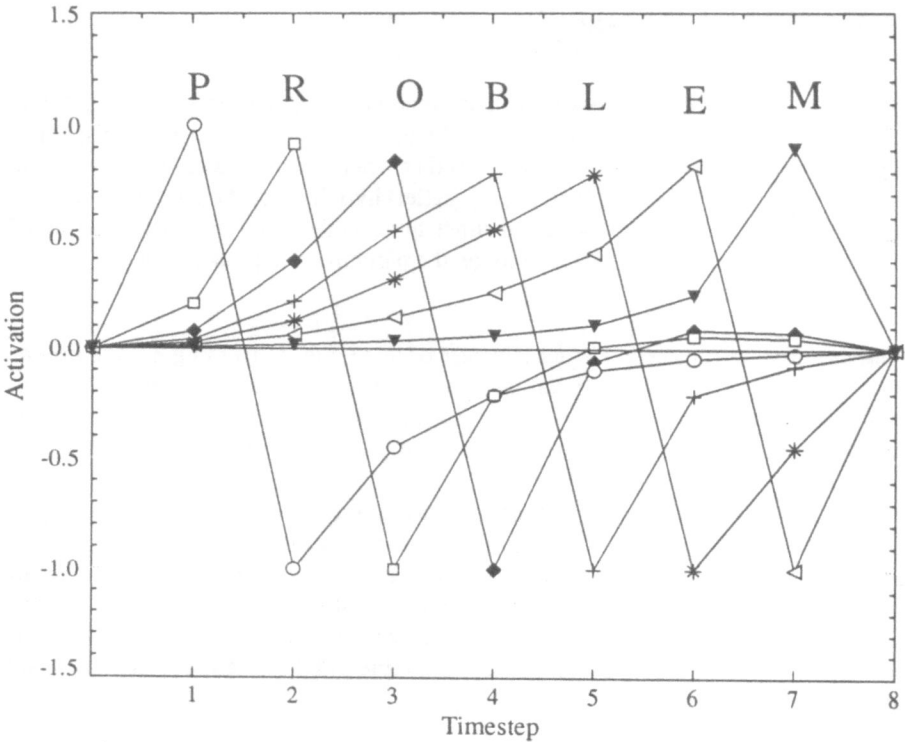

Figure 2: Activation trajectories of nodes representing letters during production of the word *problem* by a CQ system.

response preparation (parallel) from response selection (parallel mechanism, serial output).

Figure 2 illustrates this process by showing the activation trajectories of the nodes representing the constituent letters of the word *problem* during production of that word. Each curve in the figure is labelled by the letter identity it corresponds to at the point at which it wins the output competition (i.e. is the most active node). Thus the form of the recalled word can be read off left-to-right. (This figure was produced by a formal variant of the CQ algorithm described in [14]). Note that as each letter is produced, upcoming letters are already active. It is also worthy of note that the activation gap between the dominant letter and its nearest competitor narrows towards the middle of the word, and is widest at the ends.

We have applied this model to neuropsychological data from patients with an acquired spelling difficulty known "graphemic buffer disorder", (GBD; [10]; [14]). The spelling of these patients is disrupted for both real words and nonwords, and the character of the errors they make in both cases is qualitatively very similar, though more errors are made in writing nonwords to dictation. Errors typically involve mis-orderings and substitutions of letters in target words, with little discernible effects of phonology (unpronounceable spelling are produced) or lexical variables such as frequency. Thus subjects do not show the strong word/nonword dissociation patterns typical of lexical and phonological agraphics mentioned above. Because of this it has been claimed that the problem must lie in the "common path" shared by the lexical and phonological spelling routes. According to the diagram in Figure 1, these two pathways first converge at the graphemic buffer (temporary store of to-be-produced letters), hence the designation of the disorder (see [10] for further discussion and justification of this analysis). It is proposed that storage of letter identity and order in the buffer has become disrupted, leading to serial order errors.

As noted, GBD is roughly characterised by the production of serial order errors in the spelling of both words and nonwords. These errors have the following general characteristics:

1. Errors of substitution, shift, exchange, insertion and deletion.

2. Word length effects: likelihood of an error increases roughly linearly with number of letters in the target word.

3. Serial position effects: Error rates increase towards the middle of words - beginnings and ends are relatively well recalled.

4. Doubling errors: Words containing a doubled letter may be recalled with the wrong letter doubled. This error is also frequent in normal typing [16].

5. Quantitative lexical effects: The *qualitative* pattern of errors for words and nonwords is not reported to be significantly different. However, subjects are significantly worse *quantitatively* on nonword spelling.

It is worth noting that "slips of the pen" in normal subjects show many of the same characteristics, for instance the inverted-U serial position curve for errors [9].

Houghton et al. [12] were able to model many of these features of the syndrome using a competitive queuing architecture (Figure 3) in which random noise was added to the letter identity nodes activated in the queue.

The explanations Houghton et al. provide for the above data are (respectively):

Error types: Noise disrupts competition in the parallel queue allowing a variety of attested error types to occur. For instance, a shift occurs if the wrong node becomes maximally active at the wrong time. A deletion occurs if the appropriate letter node is under-active, allowing it to be overshadowed by a successor. If the missed out letter does not win the competition at the next chance (which would cause a transposition), then, as production of the word gets further from the point at which the letter should have been generated, its activation will diminish, so that it never succeeds in being produced.

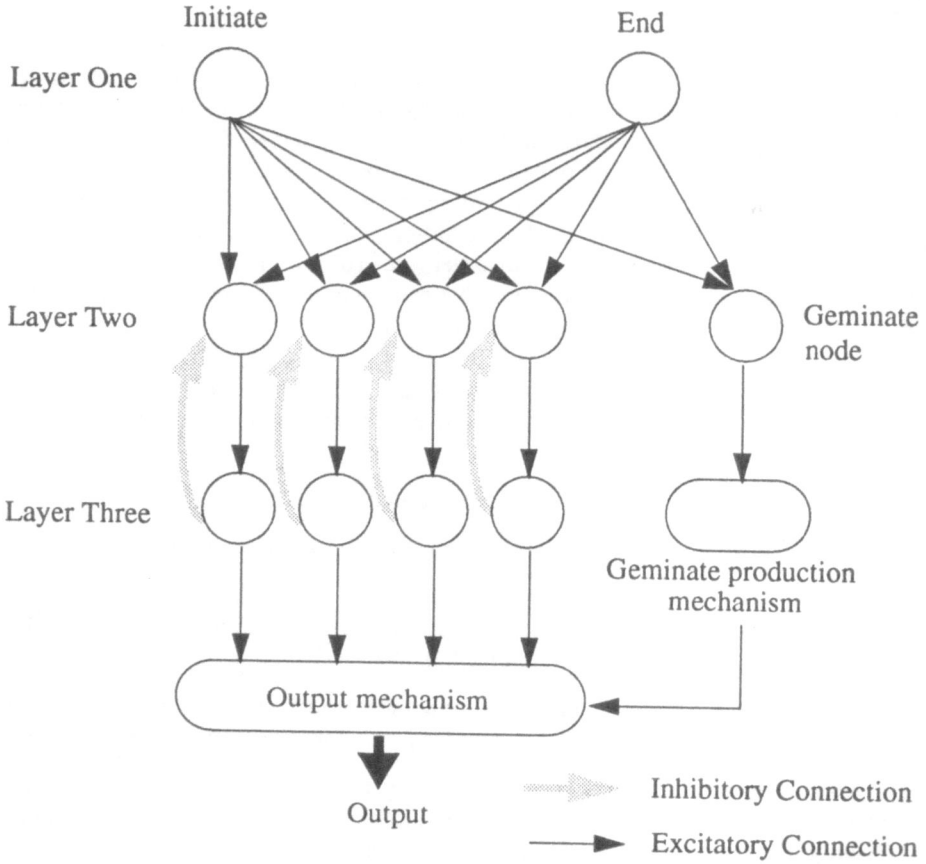

Figure 3: The lexical route model of Houghton, Glasspool and Shallice [12].

Word length effects: The chance of an error occurring increases if a word takes longer to produce. However, there is an additional factor. The CQ model used has to learn sequences of varying length with the same "resources" (fixed weight space). The more items that need to be learned in a chunk, the nearer they will be represented in the weight space. This proximity increases the degree of parallel activation and competition at recall, leading to more errors.

Serial position effects: As noted in the discussion of Figure 2, competition for output increases at medial positions (this is due to a combination of factors). This makes recall at these positions less reliable.

Doubling errors: The use of the CQ architecture makes the generation of repeated items very difficult (since items are suppressed after being generated). This necessitates the use of a "doubling schema" which acts to prevent suppression when it "fires". This schema is linked into the representation of a word during learning, and ideally will be active when the to-be-doubled letter is being output. However, the addition of noise causes it to be active inappropriately, causing the wrong letter to sometimes be doubled. This is the same account as is given by Rumelhart & Norman [16] for doubling errors in typing.

Lexicality effects: Houghton et al. follow Caramazza et al. [10] in arguing that non-word spelling involves the parallel activation of a set of letters prior to output (just as for the spelling of real words). It is proposed that a series of letters (generated by an unimplemented sound-spelling conversion mechanism) is compiled into a "spelling plan" prior to output. This plan is in the form of a competitive queue, and is hence prone to all of the above error patterns when subject to noise. This explains the qualitative correspondence between word and nonword errors. The quantitative difference is due to the rapidly compiled representation for the nonword not being as "robust" as the representations for well-learned words. This leads to the nonwords being more disrupted by the same level of noise (but disrupted in precisely the same way).

There are a variety of additional facts regarding this syndrome not accounted for by this model, and it is so far limited to words of up to about 8 letters long (the natural "span" of a chunk in the mechanism). However, there appears to be no other computational theory of serial order representation available which can account for the above range of data. Competitive queuing therefore provides a very useful basis for an account of spelling from memory.

3. The Phonological Route

The spelling process in its entirety is, as discussed in the introduction, the result of interaction between several relatively separable competencies. Given the good performance in isolation of our lexical spelling model, we decided to extend the model to enable phonological spelling using a modular format, and to proceed by investigating the problem of phoneme to grapheme conversion. Referring back to Figure 1, this process takes place on the route from the phonological output buffer to the graphemic buffer.

A conversion process on this route will only have to deal with regular spellings, so it would be reasonable to expect it to utilise regularities in phoneme to spelling correspondence in the subject's vocabulary. Barry and Seymour [17] showed that subjects do indeed tend to use the most commonly occurring correspondences when they spell nonwords. The possible spellings for a particular vowel sound can be ranked according to the probability that subjects use them in spelling a nonword. This ranking matches the relative frequency of occurrence of those spellings for the same vowel sound in the English language. Furthermore, competing spellings for a vowel sound can be primed [18]. Thus, for example, if the subject hears the word "sweet" followed by the nonword /p//r//i//t/, their most likely spelling for the nonword will be *PREET.* If instead they hear the word "treat" first, their most likely spelling will be *PREAT.*

Given this evidence, our requirements for a phonological spelling model were as follows:

1. The model should learn regularities in sound to spelling correspondence from exposure to a corpus.

2. The model should show a ranking in its choice of renderings similar to that shown by human subjects.

3. The model should be able to account for Barry and Seymour's priming data.

In the field of phonological reading, Zorzi, Houghton and Butterworth have shown that a feed-forward network, which would learn both regular and irregular word-to-pronunciation correspondences when it contained hidden layers, could learn regular correspondences only when restricted to two layers [19]. This suggests that a two layer association network may well be capable of learning the relevant statistical regularities in a corpus of pronunciation-to-spelling correspondences.

While simple pattern association networks operate in an essentially parallel manner, an essential component of our modelling approach is serial operation. However, simply presenting isolated phonemes to a network one at a time and requiring the corresponding spellings as output will clearly not produce good results, as many sound-to-spelling correspondences depend on the context in which a phoneme is found. For example, the phoneme /k/ is usually spelled *ck* when it occurs at the end of a word, but this pattern is never found at the start of a word. Instead *c* or *k* is used, usually depending on the identity of the following phonemes. If a simple association network is to give adequate performance, it must operate not on isolated phonemes but on phonemes in context.

An approach which has been used in models such as NETspell [20] and NETtalk [21] is the provision of context using a "sliding window". The input layer of the network, rather than consisting of a single set of nodes representing the currently presented phoneme, comprises several such sets of phoneme nodes. One of these represents the currently presented phoneme, while others represent phonemes occurring before and after the current phoneme. As each phoneme is processed, the phonemic representation is shifted across the phoneme sets. The output from the model at any time-step is taken to be the most active phoneme node at that step.

In the current model, we use five identical sets of 44 phoneme nodes in the input layer, each of which connects via weighted links to each of a single set of nodes in the output layer (Figure 4). The input format will change to match the output from a syllable-based model of word and nonword pronunciation using competitive queuing and based on work by Hartley and Houghton [22], but we believe that the final output

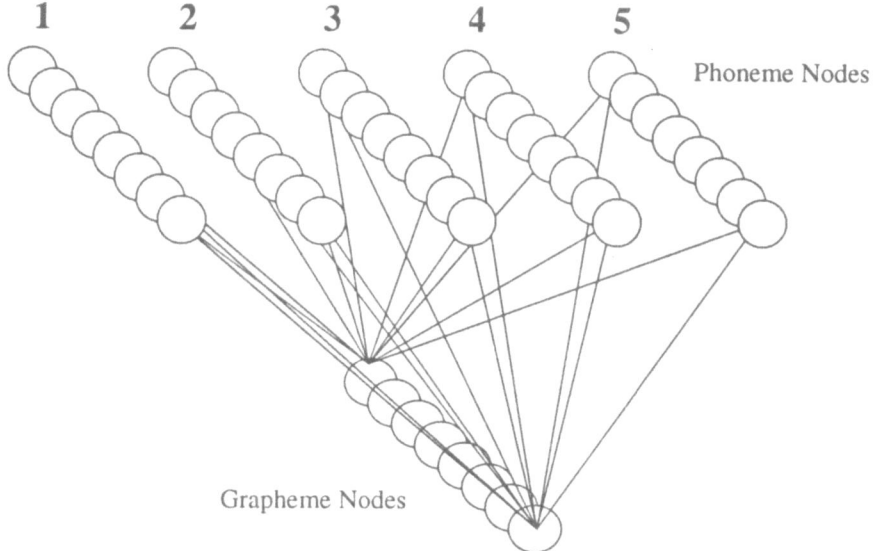

1 2 3 4 5

Phoneme Nodes

Grapheme Nodes

Figure 4: The two-layer architecture for the phoneme-to-grapheme system. The first layer contains five identical sets of phoneme nodes (1-5). The output contains a single set of grapheme nodes.

from that model will be formally equivalent to such a sliding window. The operation of the sliding window is illustrated in outline in Figure 5.

The output layer of the network consists of grapheme nodes representing "functional groups" of letters, such as *TH* and *EA,* as well as individual letters. This is primarily motivated by the priming data of [17], which suggests that entire functional groups are involved rather than individual letters. However, a secondary motivation is the fact that the performance of the model is considerably worse when functional groups are not available in the output layer. The actual functional groups used are those proposed by Venezky [23]. This choice is somewhat arbitrary, and careful selection of groups may improve the performance of the model.

The corpus used in simulations with the phonological spelling model is a set of 3957 spelling - pronunciation pairs for monosyllables obtained from the Oxford Psycholinguistic Database [24]. The delta rule is used to train the network, which reaches asymptotic performance after about 40 epochs. While development work is still in progress on this model, initial results are promising. After training, the model produces 'correct' phonological renderings for 82% of the words in the corpus. Most errors are either the result of unreliability in detecting the end of a word, and thus producing too many or too few letters, or occasional letter deletions elsewhere in the word. Scoring is carried out manually and is inevitably somewhat subjective.

1

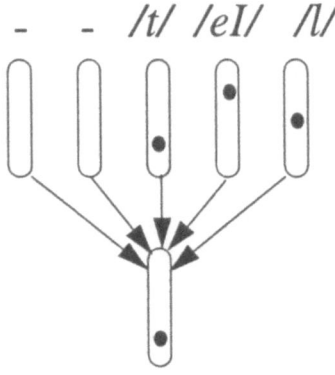

T

2

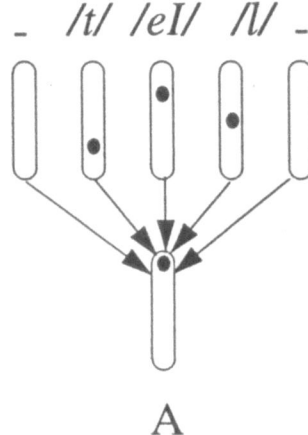

A

3

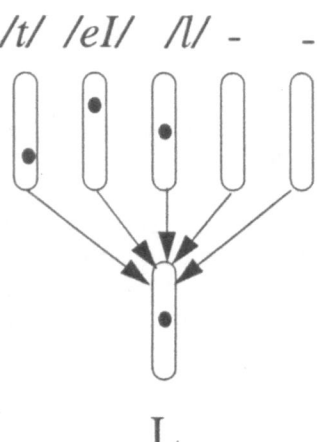

L

4

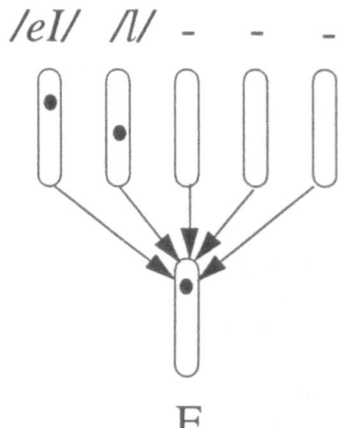

E

● = Active Node.

Figure 5: The operation of the sliding window system during production of the spelling 'TALE' for the word /t//eI//l/. The activation patterns corresponding to the pronunciation are shifted across the input window over four timesteps (1-4). At each step, the output layer must strongly activate the appropriate grapheme node.

Some typical spellings produced by the model are:

"Loon" --> *LOON*

"Hound" --> *HOUND*

"Wrist" --> *RIST*

"Slight" --> *SLITE*

These use the expected phoneme to grapheme correspondences. Furthermore, although the model's output is taken to be the most active output node at each time-step, an examination of the activations of other output nodes shows that they are ranked in activation in exactly the way that probability of use is ranked in Barry and Seymour's study [17]. For example, presenting the phoneme /i/ in the word /b//i//n/ results in the functional group *EA* becoming most active, with *EE* next most active, followed by the letter *E*. This ranking corresponds to the relative frequencies with which each spelling is used for the vowel /i/ in the training corpus. This activation ranking suggests that the addition of a small random element to the grapheme node activations would lead to relative probabilities for various spellings similar to those found with human spellers.

The lexical route model uses a representation for double letters in which a single occurrence of a letter coincides with the triggering of a separate 'geminate' node. As explained above, this is necessary if the model is to produce double letters at all, and also correctly models the human data. However, the phonemic route model does not require this representational scheme as it does not depend on the inhibition of letters following their output, and is thus quite capable of producing repeated letters with no additional mechanism. Moreover, the network is unable to learn to use a geminate node to represent double letters. Consider the vowel /i/ for example. 'ea' and 'ee' are both common spellings for this vowel, although 'ee' is slightly less frequent. Using the geminate node representation, although the network will attempt to use the most frequent spelling, 'ea', the spelling 'ee' is common enough that a strong association will exist between /i/ and the geminate node, sufficient to trigger the node. The result is that 'ea' is produced while the geminate node fires, giving 'eea'.

4. Combining Information from the Two Routes

Referring to Figure 1, if we assume a CQ - based production system for phonological word forms such as that of Hartley and Houghton [22], and the lexical route model described above, then the phonological and graphemic output lexicons will use very similar representations, both of which may be accessed in parallel, and it is conceivable that they could easily be linked or even shared. Further "down-line', however, by the time the phonological and graphemic output buffers are reached the representations have become serial and specific to speech or spelling. Clearly any interface between the two routes at this level will be more complex.

There are several major points of difference between the representation used in the phoneme-to-grapheme conversion network and that used in the lexical route model. In particular:

1. The phoneme-to-grapheme network works considerably better when functional groups are included in the output representation as well as individual letters. This representation is also implied by the effect of priming [18]. The lexical model, on the other hand, cannot use this representation if it is to correctly model the typical errors made by graphemic buffer patients, which do not respect functional groups.

2. The phoneme-to-grapheme network does not use the separate node representation for geminates which is essential for correct operation, and for correct error modelling, in the lexical route model. Simulations have confirmed that the two layer architecture does not require this representational scheme and is not sufficiently powerful to learn the required mapping.

Two further points of incompatibility concern the dynamics of spelling production in the two systems:

1. The pattern of errors produced by the breakdown of the phoneme-to-grapheme network's operation as noise is added to node activation values is quite different from that produced by the CQ mechanism of the lexical route model. CQ systems typically produce bowed serial error curves and a high proportion of order errors. The dynamics of the phoneme-to-grapheme network are quite different, however. Smooth pre-activation of grapheme nodes does not occur, instead nodes tend to suddenly become active as a phoneme combination moves into particular phoneme positions. The typical errors produced by this network are thus substitutions rather than order errors.

2. The routes operate at different rates - speech is a much faster process than writing.

We conclude that the phonemic route cannot directly control graphemic output. This raises the question of the nature of the interaction between the phonemic and lexical spelling routes. We wish to make two claims regarding this interaction:

1. **Control of spelling by pronunciation (nonword spelling) does not happen online.**

   Instead, we propose that nonword spelling proceeds as follows:

   • A motor plan is constructed by rapid learning in the lexical system, using the sound-to-spelling conversion network to produce a spelling from a phonological representation or the nonword. This process may happen at the usual speech rate, as the CQ-based lexical system is quite capable of learning at high rates and from a single presentation, and could be paced according to phonological units (e.g.

syllable-by-syllable, as in [22]).

- This motor plan is then executed at the slower rate of the spelling system, just as the motor plans for learned words are. The motor plan for a nonword is thus identical in nature to that for a known word, but is less well learned and hence less robust.

2. Phonologically mediated repair operations do not happen on-line.

Rather, repair operations require strategic control by high-level, probably conscious, supervisory processes.

4.1 Phonologically Mediated Repair

We propose that, during normal spelling of known words, the lexical system will be dominant. Where it is clear that an error has occurred, for example because a letter has failed to be retrieved, a repair process must be invoked based on the phoneme-to-grapheme system.

High-level repair processes under strategic control are not, of course, a novel idea. Such strategic processes are suggested, for example, by McCloskey et al. [25] and Jonsdottir, Shallice and Wise [15] on the basis of error data from GBD patients. Jonsdottir et al. suggest that when an error is detected during the spelling of a known word, the graphemic buffer must be re-loaded, using phonological information where lexical information is not available. The subject then needs to select the appropriate part of the phonological representation to make the repair. This involves an interactive and recursive process requiring good control and manipulative skills. A process at this level is surely conscious, and might correspond to Norman and Shallice's SAS [26].

5. Conclusions

Both the lexical and the phonological route models discussed here show encouraging performance in modelling several aspects of the psychological data, especially considering that they both involve only relatively simple, low-level processes.

The interface between the two aspects of spelling modelled here is not straightforward for two reasons: Firstly, there are mismatches between the output representations, and also between the dynamics and production rates of the two systems, as discussed above. Secondly, this is the point where the various idiosyncratic conscious spelling strategies discussed in the introduction would be expected to come into play. It seems unlikely therefore that the interface between the two models can be entirely automatic and unconscious.

As connectionist approaches to modelling mature, and models become more ambitious in their scope, we can expect to see the appearance of high-level models consisting of several interacting low-level modules. This is a natural way to proceed given the well known advantages of modularisation in complex systems from the points of view of design, implementation and theorising. Modularisation is also implied by most neuropsychological theorising, and the fact that, as more diverse connectionist architectures emerge, different architectures have been found to be most suitable for different tasks. It should be no surprise therefore to see the emergence of models such as that described in this chapter using several heterogeneous connectionist modules. Another recent example is Mikkulainen's DISCERN model [27].

Our conclusions regarding the nature of the interaction between the two routes have been precipitated by problems encountered in attempts at modelling this interaction at the same low level as the models of the routes themselves. A major benefit of low level modelling is the need to focus on this type of interface or control problem, which can be difficult to see in high level descriptions such as 'box and arrow' diagrams. It is often the case in modular systems that the interfaces between modules are more complex than the modules themselves. Descriptions such as 'box and arrow' diagrams make it very easy to focus on the functions carried out by the boxes, rather than the possibly more challenging interactions implied by the arrows.

References

1. Chomsky, N. Syntactic Structures. Mouton: The Hague. 1957

2. Shallice, T. Phonological agraphia and the lexical route in writing. Brain1981; 104, 413-429.

3. Beauvois, M., F., & Derouesne, J. Lexical or orthographic agraphia. Brain 1981; 104, 21-49.

4. Morton, J. The logogen model and orthographic structure. In Frith, U. (Ed.), Cognitive approaches in spelling. London: Academic Press. 1980

5. Shallice, T. From neuropsychology to mental structure. Cambridge: Cambridge University Press. 1988

6. Kreiner, D.S., & Gough, P.B. Two ideas about spelling: Rules and word-specific memory. Journal of Memory and Language 1990; 29, 103-118.

7. Alegria, J., & Mousty, P. On the development of lexical and non-lexical spelling procedures of French-speaking, normal and disabled children. In Brown, G. D. A., & Ellis, N. C., (eds.), Handbook of Spelling: Theory, Process and Intervention. Chich-

ester: John Wiley and Sons. 1994

8. Frith, U. Unexpected spelling problems. In Frith, U. (ed.), Cognitive Processes in Spelling. London: Academic Press. 1980

9. Wing, A.M., & Baddeley, A.D., Spelling errors in handwriting: A corpus and a distributional analysis. In Frith, U. (ed.), Cognitive processes in spelling. London: Academic Press. 1980

10. Caramazza, A., Miceli, G., Villa, G. & Romani, C. The role of the graphemic buffer in spelling: evidence from a case of acquired dysgraphia. Cognition 1987; 26, 59-85.

11. Caramazza, A. & Miceli, G. The structure of graphemic representations. Cognition 1990; 37, 243-297.

12. Houghton, G., Glasspool, D., & Shallice, T. Spelling and serial recall: Insights from a competitive queueing model. In Brown, G. D. A., & Ellis, N. C., (eds.), Handbook of Spelling: Theory, Process and Intervention. Chichester: John Wiley and Sons. 1994

13. Houghton, G. The problem of serial order: A neural network model of sequence learning and recall. In Dale, R., Mellish, C., & Zock, M.(Eds.), Current Research in Natural Language Generation. London: Academic Press. 1990

14. Houghton, G. Some formal variations on the theme of competitive queueing. Internal Technical Report, UCL-PSY-CQ1. (May, 1994). Dept. of Psychology, University College London. 1994

15. Jonsdottir, M., Shallice, T., & Wise, R. Language-specific differences in graphemic buffer disorder. (Submitted)

16. Rumelhart, D. E., & Norman, D. A.   Simulating a skilled typist: a study of skilled cognitive-motor performance. Cognitive Science 1982; 6, 1-36.

17. Barry, C. & Seymour, P. H. K. Lexical priming and sound-to-spelling contingency effects in nonword spelling. Quarterly Journal of Experimental Psychology 1988; 40A (1) 5-40

18. Campbell, R. Writing nonwords to dictation. Brain and Language 1983; 19, 153-178.

19. Zorzi, Houghton & Butterworth. Two routes or one in reading aloud? A connectionist "dual-process" model. Unpublished manuscript.

20. Caramazza, A. & Olson, A. Lesioning a connectionist model of spelling. A talk

given at Venice III: Cognitive Neuropsychology and Connectionism. October 1988, Venice.

21. Sejnowski, T. J., & Rosenberg, C. R. NETtalk: A parallel network that learns to read aloud. In Anderson, J. A., & Rosenfeld, E. (eds.) Neurocomputing: foundations of research. 663-672. Cambridge, MA: MIT Press. 1988

22. Hartley, T., & Houghton, G. A linguistically constrained model of short-term memory for nonwords. (In submission).

23. Venezky, R. L. The structure of English orthography. Paris: Mouton. 1970

24. Quinlan, P. T. The Oxford Psycholinguistic Database. Oxford: Oxford University Press. 1993

25. McCloskey, M., Badecker, W., Goodman-Shulman, R., & Aliminosa, D. The structure of graphemic representations in spelling: Evidence from a case of acquired dysgraphia. Cognitive Neuropsychology 1994; 11, 341.

26. Norman, D. A., & Shallice, T. Attention to action: Willed and automatic control of behaviour. Center for Human Information Processing (Technical Report No. 99). 1980. Reprinted in revised form in Davidson,R. J., Schwartz, G. E., & Shapiro, D. (Eds.) Consciousness and self-regulation (Vol. 4). New York: Plenum Press. 1986

27. Miikkulainen, R. Subsymbolic natural language processing: an integrated model of scripts, lexicon, and memory. Cambridge, MA: MIT Press, 1993

Author Index

Altmann, G.T.M. 19
Baddeley, R. 86, 97
Bairaktaris, D. 191
Bauer, H.-U. 107
Beale, J.M. 176
Beauvois, M.W. 155
Bullinaria, J.A. 34
Cartwright, R. 62
Der, R. 107
Dienes, Z. 19
Fyfe, C. 97
Gao, S.-J. 19
Glasspool, D.W. 209
Griffith, N. 137
Herrmann, M. 107
Houghton, G. 209
Humphreys, G.W. 62, 165
Kay, J. 117
Keil, F.C. 176
Lovatt, P.J. 191
Meddis, R. 155
Phillips, W.A. 117
Shallice, T. 209
Slack, J. 49
Smith, K.J. 165
Smith, L.S. 147
Smyth, D.M. 117
Stone, J.V. 75
Willshaw, D. 3

Published in 1990–92

Semantics for Concurrency, Proceedings of the International BCS-FACS Workshop, Sponsored by Logic for IT (S.E.R.C.), University of Leicester, UK, 23–25 July 1990
M. Z. Kwiatkowska, M. W. Shields and R. M. Thomas (Eds)

Functional Programming, Glasgow 1989
Proceedings of the 1989 Glasgow Workshop, Fraserburgh, Scotland, 21–23 August 1989
Kei Davis and John Hughes (Eds)

Persistent Object Systems, Proceedings of the Third International Workshop, Newcastle, Australia, 10–13 January 1989
John Rosenberg and David Koch (Eds)

Z User Workshop, Oxford 1989, Proceedings of the Fourth Annual Z User Meeting, Oxford, 15 December 1989
J. E. Nicholls (Ed.)

Formal Methods for Trustworthy Computer Systems (FM89), Halifax, Canada, 23–27 July 1989
Dan Craigen (Editor) and Karen Summerskill (Assistant Editor)

Security and Persistence, Proceedings of the International Workshop on Computer Architectures to Support Security and Persistence of Information, Bremen, West Germany, 8–11 May 1990
John Rosenberg and J. Leslie Keedy (Eds)

Women into Computing: Selected Papers 1988–1990
Gillian Lovegrove and Barbara Segal (Eds)

3rd Refinement Workshop (organised by BCS-FACS, and sponsored by IBM UK Laboratories, Hursley Park and the Programming Research Group, University of Oxford), Hursley Park, 9–11 January 1990
Carroll Morgan and J. C. P. Woodcock (Eds)

Designing Correct Circuits, Workshop jointly organised by the Universities of Oxford and Glasgow, Oxford, 26–28 September 1990
Geraint Jones and Mary Sheeran (Eds)

Functional Programming, Glasgow 1990
Proceedings of the 1990 Glasgow Workshop on Functional Programming, Ullapool, Scotland, 13–15 August 1990
Simon L. Peyton Jones, Graham Hutton and Carsten Kehler Holst (Eds)

4th Refinement Workshop, Proceedings of the 4th Refinement Workshop, organised by BCS-FACS, Cambridge, 9–11 January 1991
Joseph M. Morris and Roger C. Shaw (Eds)

AI and Cognitive Science '90, University of Ulster at Jordanstown, 20–21 September 1990
Michael F. McTear and Norman Creaney (Eds)

Software Re-use, Utrecht 1989, Proceedings of the Software Re-use Workshop, Utrecht, The Netherlands, 23–24 November 1989
Liesbeth Dusink and Patrick Hall (Eds)

Z User Workshop, 1990, Proceedings of the Fifth Annual Z User Meeting, Oxford, 17–18 December 1990
J.E. Nicholls (Ed.)

IV Higher Order Workshop, Banff 1990
Proceedings of the IV Higher Order Workshop, Banff, Alberta, Canada, 10–14 September 1990
Graham Birtwistle (Ed.)

ALPUK91, Proceedings of the 3rd UK Annual Conference on Logic Programming, Edinburgh, 10–12 April 1991
Geraint A. Wiggins, Chris Mellish and Tim Duncan (Eds)

Specifications of Database Systems
International Workshop on Specifications of Database Systems, Glasgow, 3–5 July 1991
David J. Harper and Moira C. Norrie (Eds)

7th UK Computer and Telecommunications Performance Engineering Workshop
Edinburgh, 22–23 July 1991
J. Hillston, P.J.B. King and R.J. Pooley (Eds)

Logic Program Synthesis and Transformation
Proceedings of LOPSTR 91, International Workshop on Logic Program Synthesis and Transformation, University of Manchester, 4–5 July 1991
T.P. Clement and K.-K. Lau (Eds)

Declarative Programming, Sasbachwalden 1991
PHOENIX Seminar and Workshop on Declarative Programming, Sasbachwalden, Black Forest, Germany, 18–22 November 1991
John Darlington and Roland Dietrich (Eds)

Building Interactive Systems:
Architectures and Tools
Philip Gray and Roger Took (Eds)

Functional Programming, Glasgow 1991
Proceedings of the 1991 Glasgow Workshop on Functional Programming, Portree, Isle of Skye, 12–14 August 1991
Rogardt Heldal, Carsten Kehler Holst and Philip Wadler (Eds)

Object Orientation in Z
Susan Stepney, Rosalind Barden and
David Cooper (Eds)

Code Generation - Concepts, Tools, Techniques
Proceedings of the International Workshop on
Code Generation, Dagstuhl, Germany,
20–24 May 1991
Robert Giegerich and Susan L. Graham (Eds)

Z User Workshop, York 1991, Proceedings of the
Sixth Annual Z User Meeting, York,
16–17 December 1991
J.E. Nicholls (Ed.)

Formal Aspects of Measurement
Proceedings of the BCS-FACS Workshop on
Formal Aspects of Measurement, South Bank
University, London, 5 May 1991
Tim Denvir, Ros Herman and R.W. Whitty (Eds)

AI and Cognitive Science '91 University College,
Cork, 19–20 September 1991
Humphrey Sorensen (Ed.)

5th Refinement Workshop, Proceedings of the 5th
Refinement Workshop, organised by BCS-FACS,
London, 8–10 January 1992
Cliff B. Jones, Roger C. Shaw and
Tim Denvir (Eds)

Algebraic Methodology and Software Technology
(AMAST'91)
Proceedings of the Second International
Conference on Algebraic Methodology and
Software Technology, Iowa City, USA,
22–25 May 1991
M. Nivat, C. Rattray, T. Rus and G. Scollo (Eds)

ALPUK92, Proceedings of the 4th UK
Conference on Logic Programming,
London, 30 March – 1 April 1992
Krysia Broda (Ed.)

Logic Program Synthesis and Transformation
Proceedings of LOPSTR 92, International
Workshop on Logic Program Synthesis and
Transformation, University of Manchester,
2–3 July 1992
Kung-Kiu Lau and Tim Clement (Eds)

NAPAW 92, Proceedings of the First North
American Process Algebra Workshop, Stony
Brook, New York, USA, 28 August 1992
S. Purushothaman and Amy Zwarico (Eds)

First International Workshop on Larch
Proceedings of the First International Workshop
on Larch, Dedham, Massachusetts, USA,
13–15 July 1992
Ursula Martin and Jeannette M. Wing (Eds)

Persistent Object Systems
Proceedings of the Fifth International Workshop
on Persistent Object Systems, San Miniato (Pisa),
Italy, 1–4 September 1992
Antonio Albano and Ron Morrison (Eds)

Formal Methods in Databases and Software
Engineering, Proceedings of the Workshop on
Formal Methods in Databases and Software
Engineering, Montreal, Canada, 15–16 May 1992
V.S. Alagar, Laks V.S. Lakshmanan and
F. Sadri (Eds)

Modelling Database Dynamics
Selected Papers from the Fourth International
Workshop on Foundations of Models and
Languages for Data and Objects,
Volkse, Germany, 19–22 October 1992
Udo W. Lipeck and Bernhard Thalheim (Eds)

14th Information Retrieval Colloquium
Proceedings of the BCS 14th Information
Retrieval Colloquium, University of Lancaster,
13–14 April 1992
Tony McEnery and Chris Paice (Eds)

Functional Programming, Glasgow 1992
Proceedings of the 1992 Glasgow Workshop on
Functional Programming, Ayr, Scotland,
6–8 July 1992
John Launchbury and Patrick Sansom (Eds)

Z User Workshop, London 1992
Proceedings of the Seventh Annual Z User
Meeting, London, 14–15 December 1992
J.P. Bowen and J.E. Nicholls (Eds)

Interfaces to Database Systems (IDS92)
Proceedings of the First International Workshop
on Interfaces to Database Systems,
Glasgow, 1–3 July 1992
Richard Cooper (Ed.)

AI and Cognitive Science '92
University of Limerick, 10–11 September 1992
Kevin Ryan and Richard F.E. Sutcliffe (Eds)

Theory and Formal Methods 1993
Proceedings of the First Imperial College
Department of Computing Workshop on Theory
and Formal Methods, Isle of Thorns Conference
Centre, Chelwood Gate, Sussex, UK,
29–31 March 1993
Geoffrey Burn, Simon Gay and Mark Ryan (Eds)

Algebraic Methodology and Software
Technology (AMAST'93)
Proceedings of the Third International
Conference on Algebraic Methodology and
Software Technology, University of Twente,
Enschede, The Netherlands, 21–25 June 1993
M. Nivat, C. Rattray, T. Rus and G. Scollo (Eds)

Logic Program Synthesis and Transformation
Proceedings of LOPSTR 93, International
Workshop on Logic Program Synthesis and
Transformation, Louvain-la-Neuve, Belgium,
7–9 July 1993
Yves Deville (Ed.)